Presto Sketching

The Magic of Simple Drawing for
Brilliant Product Thinking and Design

Ben Crothers

Beijing · Boston · Farnham · Sebastopol · Tokyo

Presto Sketching
by Ben Crothers

Copyright © 2018 Ben Crothers. All rights reserved.

Published by O'Reilly Media, Inc., 1005 Gravenstein Highway North, Sebastopol, CA 95472.

O'Reilly books may be purchased for educational, business, or sales promotional use. Online editions are also available for most titles (*http://www.oreilly.com/safari*). For more information, contact our corporate/institutional sales department: (800) 998-9938 or *corporate@oreilly.com*.

Development Editor: Angela Rufino
Acquisitions Editor: Nikki McDonald
Production Editor: Melanie Yarbrough
Copyeditor: Octal Publishing
Proofreader: Rachel Head
Indexer: Lucie Haskins

Cover Designer: Randy Comer
Interior Designers: Ron Bilodeau and Monica Kamsvaag
Illustrator: Ben Crothers
Compositor: Melanie Yarbrough

October 2017: First Edition

Revision History for the First Edition:

2017-10-09   First release

See *http://www.oreilly.com/catalog/errata.csp?isbn=0636920092391* for release details.

978-1-491-99428-3

[LSI]

For Yvonne.

Your love and energy live on.

[*contents*]

[*Preface*]

You PROBABLY KNOW AT least three languages.

I can think of two, right off the bat. You speak and write at least one formal language (you're using one to read this, right?), and you use your body (nonverbal language). You've probably honed your spoken and written language at school and work, and you honed your body language along the way, too.

Your third language, which may be less obvious, is your *visual* language: sketching, drawing, using emojis, using photos and stock images in your presentations—it's all visual communication. For most of us, we dropped our visual language early in school, and our two most valuable twins of communication—words and pictures—have been separated ever since!

I've been using visual communication in my career as a designer for many years and in many ways, mostly by sketching on paper and sketching on whiteboards. But I've found that what's become more and more important is not only sketching to show interfaces and customer experiences, but sketching to *think*, and sketching to *help others* think. My pen has become a powerful thought partner for me and my team.

I've also been teaching people for many years to bring those twins of words and pictures back together again, and use their pens as thought partners, too. I've seen sketching lift people's thinking, and I've seen sketching help people find their true direction in life.

That's why I've written *Presto Sketching: The Magic of Simple Drawing for Brilliant Product Thinking and Design*: to help you use sketching as your thought partner, too.

There are loads of books about this sort of sketching already around (and they're great!), but I want to help fill what I see as the gap between *knowing the potential* of sketching, and actually being *taught how to do it*, in understandable, incremental steps, to produce satisfying results.

I really want to emphasize that the techniques you'll read about in *Presto Sketching* are not unique; they're pretty universal and have been around forever. I don't lay claim to any of them (except some of the visual patterns presented later in the book), and like any language, they will continue to grow and change over the years. I chose the word "Presto" because to me, that's what sketching feels like: it's light, rapid, fun, and just a bit magical.

These techniques have meant so much to me, and I want to spread them from my work out to you, and to those whom you want to help. So, grab a marker, and join me as we sketch our futures together!

Acknowledgments

First, "big ups" to all the art teachers out there. You're not only teaching us how to express ourselves, but how to *see*, and that's so important. Thank you to my own high school art teacher, Donald McLean, for your encouragement (it has helped me more than you'll ever know) and for teaching me that precision matters, in so many ways.

Utmost gratitude goes to my friend and mentor Jeff Patton, not only for introducing me to O'Reilly in the first place, but for his valuable feedback, guidance, and encouragement. Oh, and that document scanner that you gave me over dinner is in regular use. There's no end to your generosity!

Huge thanks and praise go to all the interviewees in this book: Alex, Andrew, Devon, Glenn, Jacqui, John, Justin, and Matt. I've been so inspired by your stories, and I can't wait for others to be inspired by them, too; they are the heart and soul of this book. Cuddles and fist bumps to you all. We did it!

High fives and toasts of appreciation also go to my group of early reviewers: Ash Alluri, Georgie Bottomley, Ross Chaldecott, Mark Elizondo, Valter Fatia, Marti Gold, Dreu Harrison, Narelle Hooper, Alice Howard-Vyse, Ron Lui, Andrew Mackie, Kristi Mansfield, Heather Martinez,

Jay Rogers, Michelle Scott, and Ian Stalvies. Thank you for always believing that this was going to be a thing, especially in those times when I didn't.

Thanks and hugs to the gang at General Assembly in Sydney for letting me teach sketching (and test the techniques that are in this book), and to the fabulous O'Reilly team for your boundless energy, patience, enthusiasm, and brilliant can-do attitude in bringing *Presto Sketching* to life.

And finally, a huge thank you to my own family for their bucketloads of patience listening to me banging on so much about *Presto Sketching*, for their love and support, and for the well-timed words of wisdom.

Part 1

Presto Sketching Preparation

SKETCHING IS BOTH A physical and a mental activity, so consider this first section of *Presto Sketching* your physical and mental warm-up. This section will help set you up for success.

To begin, let's take some time to understand how visual communication works in our world, and how to shore up our confidence for sketching. We'll also take a look at what materials you should get your hands on.

Introduction

Boring meetings. Long, dense business presentations. Foggy strategy. Lame ideas. Confused teams. You're about to kiss all those goodbye, by becoming a *Presto Sketcher*.

Presto Sketching is a clever way of using simple drawing to better explore problems, better explain concepts, and better envision new ideas. I've helped loads of product teams and managers use simple sketching in these ways, and I've been teaching these methods for years. All of them have discovered the sheer unbridled magic that sketching can bring to their work and their lives, and now it's your turn!

In this introduction, I'd like to show you a few things:

- That you're about to discover (or rediscover?) how sketching is the gateway to better thinking

- What you'll get from this book (and what you won't)

- How to use the contents of this book to hone your sketching skills in the best way

Sketching: Your Untapped Superpower

You're probably thinking that this is a book about sketching. And it is. I want to help you be a better sketcher. I want to help you be more confident in bringing what is in your head out onto paper and into the world.

But I also want to show you how sketching is one of your greatest untapped superpowers, not just because sketching looks great, but because the very act and process of sketching makes you smarter. By developing your sketching superpower, you will think more clearly and strategically, you will solve problems better, you will have more ideas, and you will be a better communicator. And in doing that, you'll bring real magic into others' lives by helping them with their thinking, their ideas, and their plans.

But I'm getting ahead of myself. Let's get into why this book is for you, and what Presto Sketching will do for you.

Wait, There's More Than Just Sketching Wireframes?

When I was a kid, I was always fascinated by magicians and how they could quite literally produce a dove or some other thing out of thin air, all in a quick flourish.

Sketching is definitely a kind of magic, too. All forms of visual art can cast a spell on us, drawing us in, challenging us, soothing us, making us reflect, changing our view of the world. A study by the Art Gallery of New South Wales in Australia found that viewing art helped people with dementia deal with anxiety[1] because art kept them in a state of "in the moment pleasure," or what author Mihaly Csikszentmihalyi would call "flow."[2] Art sneaks up on us and helps us tap into our imaginations, which is a funny sensation for most people. There are some works of art I could sit in front of for hours, they have such an effect on me.[3]

---

1   For more on this study, see Stephanie Dalzell's article, "Art alleviates anxiety for people with dementia, new research finds," available at *http://ab.co/2cX99bI?*.

2   See his book *Flow: The Psychology of Optimal Experience* (Harper Perennial Modern Classics).

3   "Pan" (1898) by Australian artist Sydney Long comes to mind. It's a vision of Arcadian bliss, bathed in low twilight. It gives the rugged Australian landscape a more mythical, ethereal character, with the trees appearing to wave and waft in surreal shapes like smoke. I could go on about this painting for ages!

But there's also definitely something magical about seeing something come to life as someone draws it, before your very eyes. And it doesn't matter what the level of drawing ability is: watching someone else draw is a magical experience. That's why *Pictionary* is such an endearing game; it's just so much fun to watch other people draw![4]

This kind of magic happens to work amazingly well in our working lives, when we combine words and sketching (Figure 1-1) in meetings and workshops. The shared experience of turning a jumbled conversation into a crisp sketched image on a whiteboard is nothing short of extraordinary. That's synthesis in action. It's like a wizard reaching into your brain, lifting out a bunch of half-formed ideas, and breathing life into them before your very eyes, all with a flourish of the whiteboard marker and a doff of the pointy hat.

FIGURE 1-1
Words and sketching are better together: There's real magic in listening to what someone describes verbally, and then reflecting that as a clear, compelling sketch.

That's what Presto Sketching is all about: using sketching for clever thinking as well as clever communication; expressing yourself and your ideas to others through light, simple drawing; and helping others think and express themselves in the same way.

---

4   Personally, I love those times playing *Pictionary* when the person drawing renders the clumsiest thing ever, and their partner guesses it straight away, leaving an opponent— who's known to be really good at drawing—utterly dumbfounded!

There is so much more that you can sketch as a designer, product manager, or entrepreneur than just user interface wireframes. Presto Sketching is about letting your hand do more of the talking. It is such an amazing way to conjure a concept, bring something to life in seconds, bring clarity to something that's wordy and vague—all with a super simple drawing!

How This Book Will Power Up Your Product Thinking and Design

If you're reading this right now, I figure you're interested in getting better at sketching to help you think, work, or be creative in *some* way. Hurrah! No matter what you think your drawing ability is, no matter how "visual" you think you are, this book will help you in lots of areas (Figure 1-2), wherever you're at in your sketching journey.

Sketch better

Be more creative

Integrate Visuals into your work

Communicate and persuade better

Solve problems better

Help teams set and achieve goals

FIGURE 1-2
What you'll get from this book: How sketching will improve your product thinking and design.

If you're fairly new to the world of visual thinking and visual communication, *Presto Sketching* will set you up for success. By putting the techniques in this book into practice, you'll be well on your way to seeing these results:

- Greater confidence and enjoyment in sketching and adding your own images to your work

- A greater variety and number of ideas and solutions to problems

- More dynamic and persuasive presentations, reports, and other communications

- Expanding your professional skill set to include visual thinking and visual communication

- More effective and insightful meetings

- Being known as a more creative, innovative person

What You Won't Get from This Book

I should be up-front and say that if you're after a book to help you in the full range of drawing techniques, this *isn't* the book for you. *Presto Sketching* is about showing people your ideas in progress, not showing them beautiful finished pieces of art. It's also about helping people to *see themselves in whatever situation you're sketching*, not just what you think about that particular situation.

So, we *won't* be going into topics like these:

- How to do perspective and fancy orthographic views

- How to do portraits, still-life compositions, landscapes, and so on

- How to become famous as an artist

That said, if you're a student of creative and aesthetic practice, I'm sure you'll find some gems here to take into your own artistic journey. I've been teaching techniques like these for years; every class contains a range of abilities and levels of confidence, and everyone always extracts something rewarding and useful from them.

Using This Book

This book has three major sections. The first section (Chapters 2 to 4) will help you understand the place that visual communication has in your work and how to gain confidence in being a producer—not just a consumer—of visual communication.

The second section (Chapters 5 to 9) is chock-full of techniques, tips, and tricks to give you a foundation that you can adapt to your own work. The third section (Chapters 10 to 14) helps you apply these techniques in specific areas of product strategy, management, and design.

Each chapter has some exercises to help you put the lessons and techniques learned into practice. The exercises build on one another and become more difficult, but also more fulfilling and more Instagram-worthy. You'll notice that each one has a difficulty setting. This is also a great way to dip into the book from time to time, depending on where you're at.

Most chapters end with some questions to help you consider your progress and establish where you want to go in your sketching journey. Treat them as mentoring tools, to help you stretch yourself where you want to be stretched. No matter where you are on that journey, I guarantee you that there are ways you can stretch yourself, whether by honing your execution, influencing others, getting out of a rut, or trying new things.

You'll also find some interviews with different people throughout the book. Each person is at a different stage in their journey of visual practice, but their stories are all fascinating, as are the individuals behind them. I've been greatly inspired by them, and I hope you are, too.

And if all the techniques, exercises, questions, and interviews (Figure 1-3) aren't enough, there are also some libraries of different images to help you along, such as icons, visual metaphors, and conceptual illustration patterns.

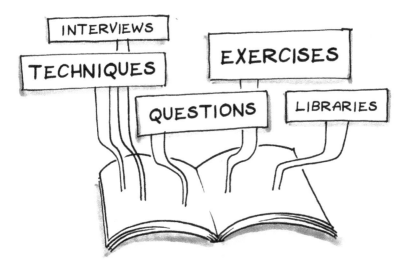

FIGURE 1-3
What's in this book: You can dip into any part of *Presto Sketching* to pick up tips on technique, exercises, questions, interviews, and libraries of various types of sketches.

Enjoy the Ride

Presto Sketching is going to take you on a journey into your own thinking and creativity as well as into a larger world of visual thinking and visual communication. I've enjoyed this ride immensely in my own life and seen so much benefit from it; I hope that it helps you and expands your world, too.

I'm often reminded of the notion that you don't need to change the world, you just need to change the world for the person in front of you, and that's okay. Perhaps sketching can help you change how you see a problem, think up solutions, communicate your ideas, and reimagine your world. If you do that, you can in turn help that person in front of you, that team meeting, that room of people to see a problem, think up solutions, communicate their ideas, and reimagine their world.

Let's go.

EXERCISES

EASY **Exercise 1-1: Warm-up process sketch**

Take three minutes and draw how you make a pizza. Hang on to your sketch because later on in the book I'm going to ask you to draw this again. It's going to be fun to see how you've grown in confidence and ability.

EASY **Exercise 1-2: Get someone to share your journey**

As you might have picked up on by now, I'm really into helping others help themselves get better at sketching. As anyone knows who has tried to succeed at a diet or exercising, it's worthwhile doing it with a friend. It will be more fun, and you'll be more motivated. So, go ahead and find someone with whom you can read *Presto Sketching* and do the exercises.

SOME QUESTIONS FOR YOU

What are your goals?

What would you actually like to achieve, when it comes to sketching? What would you personally like to get out of reading this book? Write down three goals you have, and keep them together with your afore-mentioned first sketch of how to make a pizza.

You might not have any specific goals at this point, and that's fine. Here are some examples that might help:

- To increase my drawing ability, beyond just being able to draw a random box and stick figure
- To boost my confidence in sketching in front of others
- To use whiteboard drawing more in my meetings at work

Interview with Alex Riegelman

Alex Riegelman started as an industrial designer and is now a lead designer at Atlassian, where he applies conceptual modeling to solving complex problems. We all might not have Alex's industrial design drawing chops, but anyone can take on his approach to using sketching as a way to sell ideas.

AR: The thing that I really enjoy about design is thinking about big complex systems with lots of moving parts; that's what gets me out of bed in the morning. I take a perverse satisfaction in trying to hold in my mind how all those parts fit together. It's one of my strengths as a designer. Visual design? Not so much.

The work that I've been doing for the last year is not about the details of interfaces or buttons or pages, but how we can change the whole conceptual model, to improve the software. I need the buy-in of 20 or so stakeholders who know what they have and who are skeptical of change, and I have to convince them somehow to devote time and resources to make this change.

I find sketching really valuable for communicating that kind of complex idea. Simplifying all those parts and connections I hold in my head to provide a shortcut for people like those stakeholders, who don't have the same desire, capacity, or time.

You can always draw boxes and arrows, but when things get to a certain scale and complexity, boxes and arrows lose their ability communicate; it just looks like a giant lot of spaghetti. It can also be tempting to show lots of wireframes, but it's still asking the audience to hold too much in their head. You need some level of synthesis or abstraction on top of a strictly representative diagram, and you need to use sketching to convey emotion. Start with, "Here's how it *feels*." I've been having more and more success with that.

If I were to draw a diagram of a system before and after a proposed change, and the second drawing has 20 percent fewer boxes and arrows, everyone will shrug and say "Yeah, that one has 20 percent fewer boxes..." but they won't emotionally connect with it.

It's important to match the medium to the audience. Sometimes a sketch in a sketchbook is enough. I can bring it out from time to time in conversation and use it to say, "If we do that, this is the emotion that customers will have," or "This is a possible future that we may end up with." That works if it's a small group of people. But if it's going really broadly, I'll polish it in Illustrator. If it's just a hand-drawn sketchy thing, it'll only suit people who are *in* the problem, and who communicate that way, too, because they accept that the sketch—and the *thinking*—doesn't feel finished. But if I polish it, it conveys a level of confidence. People are more willing to accept that this person (or group) has done the work to understand and solve the problem, because what they're viewing has the appearance of being complete, just like the *thinking behind it* is complete.

I like to use a lot of visual metaphor in my work, especially ones that are grounded in a three-dimensional space. This is probably because of my education as an industrial designer. I'm all about the physical world. It's a universal reference, everybody lives in the physical world, so everyone can relate. If I want to convey a huge challenge, I sketch a cliff. But it's a cliff that is in three-dimensional space; you can't get over it (Figure 1-4). It's somehow more resonant than just showing two-dimensional icons or objects floating around in space.

FIGURE 1-4
Alex on adding impact with visual metaphor and 3D space: "I like to use a lot of visual metaphor in my work, especially visuals that are grounded in a three-dimensional space."

Even if sketching is not something that you enjoy doing, there are people who learn best through this kind of communication. Even if it's not your forté, it can be a really powerful way to communicate with others. And if you can combine visual communication and writing into an activity, that's even better!

> Start with, "Here's how it *feels*." I've been having more and more success with that.

Winning in the New Visual Age

ONCE UPON A TIME, visual languages ruled the world, from the haunting animal paintings on cave walls in Lascaux, France, to the hieroglyphics of the Egyptians and Mayans. These days, it looks like we've come full circle, with images once again all around us and the new visual languages of infographics and emojis filling our screens.

We're in the middle of a new visual age, and images of all kinds are competing for our limited attention. We now owe it to ourselves, our ideas, and those we communicate with to not just be consumers of images, but producers as well.

In this chapter, I want to show you why this is so important, and why sketching is everybody's job.

Words Fail

Imagine for a moment that the only means we had to express ourselves was with words. Spoken and written words, as depicted in Figure 2-1. There would be no paintings, drawings, or visual art of any kind. There'd be no music, no infographics, and no mime artists.[1] There'd be no maps, and thus weather reporters wouldn't have much for us to look at while we listened to them rattle off tide times, barometric pressures, and whatnot. And I hate to say this, but business presentations would be even longer and even more boring, with no charts or stock photos of any kind.

FIGURE 2-1

She's missing the mysterious smile: Imagine if we could express ourselves only with words...

---

1 Not a great loss, I guess, but they do have some olde worlde sad-comic appeal, don't they? Seriously, apologies to the greats, like Marcel Marceau and Harpo Marx.

My point? Of course, we need words, but by themselves they're just not enough. Sometimes, there are things that need communicating—like with maps and charts—that words alone simply can't capture.

But words are easy. Talk is cheap, as they say, and we're churning out (and being inundated by) unprecedented volumes of it. A 2011 study showed that we were already consuming five times the amount of information then as we did in 1986.[2] Americans were exposed to waves of roughly 34 gigabytes of information a day (*not* including information at work), which is roughly 100,000 words, or the length of an average novel.[3] With the amount of posts, tweets, ads, emails, instant messages, and so on that hit us daily these days, those waves are growing bigger and bigger.

"So what?" you might say. We can all choose to be more judicious in our daily information diet. But no matter how many of those "37 Gruesome Celebrity Plastic Surgery Nightmare Photos That Will Make Your Jaw Drop"[4] listicles you stay away from, there are two huge consequences of this word glut that are holding us all back: it's making us dumber, and it's suffocating our communication.

The Tsunami of Words Is Making Us Dumber

I'm not resorting to hyperbole here. Daniel J Levitin, author of *The Organized Mind: Thinking Straight in the Age of Information Overload*, puts the impact of all this information on us best:

> Every status update you read on Facebook, every tweet or text message you get from a friend, is competing for resources in your brain with important things like whether to put your savings in stocks or bonds, where you left your passport, or how best to reconcile with a close friend you just had an argument with.

---

2 See Richard Alleyne's article, "Welcome to the Information Age – 174 Newspapers a Day," available at *http://bit.ly/1Eh9Ra9*.

3 These figures come from *The Organized Mind: Thinking Straight in the Age of Information Overload* by Daniel J. Levitin (Dutton). *To Kill a Mockingbird*, one of my favorite books of all time, has 99,121 words.

4 No, come back! Please don't go Googling that.

Our brains have limited bandwidth, and when we fill it with everything from instant messaging to Medium posts to podcasts, we're filling that bandwidth with a swath of tiny trivial decisions our brains must make and crowding out the more significant decisions that need to be made, as illustrated in Figure 2-2. We can't get our heads around the things that matter, like better parenting, counseling friends, and critically assessing biased media reports, because we're too busy exhausting our brains with things like what someone we don't know had for lunch yesterday. We are making ourselves dumber.

FIGURE 2-2
You're taking in too much information! Your finite resource of attention is being hammered by an infinite amount of information and stimulation.

Software Is Killing Our Communication

All of the software we use, not to mention a huge array of social media, collaboration and publishing platforms, makes it easier and easier to spout out as much text as we like. We're even at the point where robots are writing the news we read, instead of humans.[5]

---

5 *Wordsmith* is an artificial writer developed by a company called Automated Insights. It is used by many news producers, including the Associated Press and Yahoo!. In 2015 it produced more than 1.5 billion pieces of content, up from 300 million in 2013. Yep, let that sink in. Are you sure your news isn't written by a robot?

It's all too easy to share another post on Facebook, send another instant message, and add another 10 slides to that PowerPoint presentation. It's all too easy for the Internet of Things to generate more and more tera-bytes of big data. On top of all this, software actually makes it easier for *other* software to add more features, which is partly why every app these days has its own messaging feature. All this content and conversational traffic is clogging, not helping, communication.

We Need Synthesis

Now, don't get me wrong: I'm not hating on words and software. I read books, and, yes, there certainly are words in this book. I like an engag-ing TED talk as much as the next person; listening to a great speaker can be absolutely enthralling, and verbal storytelling is a kind of magic, too. And I couldn't do my work without software. But words and soft-ware are not enough.

With this ever-increasing avalanche of words hitting us, and with the same finite amount of attention that we all have, the last thing we need is easier ways to spout more words. We need *synthesis*.

But what is synthesis? Synthesis is about reflecting on information and data, classifying and grouping it, finding patterns and trends, distilling large volumes of guff into succinct meaningful insights and conclu-sions, and deepening understanding (Figure 2-3).

FIGURE 2-3

Be wise and synthesize: We need to develop our superpower of synthesis to deal with content overload and brain fatigue.

Synthesis is what happens when you "read between the lines" of some-thing. Synthesis is what happens when you connect concepts together in your mind, and come up with an "a-HA!" moment. Synthesis is what happens when someone in a meeting comes out with a pithy insight that clarifies everything for everyone in the room, after listening to the conversation.

And synthesis feels pretty good! Brandy Agerbeck, in her book *The Graphic Facilitator's Guide* (Loosetooth.com Library), puts it really well:

> Synthesis is about combining pieces from different sources and making something whole—and new—from them. This whole allows you to see the original sources from a different perspective and make new meaning.

That different perspective gives us so many advantages when it comes to exploring, explaining, and envisioning. It helps us to bust long-held assumptions, it helps us to communicate much more clearly and compellingly to audiences who have shorter and shorter attention spans, and it help us to direct people on how to take action.

We need more synthesis. And we need to see that we're not just authors and readers, but synthesizers, too.

But synthesis is difficult. And I don't mean just baking a good soufflé difficult:[6] I mean marathon running difficult. Synthesis has to come from your own reflection, thinking, and connection making. No amount of "gramming"[7] and blog post reading and step counting and lakes of big data will do it for us. It's really challenging, but it is a gift we all have that we need to exercise more.

Visuals Stick

It probably comes as no surprise to you that we're much better at processing visual information than any other type of information. We are hardwired to receive and process visual information ridiculously faster

---

6 Seriously, have you tried? I hear that two top tips are to use fresh eggs at room temperature, and to not whip the egg whites into the base mixture. You're welcome.

7 *Gramming* (n.): the act of passively and endlessly scrolling through your Instagram feed on your device. I learned this from my cousin recently, who picked it up from a 19-year-old #ontrend #hip.

than text,[8] and we're hardwired to see patterns in inanimate objects everywhere, whether it's bunny rabbits in your bathroom tiles, or a face in a cheese toastie[9] (Figure 2-4).

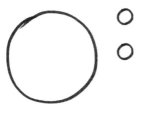 

FIGURE 2-4

Face up to it: Brain studies have repeatedly shown that we're incredibly good at seeing faces in things where faces don't exist. Not only do we instantly recognize three circles and a line (left) as a face (right), but we also can't help trying to work out the mood of the "face" (in this case: unimpressed?).

Cartoonist and visual communication maestro Scott McCloud says it best in his book *Understanding Comics: The Invisible Art* (HarperCollins):

> Pictures are *received* information. We need no formal education to "get the message." The message is instantaneous. Writing is *perceived* information. It takes time and specialized knowledge to decode the abstract symbols of language.

Thankfully, we can enjoy the best of both worlds and combine verbal and visual communication, or words and pictures (Figure 2-5). Visuals supercharge the ideas and thoughts that we're trying to get across, and the receiver of the information gets two inputs instead of one.

---

8 "60,000 times faster" gets bandied about the internet a lot, but with no cited references. So I'm just going to go ahead and say that processing visuals is faster than processing text because you have to actually *learn* written language, which takes more brainpower than processing visuals.

9 A bit of actual science for you: this is called *pareidolia*, a phenomenon by which the mind perceives familiar patterns of something where that thing doesn't actually exist.

FIGURE 2-5
Talking and drawing are better together: If we just talk about an idea to each other (left), it goes from brain to mouth to ear to brain, and a lot can be lost in translation. When visual communication is involved (right), there are two inputs that the receiver can process, leading to clearer communication.

The thing I'm really excited by is that the act of *creating* visuals—the act of sketching—also helps us to synthesize. You'll be very pleased to know that using sketching as a tool to help you think, rather than just as a way of showing a final nicely rendered solution, will make synthesis much easier for you. And let's face it: we have to tackle more and more complex problems these days, and if you keep just using your head you'll just become more and more muddled, which leads to things like stress, forgetfulness, and poor life choices, like watching *The Bachelorette*, buying lottery tickets, and so on, and nobody wants that.

Everything Is Going Visual

Not only are visuals a more economical way of expressing ourselves and retaining information, but they are rapidly becoming the *preferred* conduit for a lot of what we express and retain, in all areas of our lives. As we spray more and more information at one another day after day, and as more and more things compete for our attention, we are opting for visual vocabularies more often—and software is making that easier, too.

A great example of this is emojis. According to research, there are about 2.5 billion smartphone users worldwide,[10] and we are sending over 60 billion messages[11] and well over 5 billion emojis every day.[12] Ev. Err. Ree. Day.

We're also witnessing the rise and rise of infographics and data visualization. What started as humble bar charts and pie charts has matured into an entire world of visual representations to reveal insight and stories from numerical data (Figure 2-6).

FIGURE 2-6

The rise and rise of visual communication: The volume and variety of images we use in generating and receiving communication have grown massively over recent years.

Just as software and apps make it easy to generate text content, it's becoming easier to generate visual content, too. But notice that it doesn't go beyond the basics: worthy but generic emojis and icons, overused clip art, and clichéd, contrived stock photography. At best, this stuff is bland and doesn't truly capture your idea the way you really want it to. At worst, it's cringeworthy and will distract people from the idea that you're actually trying to communicate.

---

10 See the 2016 eMarketer report "Worldwide Internet and Mobile Users: eMarketer's Updated Estimates and Forecast for 2015–2020," available at *http://bit.ly/2wWoctn*.

11 From the Pew Research Center—U.S. Smartphone Use in 2015: *http://www.pewinternet. org/2015/04/01/us-smartphone-use-in-2015/*.

12 That's just Facebook alone. Facebook released figures to coincide with World Emoji Day (July 17, 2017), showing an average of 5 billion emojis sent each day on Facebook Messenger. That's on top of a mere 60 million emojis sent on Facebook.

Bottom line? We are replacing more and more words with pictures, and consuming visually more than ever before, and this trend will only continue to grow stronger. Advertisers know it, teachers know it, and the best public speakers and communicators know it. Here's what the academics are saying:

> We have noticed a decrease in the amount of anchoring copy used in visual metaphor ads...We theorize that, over time, advertisers have perceived that consumers are growing more competent in understanding and interpreting visual metaphor in ads.[13]

It's Time to Be a Visual Producer, Not Just a Consumer

Now I'm sure you're nodding sagely. Yes, visual communication is more important than ever before. But consuming, exchanging, and being surrounded by visual information is not the same thing as being visually literate.[14] Visual literacy means *creating* visuals, too (Figure 2-7). Martin Eppler, a Swiss researcher at the University of St. Gallen, even claims that this visual literacy is crucial for modern management today. And I'm with Martin on that—*big time*.

FIGURE 2-7

Be a producer, not just a consumer: Creating your own visuals with sketching means that you're not just a consumer of others' content and ideas, but a producer of content and ideas, too.

---

13 Barbara J. Phillips, "Understanding Visual Metaphor in Advertising," in *Persuasive Imagery*, ed L. M. Scott and R. Batra (Erlbaum).

14 See Eva Brumberger's article, "Visual Literacy and the Digital Native: An Examination of the Millennial Learner" (*Journal of Visual Literacy.* 30(1):19–46).

The message is clear: there's an amazing Visual Thinking Train that has pulled up at your stop, and it's time to get on board. Why wait for others to broadcast their ideas more powerfully than yours? And why let your own thinking be formed by everyone else's visuals, when you could (and should!) be that agent of change for others?

The good news is you don't need a marketing degree or a master's degree in communications to get started. You don't need sophisticated software and an army of designers. All you need is a pen and paper, and the will to make your mark.

And it's this will—this way of thinking and mark making—that we'll turn to in Chapter 3.

EXERCISES

EASY **Exercise 2-1: Your information 'input' map**
Write your name in the middle of a sheet of paper and then draw a circle around it. This is you. Now, think of all the different content/information sources you take in every day—at home, at work, at school, in transit, wherever—and write each one around the edge of the paper. Draw a circle around each one. Next, draw an arrow from each one to you in the middle.

There's probably a fair bit going on! Take a look at this information input map, and think about whether there are some sources that you want to dial down. Or maybe there are others that you want to increase in some way. And are there any content/information sources that you want to have, but are missing?

EASY **Exercise 2-2: Your turn with the pen**
As we've seen, visual literacy means creating visual content, not just consuming it. Take another look at your information input map. What's one thing you would like to generate, in response to all the content and information you take in, that you haven't before?

SOME QUESTIONS FOR YOU

What's your information diet like?

Remember that old "food pyramid" picture about the proportions of different foods we should have in our diet? Imagine that was types of information, as presented in Figure 2-8. What is the largest "layer" of information you take in? And the next? What's at the very top (i.e., the smallest amount)?[15]

FIGURE 2-8

What's your information diet? A completely fictional but representative "information diet" pyramid.

---

15 Honest, this is totally not a representation of my own information diet at all. Okay, yes, I might sneak in an episode or two of *Black Mirror*, and I never asked for all those vague motivational quotes to appear on my Facebook feed. Who's actually making those, anyway?

What could you drop to make time to sketch?

The truth is, there's probably some activity we can all drop—or do less of—to free up some time to sketch. What specific information-consumption actions could you drop?[16]

Interview with Glenn Stephenson

As a scribe for hire, Glenn wields his markers with skill and devotes himself to his craft. Here he shares how to go from good to great in the visual communication discipline.

GS: I've been a full-time visual practitioner for the past three years, and similar to others in this industry, I found my path here through a suggestion from a friend.

I needed new challenges in my life after a long career in the hospitality industry, so I returned to university, where I studied and graduated from RMIT University's [Melbourne, Australia] Industrial Design Program. Through this program I made a good friend who had previously experienced graphic facilitation. She suggested this sort of work could be a good fit for me due to my visual skills in drawing and prototyping. I had a short introductory stint with Capgemini, and shortly thereafter connected with PwC's "The Difference." The rest, as they say, is history where we maintain a great professional relationship today.

Visual thinking and visual communication for me is about enabling clients to find clarity and purpose in situations often lacking this necessary clarity and/or are emotionally driven. I liken it to helping to guide a team along their clearest path forward. Through the visual medium, we allow conversation to evolve, eliciting group understanding of not only accomplishments, but highlighting and allowing focus on any challenges ahead (seen to great effect in Figure 2-9).

There are two big challenges for me in visual thinking and visual communication. The first is the need to hear a group conversation or presentation well. As Graphic Recorders, we need to not only hear the

---

16 Here's one thing that works well for me: instead of saving stuff to Pinterest or taking a screenshot of a web page I like and saving it to a folder on my computer, I copy it in my sketchbook. I refer back to my sketchbooks a lot more than some folder buried on my computer. Plus, the physical act of sketching a copy makes me go through at least some of the little design decisions that the original artist or designer went through.

presenter, but also any questions or statements from the audience or group that further add layers of richness to the conversation. I want the best result for my client, and ensuring that I am firm with my positioning in the room is critical.

The second challenge is recording the content in a way that is useful for the client and in a language they will understand.

I find that in the heat of the moment, it is easy to get carried away with a graphic simply because it may look great, however holistically this graphic may not actually assist comprehension of the capture after the fact. Representing the spoken content using a client's common language and acronyms will ensure the artifact lives to have a purpose outside of merely 'wowing' an audience with your ability to draw.

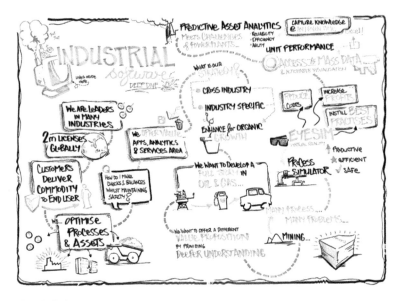

FIGURE 2-9

Glenn on finding clarity and purpose: Visual thinking and communication is "like helping to guide a team along the clearest path forward, through what is often wild terrain dotted with border crossings, steep ravines, and marshlands."

It's really important to always be thinking about how to improve what you do. One way is to find great people to team up with and learn from. I had the opportunity to work alongside Kate Baxter, a great practitioner within this field, and we got talking together about what we both felt was integral to producing great work in environments that are often demanding, both physically and mentally.

Not only must we remember to work in a way that does ourselves justice, realizing our skills are valuable and useful, but we must save time for "magic." Passively churning out work does no one any favors; you have to give yourself space to develop yourself outside of time with clients. You have to make time to improve your own skills, try new things, and explore other methods to then bring into your own practice. This is something I value highly!

Connecting and teaming up with other visual practitioners allows for developmental conversations to grow. We continually refine our practice and embrace the opportunity to bounce ideas and techniques off each other. The buzz of working with a great team over the course of an intense four or five days is unbeatable!

> We must save time for "magic"...Give yourself space to develop yourself outside of time with clients.

[3]

Building Your Confidence

OKAY, SO NOW YOU know that sketching is not someone else's job, it's your job, too. At this point, you might be raring to go, marker in hand, singing "Climb Every Mountain." Go you! Or, if you're like most people, you're somewhere further down the confidence scale, wondering how to begin, or frustrated that you're not able to sketch to the standard you want.

Help is here! We need to pull this confidence thing apart first, to become more self-assured. This chapter will help to connect you back to when you drew like you didn't care what others thought about you. It will help you to understand the way you think when you sketch so that you can tackle that process of getting what's in your head out onto paper and into the world.

We'll also look at ways in which you can prevent your body and your mind—that inner critic—from betraying you and holding you back. And then you'll be singing "Climb Every Mountain," just like those sketching show-offs.

Rightio! Let's awaken the Picasso within.

Rediscover Your Pony

I like asking people what they used to draw when they were young. What's always interesting is not only the things that they used to draw, but the *way* people talk to me about it. You can probably imagine the vast spectrum of responses: everything from blank stares, polite smiles, and slowly backing away to a half hour of nostalgic enthusiasm.[1]

I actually ran a highly informal, unscientific survey asking people what they used to draw as kids, and then I drew the results, which you can see in Figure 3-1. I wonder if you see anything in here that you used to draw?

FIGURE 3-1

What did we draw as kids? This is a sketch I did showing the main things that people used to draw as kids, according to my highly unscientific survey.

There is this one friend of mine who confessed that she used to draw ponies as a little girl. She loved horses (and still does), so she used to try drawing them. The thing is, they came out looking chubby and short, like ponies, but she was still happy with them looking that way, so she

---

1 Alright, if you must know, I drew a ton of those little flipbook animations in the corners of my textbooks. They were usually little figures getting cut in half, blowing up, and so on. Like a lot of kids, I went through a superhero drawing phase and a skull drawing phase, too. Awesome fun!

just stuck to drawing ponies. She'd adorn her pencil case and school-books with them, and she'd dress them up with massive manes and tails sometimes.

When she told me this story, she hurriedly told me that she didn't do it for long, as if she were a bit ashamed, and that she doesn't draw at all, now. But there was another look that lit up her face when she shared that story.

It was enjoyment. Unbridled, zealous, in-the-zone, dancing-like-no-one's-watching enjoyment.

I wonder if you have a similar story. My hope for that friend of mine—and for you also—is that *Presto Sketching* will connect you again with what it was like to draw for your own pure enjoyment. I hope you can rediscover whatever your equivalent was of the pony, and sketch again like you don't care what others think.

Sketching Lets You Be the Creator You Used to Be

I hope Chapter 2 got you to see how important it is to switch from just being a consumer of the tsunami of content around us to being an active agent in the ideas economy by producing content yourself, too.

The thing is, you used to do all your own visuals. If you're like most people who have access to this book, making marks came really easy to you when you were young. But by the time you started high school, the world around you made it clear that if you weren't into art or design, you should put the pencils away and focus on words instead (Figure 3-2).

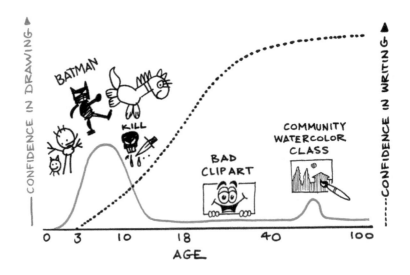

FIGURE 3-2

Confidence in drawing versus writing: Here's a rough chart of confidence and competence in writing (black) as opposed to drawing (blue) over time, for most people. Whereabouts are you on this chart? (Adapted from Sunni Brown, *The Doodle Revolution* [Portfolio].)

And by the time you hit the workforce or university, the world around you told you that the very act of picking up a pencil to draw was *risky*.[2] If you weren't on your way to being a successful artist, designer, or architect, anything to do with drawing was for your personal pleasure only. A hobby. Not for real work. You drew at your own risk and on your own dime.

Awful, isn't it? What that did to you, and to countless others, was to embed two unspoken assumptions in you. The first assumption was that anything visual was for *aesthetics only*; it belonged in art class, as opposed to all the other school subjects that were about mental rigor and knowledge. At least English gave us some room for creativity, but the idea of visuals helping with critical thinking? Forget it.

---

2   Interestingly, drawing and asking questions drop off at about the same time in life. According to Warren Berger (author of a favorite book of mine, *A More Beautiful Question* [Bloomsbury]), children start out asking hundreds of questions a day, but then questioning "falls off a cliff" as kids enter school. So much of our education and business culture rewards rote answers over challenging inquiry. I'm convinced that drawing and asking questions are tightly related, but that's something for another book.

The second unspoken assumption was that whenever it *was* time to do something visual, you could just reach for someone else's visuals, or something that your computer could give you, because you thought you didn't have the ability and speed to do it yourself. You thought you weren't qualified.

Well, you do, and you are. No matter who you are or what you do for a living—even if you *are* an artist, designer, or architect—you should reach for the pen to express yourself as often as you reach for the keyboard. We don't need perfection, but we definitely need your ideas and plans.

Let's bust those two assumptions, and take a look at how sketching is in fact a powerful thinking device that will actually make you smarter. By smarter, I mean able to better explore problems, better recall knowledge, better generate ideas, and better communicate. Being smarter also means being able to synthesize better—that skill we touched on in Chapter 2, about being better able to distill essence and insight.

Sketching Is an Extension of Your Mind

I want you to realize that sketching is a way of *thinking*, as well as a way of communicating. Just like anything you do repeatedly builds up "muscle memory" in your hands, so too it is with sketching. And the more you put the inner critic back in its playpen, the more you will free up your hand to be something like a second brain and think for itself.

You will find great value in externalizing your thoughts and ideas as sketches, just meant for yourself and nobody else. Making the intangible tangible is one of the most powerful things about sketching.

Graphic facilitator extraordinaire Brandy Agerbeck talks about this tangibility in her book *The Idea Shapers: The Power of Putting Your Thinking in Your Own Hands* (CreateSpace Independent Publishing Platform):

> Once you place your internal thoughts and feelings into a drawing, you've made them tangible and visible, and you can see them from a new perspective. This tangibility gives you distance and separation from the problem you are trying to solve.

I'm going to go one step further and say that this action of making the invisible visible is a crucial step in the *cycle of synthesis* (Figure 3-3). By the cycle of synthesis, I mean making your invisible thoughts visible, looking at them, letting the picture enrich your understanding of whatever it is you're thinking about, thinking about it again in a clearer way, and repeating. This is much more powerful than simply keeping all those thoughts in your head. It's like your brain is having a fabulous conversation with your hand at the Coolest Ideas Party in Town, rather than sitting by itself in the corner.

FIGURE 3-3
The cycle of synthesis: When we keep all our thoughts, problems and ideas in our heads, they remain invisible, hidden, and untested. When we make them visible by sketching, our eyes can see them, and we can think more clearly.

A QUICK EXAMPLE

Let's try a quick example. Grab a marker and a piece of paper and take a few minutes (not too long!) to sketch *how you make a cup of tea*, from start to finish. It's worth it. Go on, I'll wait—in fact, I'm going to go make myself a cup of tea.

Finished? I've done this quick exercise with loads of classes, and based on this, I'm pretty sure you've drawn something that looks a bit like a flowchart, with a combination of a cup, a tea bag, a kettle, and some boiling water, all linked in sequence with a set of numbers or arrows. Yours might look a bit like mine (Figure 3-4).

FIGURE 3-4

My take on a sketch about how to make tea: Note that there are some recurring elements (e.g., the cup), and each set of elements is linked with arrows, conveying a sequence.

Let's take a look at what happened in your mind when you did that exercise. This is important because it will help you to understand how you can harness sketching to make you smarter.

First, you considered whether you understood the task—sketching how you make a cup of tea—in the first place (Figure 3-5). Then, you reached into your memory banks and you imagined a cup of tea, according to your experience. Some people really do "see" a cup of tea in the mind's eye, if they're particularly visual thinkers, whereas others just have a clear concept of "cup of tea" in their minds. Let's call this first phase *Understanding*.

FIGURE 3-5
Understanding: The first thing your brain does when it receives input is to check that it understands what it needs to do, and then it imagines the result for which it's aiming.

Next, your clever brain asked itself a bunch of questions about how to solve the problem of *making* the cup of tea. You had to pull the first concept apart into pieces (water, kettle, cup, and so on), you had to think about the process (boil the kettle, *then* add the hot water to the cup), and maybe you had to think about what you *wouldn't* include in the process (putting the tea bag in the trash). In other words, you had to pull apart, sort, and perhaps prioritize what to include. Let's call this second phase *Synthesizing* (Figure 3-6).

FIGURE 3-6
Synthesizing: The questions your brain asks as it analyzes the task, breaks it down, and distills it into steps.

And while that was going on, something else truly extraordinary happened. Something that occupies countless scientists, neurophysicists, psychiatrists, psychologists, and philosophers.[3] Your clever brain asked itself: "How will I communicate this as a picture?" This is where the brain flips into the *Translating* phase (Figure 3-7).

FIGURE 3-7
Translating: The point where the brain flips from Synthesizing and uses recall and imagination to convert its answer into something it can communicate, in words, pictures, or any way at all.

You used your memory and imagination again to recall what visual patterns and conventions you know about, to convert the synthesized view of a cup of tea into something that you could draw. And then you made a series of decisions to convert all that cached information into electrical signals to (I'm assuming) your hand and rendered that sequence as a picture.

And I think that is nothing short of magic.

In essence, you used your powers of *understanding, synthesizing, and translating*—or UST—and then fine motor skills to turn the initial problem into a sketch. Brilliant! What is truly fascinating is that you use roughly the same cycle of thinking—this UST model of thinking (Figure 3-8)—for just about any problem, task, or conversation you experience.

---

3 And—ahem—people who are really into learning how sketching can make us smarter.

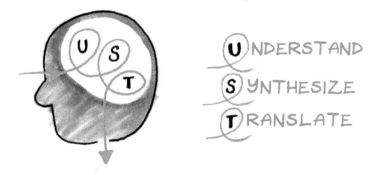

FIGURE 3-8

The UST model: The UST model is a simple way to understand how we think when we're given a task, problem, or conversation to which to respond.

This model is based on a framework called Bloom's Taxonomy,[4] as well as my own observations about how people process questions, tackle problems and creative challenges, and communicate their ideas. Bloom's Taxonomy is popular among teachers, and gives them a structure to organize questions and activities to foster deeper learning and application in students rather than just superficial rote learning.

It's important to note that the three loops of understanding, synthesizing, and translating aren't strictly linear and sequential; the thinking process can cycle around in one of those loops for a while before moving on, or double back on itself.

Using the UST Model to Improve Your Confidence

"So what, Ben?" you might be thinking. "What's so great about three loops in a head?"

This is useful because it helps you focus on where—what part of your own thinking and sketching—you want to develop your confidence and capabilities. You might be like most people, for whom it feels easy to

---

4 *Bloom's Taxonomy of Educational Objectives in the Cognitive Domain* was developed by Benjamin Bloom and others in 1956. It has since been refined and updated according to new research. You can find out more in Lorin Anderson et al's *A Taxonomy for Learning, Teaching and Assessing: A Revision of Bloom's Taxonomy of Educational Objectives* (Longman). Others rightly debate that even the revised taxonomy is a bit simplistic and tricky to apply; a good resource for this is *Making Thinking Visible* by Ron Ritchhart, Mark Church, and Karin Morrison (Jossey Bass).

go through the Understanding loop but who barely fire any neurons in Synthesizing (shown as a reduced middle loop in Figure 3-9), before leaping to the Translating loop to get your words and actions out.

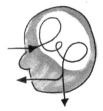 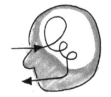 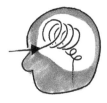

FIGURE 3-9

Applying the UST model: Here are some variations in how people think, according to the UST model. Left: not much synthesis and jumping to conclusions. Middle: not much synthesis and not much translation, ending up on the easy path to just talking more. Right: always consuming and turning things over in the mind, and never generating anything as a result.

You might see this happening around you, where people leap to conclusions, or leap to solving a problem with a quick and easy solution rather than taking the time to analyze the problem more fully. If that's the case, you might want to think about how to use sketching to develop your Synthesizing loop a bit more, or how you might use sketching to help others to develop theirs.

Of course, there is an absolute wealth of neuroscience and psychology that I've skipped over in this model, but this point about developing the skill of synthesis is too important *not* to show as a synthesized model!

GETTING MORE CONFIDENT IN TRANSLATING

Alternatively, maybe it's not so much the Synthesizing part you're hung up on, but the *Translating* part. In fact, I suspect that this is where the root of the confidence problem lies for most people: being able to convert that mental image into something you're happy with on paper (Figure 3-10).

FIGURE 3-10
Lost in translation: Has this happened to you? You can "see" what you want to express in your head, but can't move it from your head to your hand? Learning visual languages will help you build the confidence and capability to translate that picture.

Translating mental pictures into physical pictures is just like any other act of translation: we need to be more familiar with *what type of mental picture it is* and then be more familiar with *what visual language to use to translate it.*

It often helps me to think about translating thoughts into physical pictures in terms of four types (Figure 3-11):

Literal representation
  Pictures that are meant to look like objects, actions, and situations that exist in the real world

Metaphorical representation
  Pictures that explain a particular concept by using one or more other real-world concepts

Diagrammatic representation
  Pictures that explain something by showing it in a way that doesn't actually exist in the real world

Conceptual representation
  Pictures that explain abstract concepts

Let's look at each of these in more detail. This will help you think about what it is exactly that you want to get more confident in sketching, and which parts of this book will help you more.

 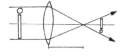

FIGURE 3-11

The visual communication spectrum: From left to right: literal representation, metaphorical representation, diagrammatic representation, and conceptual representation.

LITERAL REPRESENTATION

Literal representation is what most of us think about when we think about sketching: being able to sketch a picture of a real thing more confidently.

This is where you see literal representation in product and service design and strategy:

- Storyboards

- Icons

- Wireframes

- Low-fidelity and high-fidelity prototypes

Most of the techniques I'll show you in this book will help you with literal representation.

METAPHORICAL REPRESENTATION

We speak in metaphors and similes all the time. Both are about using a familiar thing to explain an unfamiliar thing. A simple example of a metaphor is using a picture of a light bulb to represent "idea" ("A light bulb went on over my head"). Similes use words like "as" and "like" to make the comparison a bit more explicit ("Life is like a box of chocolates").[5]

---

5 I'm going to come out and say that I have never understood the whole "life is like a box of chocolates" thing. Whenever you get a box of chocolates, it *always* tells you what's inside each of the chocolates, so there's no mystery at all. Who's with me?

This is where you see metaphorical representation in product and service design and strategy:

- Illustrating research insights and recommendations

- Customer journey maps

- Icons

Make sure you dig into Chapter 7, which is all about visual metaphor and contains a library of 101 visual metaphors for you to use.

DIAGRAMMATIC REPRESENTATION

Diagrammatic representation is great for explaining how things work or how to do something. Examples include cutaway diagrams of complex machinery, or the step-by-step pictures you see in product instructions.[6]

This is where you see diagrammatic representation in product and service design and strategy:

- Product installation, maintenance, and repair instructions

- Product cutaway diagrams

- Weather maps and geographic maps

- 3D building floor plans and street projections

These sorts of pictures are indispensable for explaining things because they usually show us the object or concept from a perspective that we would never otherwise have. Consider how maps help us understand where we are and how to get somewhere, or those molecule and lens refraction diagrams from school that helped us understand our world at a scale beyond what our eyes can show us.

---

6   I know it's cool to have a dig at IKEA furniture and how difficult it is to put together, but how cute is that little IKEA cartoon character? And the way those instructions are designed to work *with no words at all* is pretty clever.

CONCEPTUAL REPRESENTATION

Conceptual representation is all about illustrating abstract concepts like processes, changes in things over time, or relationships and comparisons between intangible entities. You're more familiar with conceptual illustration than you think: examples include weather maps, charts, and process diagrams.

This is where you see conceptual representation in product and service design and strategy:

- Customer journey maps
- Boxes-and-arrows process diagrams
- The Lean mindset cycle diagram of "build, measure, learn"
- System architecture diagrams and site maps

Learning a new language typically means learning a new set of words and sounds, and a grammar of rules to put those words together for meaningful communication. Learning visual languages is the same: you can learn how to draw simple objects and elements ("words")—like people, cars, and arrows—but you also need to learn the grammar of putting those elements together.

If you can understand and apply *visual grammar*, you can translate the concept that is in your head visually much more easily and confidently.

And don't worry. When I say "grammar," I'm not about to throw the visual equivalent of complex verb conjugation tables at you; it will be much easier and more fun than that. Think of visual grammar as a set of simple patterns and objects that your brain and hand can share when they're having those fabulous conversations at the Coolest Ideas Party in Town. The more they speak together (i.e., the more you practice), the better the conversation flows.

And guess what? Visual grammar has nothing to do with drawing ability. So you'll have that over all those drawing show-offs.

I hope some little fireworks are going off in your head now, learning that sketching is an extension of your brain, your thinking, your cleverness. But it gets better still: sketching is also an extension of your voice and your character.

Sketching Is an Extension of Your Voice

I was at a design conference once where two people were showcasing a particular project and the lessons they'd learned. One of them spoke with an affable ease, but the other person was a tightly knotted bundle of nerves. Every breath was small and rapid, and each word couldn't race out of her mouth fast enough. Everything about her manner and body language just screamed silently, "I am freaking out right now!" It was so palpable it affected the entire room. Everyone was on her side, though, and we all just wanted her to RELAX.

You might have had a similar experience seeing someone like that. Or maybe that was you up there. Don't get me wrong, I take my hat off to anyone who gets up and speaks in front of a room full of people, but our bodies can betray us, and we can get in the way of our own message, can't we?

Sketching is the same. Our bodies can betray us when we sketch in front of people, too. You might have been in a meeting in which someone is scrawling something so fast on a whiteboard that it seems like the building is on fire and the person has to blurt their guts out onto that whiteboard before fleeing down the fire escape. Everyone—including the poor soul who happens to be drawing—looks at the strange glyphs of dry erase ink spread all over the whiteboard in such a chaotic fashion and wonders: what on Earth is it meant to mean?

Slow down.

Just. Slow. Down. If this is you, just take an extra few seconds to draw whatever it is that you're drawing on that whiteboard (Figure 3-12). You see, drawing in front of people is exactly like speaking in front of people. Your hand is an extension of your voice, so speak with your hand the way that the good folks at Toastmasters tell us to. Be measured. Pause for emphasis. And draw with confidence.

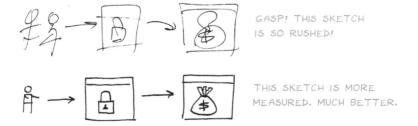

GASP! THIS SKETCH IS SO RUSHED!

THIS SKETCH IS MORE MEASURED. MUCH BETTER.

FIGURE 3-12
Sketching is like public speaking for the hand: Rather than rushing through your sketch on a whiteboard (top), take an extra few seconds when you sketch and be a little more deliberate with each line (bottom). The result will be much better!

When people witness that magic come out of your hand with confidence, they will sit up and take notice of you, and they will take notice of your ideas. And they will remember your ideas far more easily than others' ideas.

Sketching Is an Extension of Your Character

By now I hope you're realizing the power that sketching has in extending yourself. It extends your thinking, it extends your presence, and it also extends your character. By that I mean that your sketching speaks for you when you're not in the room. Every sketch you leave on a whiteboard in a meeting room, every sketch you put up on Instagram, every sketch you put into a business presentation that others will probably copy and include in their presentations is a piece of you that you leave behind.

This is how you scale yourself when you're not around. If that thought is uncomfortable for you, and you don't think your sketches are good enough, ask yourself this: what makes you confident enough to send emails, or to do a PowerPoint presentation? The answer to that question will give you insight into how to build confidence in sketching. There was one day in the past (I'm guessing) where you did your very first PowerPoint presentation. How did you learn? Did you use a copy of someone else's? Did you run it by anyone for feedback? The steps you took then will likely work for you in developing confidence in sketching.

It's true that you can hide behind a lot of stuff that PowerPoint (and other software) already has: slide templates, style templates, and so on. And you can feel pretty naked when it's just you and a pen (Figure 3-13). But there is such a character and authenticity to sketches that can't be ignored! Yours are unique, no matter what level of skill you think you have. So come out from behind that software, and embrace your own sketching style. Sure, as you get better at sketching you'll refine that style, but it will be undoubtedly, authentically you.

FIGURE 3-13
Come out from behind the slide deck: Unlike when using software, it can be pretty revealing when it's just you with a pen in front of others! But it's immediate and authentic, and that's what people respond to the most.

Sketch Your Way to Confidence

Now that we've looked into how to think about sketching, it's time to put it into practice. You can't *think* your way to confidence, in sketching or in any other endeavor; you need to *do* it. You won't become confident first, and then suddenly turn out beautiful, clever sketches.

So here are three things I'm asking you to keep in mind as you do the activities in this book: focus, silence the inner critic, and persevere (Figure 3-14). The more you're aware of these, the more you will gain confidence in sketching.

FOCUS   SILENCE THE   PERSEVERE
                INNER CRITIC

FIGURE 3-14

Focus, silence the inner critic, and persevere: If you keep these three things in mind as you sketch, you'll increase your confidence in no time at all.

Let's begin with *focus*. Whenever you decide to do some sketching, take some time to clear your mind of anything else that is going to get in the way between you and the thing you want to sketch. Put the phone away, close your email client, do whatever it takes to hold the noisy world at bay at least for a little while to give you the mental room to sketch.

Focus is a physical thing as well as a mental thing. Pay attention to the environment you're sketching in, and ensure that there aren't any visual distractions for you. They could be pleasant distractions (it's impossible for me to sketch when there are donuts in range), or unpleasant distractions like a messy desk, too many other people around, or an overly insistent cat wanting attention.

Think about actively *silencing your inner critic*. Realize that everyone around you is perfectly fine with your level of ability.[7] And they're probably on your side and want you to succeed. Our worst critics are ourselves, after all.

Be honest about calling out that critic inside: turn that vague whisper into something more real. Name the fear. Then say, "So what?" So what if you stuff up a drawing? You can do another one. So what if you spent 10 minutes trying to sketch a concept that still doesn't make sense? It takes time and repeated tries. So what if the scrawl you just did on the whiteboard in front of your boss looks like roadkill rather than the

---

7   Except maybe your annoying big brother, if you have one of those. But let's face it, it's his mission in life to undermine everything you do. There are other books around to help you with that issue.

pithy insight you have in your head? I guarantee you that visualizing that insight in any way at all has been a catalyst for richer thinking, *for both you and your boss.*

So, put the inner critic back in its playpen. Ain't nobody got time for that.

Next comes *perseverance.* I'm not going to bore you with lots of sporting analogies and clichés: you know them already. The bottom line is that you're going to need to practice if you expect to become better. Progress is better than perfection.

Might I suggest the time-honored method of setting out small, achievable goals, and then rewarding yourself when you achieve each one? Accept that there are going to be times when your sketches don't look as amazing as you'd like. But it's worth it. My goodness, it's worth it.

If you're mindful of these three things, not only will your sketching improve, but the results will set up a lovely reinforcement loop (remember the cycle of synthesis in Figure 3-3!), and your focus, honesty with yourself, and perseverance will improve, too.

And here's the bonus part: the work you put into your focus, honesty, and perseverance in sketching will pay off in *all areas of your life.*

Let's Get Our Sketch On

So, are you ready to unleash your ideas and plans on the world? Are you ready to sharpen your own thinking and improve your own communication? And are you ready to help others sharpen their thinking and help them communicate?

I thought so. You look ready. In the next part of the book we'll get into what materials you'll want to use, and then how to use them—but first, a few exercises.

EXERCISES

EASY **Exercise 3-1: Fail!**

Grab a pen and paper, and draw the worst chair you possibly can. I mean it. Make it impossible to sit on, and wildly terrible. Now draw the worst cat you possibly can. No one is ever going to rescue *that* cat from the animal shelter. Give yourself permission to fail in the most spectacular way possible, and get some fear out of your system. Feels good, dunnit?

EASY   Exercise 3-2: Draw your inner critic

Think about your inner critic. What does he or she actually look or sound like? (Let's not dull the identity of your inner critic by calling it "it"). What nasty habits does he or she have? Think about the times your inner critic has held you back from something, anything. Now sketch that critic in all his or her miserable glory. Write a name there too.

Take a good look at that inner critic that you have now made real on a piece of paper. Say to that critic out loud that he or she is not welcome, and you're not going to listen to him or her anymore. Then scrunch up that piece of paper and toss it in the wastebasket.

SOME QUESTIONS FOR YOU

What's your "confidence" goal?

Having read this chapter, what's one thing that you want to be more confident at over the next couple of weeks? What could you do to achieve this goal?[8]

What will you say to your inner critic?

What is your inner critic saying now? Try actually writing it down and saying it out loud. Now, what would you say back to this critic? Write that down, too, and say that out loud. You might want to repeat this regularly (although not on public transport...that's a bit weird).

Who are you comparing yourself to right now?

Do you know someone who can draw better than you? Maybe that question is taking you back to your school years. Maybe you're thinking of that little show-off who could draw trains and horses much better than you. Or, maybe you're thinking of someone else on your team at work, who draws amazing things on whiteboards with effortless grace.

---

8 Spoiler alert! There's a sketch to help you with this called the *Superhero Booth* sketch, which you can see in Chapter 11.

Are you comparing yourself to them? Every time you compare your abilities to someone else's, you put a dent in your own confidence. So how might you stop comparing yourself to that person?[9]

What can you do to encourage someone else?
Who else do you know who might be thinking and feeling the same as you? How might you give them a boost about their focus, confidence, and perseverance this week?

Interview with Jacqui O'Brien

From simple icons to rainbow grannies, Jacqui and her team go to great lengths to help clients find their visual voice.

JO: I've been creating marketing content and presentation content for about six years now. I started as a freelance designer in Melbourne, but these days I lead a team of designers and content strategists at The Job Creative in Sydney. We design infographics, explainer videos, and presentations to help clients market their products, services, and brands, especially where customers are evaluating those products and services. Or sometimes they're for internal audiences within large organizations, such as presentation designs for company strategies.

I could see the market shifting in 2011 toward infographics, and I thought that there was room for more time and effort into being clever with the storytelling component rather than just having data plonked on a page.

There were also lots of opportunities to take a lot of existing material and simplify it. For about two years I reduced one client's set of hideous 3D icons to a stripped-back thin icon style, and created about 400 icons! It was good to distill complex ideas into a really clean minimal style, like a simple dotted line instead of a bird carrying an envelope from one telecommunications tower to the next, just to illustrate "messaging."

---

9   Here are a few things that have helped me that you might want to be more conscious of and try for yourself. Be more thankful for what you have, rather than wanting something that you don't have. Consider that this is a journey; others are just further along in the journey than you are, and isn't it great that they're around for you to learn from? Finally, realize that you need to get off the hamster wheel of always wanting more. What you have right now is actually already enough. Go ahead, say that to yourself: "What I have is already enough."

It also taught me how to look at the detail of other designers' work, not only for learning how other designers' thinking is different from mine, and to see if there's a quicker process, but also checking my team's work. I could always pick a line that was thicker or thinner than it should be. I think women do attention to detail better!

FIGURE 3-15

Clarity is big business:"I thought that there was room for more time and effort into being clever with the storytelling component, rather than just having data plonked on a page."

We're often given massive decks of stuff to work on, and often with only 24-hour turnaround timelines, so we have to be pretty ruthless in the distilling we do. We go through the client's content with a fine-tooth comb and work hard at understanding what the key insights and statistics are that they want to convey, and then distill those down and focus on the most compelling one.

We rearrange, we cut, we cull, and we reimagine that content into a new visual language. Visual analogies can be quite effective: if we need to illustrate something like scale, we might use an elephant and a mouse at opposite ends of a scale, or a dial (like an odometer), or even just a simple plus and minus sign.

Sometimes, one visual element can become a metaphor throughout the whole piece: the elephant at the top can now represent anything that's large, and then make appearances in different ways throughout an infographic.

Every now and then we'll pitch a crazy idea to a client. There was this one presentation we had to improve, that was all about where a particular company had been, where they had got to today, and what they needed to do to reinvigorate the team for the future. We pitched this lovely reinterpretation involving an elderly woman who goes from knitting boring gray sweaters to popping into an alternate universe, discovering a rainbow of colors, and then popping back out again, with a bit of rainbow hair and full of revelations about what her customers really needed.

That story didn't fly with the client at all! Popping into alternate universes was too much for them, but the rainbow granny story loosened up their thinking, and allowed us to get more oomph out of the narrative and to create more exciting visuals that were slightly quirkier than what they were already thinking of.

Everyone's got a message, an idea, a brand, a story to convey. I guess we just try to find the message's *visual voice*; we just try to amplify that in different ways. Finding the visual voice in the material that clients give us is about finding the main message in all those words, bringing that message to life, and championing that message in a visual sense. That's what inspires people, and motivates change.

I guess we just try to find the message's visual voice; we just try to amplify that in different ways.

[4]

Getting the Right Materials

I'M GOING TO MAKE a confession: I've read loads of books on drawing and painting, and guess what section I always gloss over and never read? The "materials" section. I know I'm probably not alone in this, but as a Presto Sketcher, you need to be smart about the materials you use for different occasions. So I hereby present to you: The Materials Section That You Will Actually Read.

The Materials Section That You Will Actually Read

There's an ever-widening array of sketching materials to choose from these days, not to mention some pretty snazzy digital materials on offer. It pays to think about what you're like as a sketcher and how you want to incorporate sketching into your work; this will steer you toward a more satisfying set of tools. The good news is that anything you draw *with* and draw *on* is fine for Presto Sketching. But isn't it good to know the advantages and disadvantages of different materials, to bring out your best sketching? With that in mind, let's take a look at the following:

- What Materials Star Sign are you?
- Which markers, paper, and sketchbooks to use
- Dealing with whiteboards
- Digital surfaces
- Blending the traditional and digital

What Materials Star Sign Are You?

The MacGuyver Sketcher

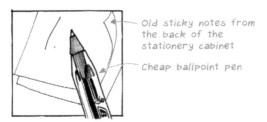

Old sticky notes from the back of the stationery cabinet

Cheap ballpoint pen

You'll sketch with anything and on anything that's nearby, whatever it takes to get the job done.

Go ahead and grab that old blue biro and that unused Filofax from 1992, or some ratty sticky notes where the sticky back bit is all clogged up with dust and last month's potato chip crumbs. They'll do just fine. But know this: sooner or later your creative instincts and resourcefulness will land you in front of the top brass, and they're going to want to see some polish, *capisce?*

The Earnest Sketcher

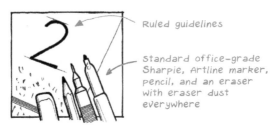

Ruled guidelines

Standard office-grade Sharpie, Artline marker, pencil, and an eraser with eraser dust everywhere

When it comes to sketching, why do 1 line when you could do 20? Hopefully one of them will be right.

Oh, the joy of producing something that's perfect in every way... in form, function, and feedback from others. Sure, it takes a lot of time, paper, and pencils, and there's so much of that eraser dust on the paper, desk, and floor that it looks like a herd of dandruff fairies skipped past, but that's the cost of perfection. Might I tempt you to be a little reckless: hop on the Harley Davidson of stationery for a while, and use ink without—gasp—a pencil and an eraser? It will be faster and more exhilarating. You'll make mistakes, but your confidence will go through the roof.

The Executive Sketcher

Your sketches are always going to be glorious, because they're rendered with a Mont Blanc fountain pen on 600 gsm organic cotton archival paper.

You have an eye (and a wallet) for the most expensive gear. You never fail to impress others with your first-class style, so why should your sketching be any different? Between you and me, I applaud your contribution to the stationery manufacturing industry, but you might want to practice a bit with a humble Sharpie and some letter-size printer paper first. Go ahead, I won't tell anyone.

The Presto Sketcher

You're never without a marker and are always ready to use it to make your idea or someone else's idea tangible.

Ideas won't wait for the perfect time, the perfect place, the perfect pen, or the perfect audience, so you have to go with whatever is handy, wherever you are. Still, there's nothing wrong with having the right marker for the right scale. The value is in the way you visually express the idea: clearly, quickly, confidently, and compellingly. And with a bit of panache.

Whatever your sketching star sign is, the more you do the activities in this book and the more you sketch in the wild with your friends, clients, and colleagues, the more you'll turn into a Presto Sketcher. Because Presto Sketching is light, simple, and often done impromptu, any materials are good materials. It's important to move at the speed of your mind and hand, not your materials. So, use what you like, always keep them fresh, and always keep them close by.

Markers

Think about the scale of your sketching. If it's just for you, a simple fine-line marker is great. If it's for a group of people, or to be viewed from around a large room, make sure you use a thick marker (take a look at the visual effects of different lines produced by the markers in Figure 4-1). The finer the marker, the more precision you have, but try not to be wooed by precision: going for the perfect line will slow you down and inhibit your thinking.

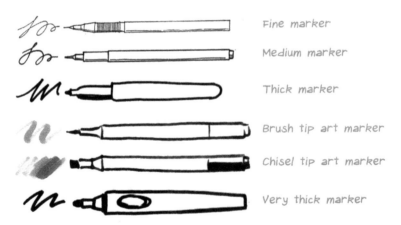

FIGURE 4-1

Try a range of markers: Try different marker brands, thicknesses, and point types to see what's right for you.

If the sketching you're doing is meant to last beyond the immediate conversation, think about the best way to render it and capture it. Is it going to carry more authority if done with a colored tint marker or two, or perhaps in your organization's corporate colors? Would going straight to digital and using a tablet help you reuse and repurpose it later on?

I tend to use a humble black Artline or Staedtler medium marker for most of the sketching on paper that I do. Indeed, most of the sketches you'll find in this book are done with a medium black marker. I use thicker markers like whiteboard markers, Sharpies, and Neulands when I'm sketching with others so that they can see them from across a room.

I'm a huge fan of alcohol-based color markers (or art markers) like Copic, Prismacolor, and Letraset. These color markers are popular with comic artists, architects, graphic designers, industrial designers, and calligraphers. The grooviest thing about them is that you can vary the tint of the color by going back over your strokes again and again. Look for ones that have both brush-tip and chisel-tip ends. The best ones are also refillable, with replaceable nibs, too.

If you want strong, gutsy color, go no further than the Posca and Ironlak paint markers. These are becoming more popular, and with their easy-on opaque intense colors, it's easy to see why.

Paper and Sketchbooks

The main thing to keep in mind when choosing paper to sketch on is the life it will have after you're done sketching. If it's made to share or stick up on a wall or whiteboard, loose-leaf blank office paper is perfectly fine. Loose leaf tends to be easier to scan, too.

If it's anything that you want to hang on to for a while, invest in a decent sketchbook (Figure 4-2). This is especially important if you're practicing your technique over and over, or if you're in the habit of observing and sketching while you're out and about.[1] This is something I learned the hard way: the more sketching I did on loose-leaf paper, the more disorganized I became, and the more I kept losing my sketches. Keeping a sketchbook is one of the best habits a Presto Sketcher can develop.

---

1   Two habits, of course, I highly recommend to all my students!

FIGURE 4-2

Paper variety is important: Blank office paper (left) is perfectly fine to sketch on, but try different kinds of sketchbooks, too. Hardcover ones with an elastic strap are great (middle), but avoid spiral-bound sketchbooks (right), because the metal can be uncomfortable on your hand...especially if you're left-handed!

Sketchbooks range from inexpensive, pocket-sized units to thick toothy A3 pads, and everything in between. I prefer A4 (letter) size (about 220 mm x 300 mm) and 100 to 110 gsm, because I can draw something fairly large, but they're still small enough to be portable. I don't tend to like tiny sketchbooks, but I know others who swear by A5 size (150 mm x 210 mm), or even pocket size.

Variety is important! Make sure that you try different types and brands, from Rhodia's dreamy silky-smooth paper, to Whitelines's light-gray paper with—er—white lines, to Khadi Papers's 210 gsm thick textured cotton paper. Bleed-proof paper pads are brilliant if you sketch with alcohol-based markers like Sharpies and Copic markers, and these days you even can get waterproof paper.[2]

Now, a word of caution! Sketchbooks are a gateway drug for many people who—ahem—have a healthy appreciation of fine stationery. There are tribes of people out there who make it their life's mission to find and collect the most exquisite notebooks and sketchbooks as well as

---

2   Nu Stone makes "tradie notebook" waterproof paper pads, and the pages are practically indestructible. Hard to tear, waterproof, and bleed-proof. It feels a little weird to draw on, but perfect with a pencil.

making delicious sketchbooks with detailed leather-bound covers by hand. Whatever your poison, just make sure you actually sketch in them.[3] Here are a few other tips for sketchbooks:

- Always check first to see if your marker will bleed through the paper.

- Steer away from using notebooks with lines on every page (Figure 4-3). Lines constrain your hand, and constrain your mind!

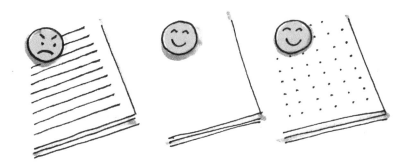

FIGURE 4-3

Avoid regular lined paper: Avoid regular lined paper (left); lines constrain the mind! Blank paper is perfect (middle), and dotted or gridded paper is fun (right).

- Mix it up by trying paper with dot grids and line grids. Rhodia and Moleskine have great sketchbooks and notebooks with grids.

- Avoid buying notebooks with templates in them (e.g., storyboard templates, large screen and mobile screen templates). You're better off drawing these by hand.

- Always date your sketches so that you have a record of how you improve your technique and what sorts of themes and phases you go through.

- Try annotating your sketches using a set of color-coded shorthand reference icons (Figure 4-4), so it's easier to keep track of different topics and themes you sketch.

---

3   Just to pique your interest, head on over to The Perfect Sketchbook (*http://www. theperfectsketchbook.com*). If you're using this sketchbook, you're using cotton paper from the original Fabriano Papermill, which—I kid you not—was a favorite of Renaissance artists like Michelangelo Buonarroti.

FIGURE 4-4

Sketchbook annotations: Include little annotations next to your sketches to keep track of different themes and topics. These are ones I use: from left to right, screenshot, random idea, problemsolving, schematic diagram, and team-based sketching.

Presto Tip: Beware the Bleed!

Watch out for markers that bleed, or go through the page you're sketching on, leaving marks and splodges on the pages underneath. The culprits are usually alcohol-based markers like the popular Sharpie markers.

But it's not just the markers! Check the type of paper that you're using as well, because the density of the paper can affect how much a marker's ink will spread across it and through it.

Always experiment a little before committing to a sketch on paper!

Whiteboards

I know some people harbor a morbid terror of having to draw on a whiteboard. I mean, it's such a hard, smooth, unforgiving surface, isn't it? And it's up on the *wall*, for crying out loud, for everyone to watch every single line you draw and mistake you make! What a cruel invention!

But trust me, the whiteboard is your friend. Think of a whiteboard as another voice in the room; you have the opportunity to let it reflect and condense whatever the conversation is.

There's no harm in practicing what you're going to draw on a whiteboard well before the meeting gets underway, or at least drawing something on the whiteboard ahead of time, so it's ready for when everyone else enters the room for the meeting.

Whiteboards are generally fairly large, but you also can get smaller portable ones.[4] Betabook is a great example of a portable whiteboard that folds in half like a book, to about A4 (letter) size.[5] I began using a Betabook a while back, and I find it super useful in meetings—especially online videoconferences—where I want to quickly draw something simple to show others and there's no other writable surface around.

Digital Surfaces

Some people are purists when it comes to sketching *only* with paper and markers, or *only* with their tablet, but I think variety and flexibility are great, and both digital and traditional media have advantages and disadvantages. What's most important is that you try different media for yourself to see how they work for you, your abilities, your workflow, and the style you're after.

Here's a synopsis of different types of digital surfaces, some advantages, and some things about which you need to be aware.

---

4   A cool little trick is to cover the front of your laptop in whiteboard paper, which then doubles as a mini pop-up screen to show others!

5   The Betabook website (*http://www.betabook.co*) has lots of ingenious uses that you might not have thought of.

GRAPHIC TABLETS

Graphic tablets (Figure 4-5) let you draw with a stylus onto a plain surface, capturing and sending whatever you draw to software on a computer, like Adobe Photoshop or Autodesk SketchBook.[6] Graphic tablets are also pressure-sensitive, which allows you to vary the thickness of your digital sketching stroke in really interesting ways.

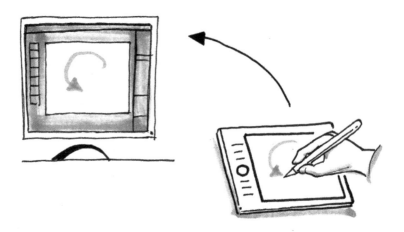

FIGURE 4-5

Graphic tablets: Some people like using graphic tablets, because they can draw directly into their preferred graphics software (like Adobe Photoshop or Autodesk SketchBook).

The trickiest thing about this way of digital sketching is that the sketch itself appears on the computer screen and not on the surface on which you're drawing, and often with a little bit of a delay. This can be a bit disorienting, but it's well worth sticking with it if you want to become fluent in digital sketching.

Another disadvantage for you might be the different feel of a stylus on a smooth synthetic surface. To overcome this, try just sticking a piece of regular paper to the tablet, and sketching with the stylus on that.

---

6   Other good drawing software products are PaintTool SAI, Mischief, and Krita.

EMBEDDED LCD GRAPHIC TABLETS

If watching your sketch magically appear on a screen while you're sketching blind on a surface is a bit weird for you, you might want to try an embedded LCD tablet (Figure 4-6). These tablets essentially let you draw directly on a large touchscreen. They tend to have similar resolution as regular computer screens, plus they're pressure-sensitive.

FIGURE 4-6

Embedded LCD graphic tablet: This is Jess, from strategic consultancy Second Road, working up a digital sketch on an LCD graphic tablet, using her paper sketches as a reference.

TABLETS AND APPS

These days, iPad and Samsung tablets offer a pretty sophisticated digital sketching experience for much less money than what you have to pay for big LCD graphic tablets. So, if you don't need the larger-sized LCD graphic tablets, an iPad or a Samsung tablet is perfect.

You can have a lot of fun sketching with your finger on a smartphone, and there are many apps around—including apps that come out of the box with the smartphone—that let you turn out a reasonably nice sketch. But I much prefer digital sketching with a stylus on a tablet.

And, oh my word, the sketching apps for tablets are getting better and better! There are new variations coming out all the time, so I'm not going to recommend one app over another.[7]

You even can have the best of both worlds by using the Astropad app. Astropad lets you sketch on your iPad and mirror it wirelessly to your Mac, into software you might be more familiar with, like Adobe Photoshop.

Whatever tablet and app you use, it's important to fully embrace the advantages that the digital sketching experience gives you, rather than just trying to do exactly the same thing as you would with a marker and paper.

Here's an example of what I mean. There are precious few moments in my life that I can recall when technology had a wonderful, massive, mind-blowing effect on me. The first was discovering the *Star Wars* arcade game in my local corner store. Another was the first time I used JavaScript and CSS to create a dynamic style switcher on a website, where the entire website would change look and feel at the click of a link.[8] Add another such moment was the first time I used Procreate on an iPad, and I sketched in layers.

In layers! I could preserve different parts of my sketch in layers! I could sketch "under" my existing sketch! Honestly, I have goosebumps right now, just thinking about it.

This layers function can definitely open up—dare I say it—a new dimension to your sketching (Figure 4-7). For example, here's a nifty little trick that my friend Justin Cheong does in Procreate for his conference sketchnotes: he imports a photo of a conference speaker, traces over it, and then removes the photo, leaving an impressive sketch of the speaker.[9]

---

7   And by the time you read this, I'll probably be using a different app anyway. But if you're curious, look no further than Procreate, Penultimate, Paper by 53, or Tayasui Sketches. If you regularly use the Adobe Creative Cloud suite, Adobe Illustrator Draw is really nice, and integrates tightly with your other apps and devices.

8   Does anyone remember CSS Zen Garden?

9   You can find out more about Justin Cheong in his interview, on page 70.

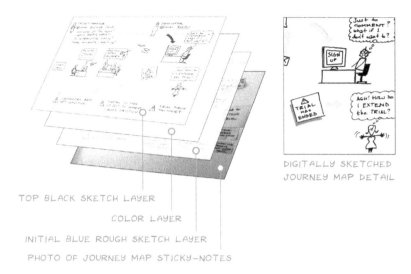

DIGITALLY SKETCHED
JOURNEY MAP DETAIL

TOP BLACK SKETCH LAYER

COLOR LAYER

INITIAL BLUE ROUGH SKETCH LAYER

PHOTO OF JOURNEY MAP STICKY-NOTES

FIGURE 4-7
Digital sketching in layers: Several tablet apps let you sketch in layers, which opens up more sketching methods, such as tracing over a photo (in this case a photo of some journey map sticky notes), a rough sketch layer, and a color layer.

TAKE ADMIRAL AKBAR'S ADVICE

I must press upon you one warning about digital sketching, however. It's all too easy to keep using the Undo function as you sketch, in an attempt to create that one perfect picture. But as Admiral Akbar sagely shouted in *Return of the Jedi*, "It's a trap!" That Undo function can actually smother your creative spirit and hamper your way to developing your own natural visual style.

Blending Traditional and Digital Media

There's no end to the blending of the traditional world of pens and paper together with the digital world, and there are exciting new technologies and blends emerging all the time. Here are a few that are worth trying:

LiveScribe pens
These "smart pens" use special paper infused with patterns of microscopic dots to digitize your notes and sketches, and map what you're sketching to any audio that's recorded at the same time. This is perfect for situations like customer interviews and workshops.

Evernote Moleskines and Evernote Post-It Notes

Evernote has been busy doing its best to integrate the paper-to-digital workflow, with the Evernote Smart Notebook and Evernote Post-It Notes. They essentially use your smartphone's camera and OCR to index, classify, and organize the information you sketch and write.

Wacom Inkling

The Wacom Inkling solves the problem of using only a certain type of "smart" pen or "smart" paper to get your sketches into your computer. It's a little box that sits at the top of your sketchbook that uses infrared signals, centaur eyelashes, or goodness knows what magic to digitize your sketches straight to your computer.

Sketching Materials at Work

The sketching materials you use at work will depend on how you want to bring sketching into your workflow (Figure 4-8). If you needed sophisticated accounting functionality in your job, you wouldn't struggle on just using a calculator, would you? You'd ask your workplace to get the right accounting software. The same applies to sketching materials: you needn't be shy about asking your workplace for the right stationery, or a whiteboard.

Sketching alone   Sketching in groups   Sketching for others

FIGURE 4-8

Materials differ depending on what mode you're sketching in: You'll need different materials when sketching for yourself, sketching with a group, or sketching for others.

SKETCHING ALONE

If the sketching you're doing is mainly for your own thoughts, learning, and practice, go for a sketchbook. If you're sketching anything that you're likely to scan and share, a sketchbook is still your friend, but consider a larger one so that you can get into the habit of sketching at a larger scale.

If you're sharing sketches as you draw them with a team (like user interface sketches, storyboards, and so on), humble office paper is perfect.

SKETCHING IN GROUPS

If you're sketching with a small group of people, a whiteboard is your best friend. Whiteboards are probably the best co-sketching surfaces there are—especially floor-to-ceiling boards, or the 6-foot boards on wheels. If I had my way, I'd make sure every meeting room and office break-out area in every office building had a floor-to-ceiling whiteboard. If sketching is a better way of working, the wall is the new desk.

As I mentioned earlier, however, drawing on a whiteboard can be rather daunting for some people, and it can hold them back from taking part in sketching in a meeting, so keep this in mind if you're expecting a group to jump in and sketch together.

If you're preparing materials for a small group to sketch with, consider the large pads of sticky tear-off flipchart paper, too. Careful, though: it's easy to burn through them, and they're not cheap.

Lots of really interesting digital options for co-sketching have been emerging over recent years. If you're lucky enough to have an interactive whiteboard (IWB) at your workplace or school, you'll know the delight of drawing with your finger on a wall and seeing pixels appear like magic. Many teams are spread across different locations and countries these days, which is where digital co-sketching options are essential. I really enjoy using Mural, and Google Suite has just released JamBoard. These digital options save your work online, so it's really easy for a team to work together from different locations and pick up where they left off seamlessly.

SKETCHING FOR OTHERS

The BASE jumping equivalent of sketching is graphic facilitation,[10] or sketching for others in real time, reflecting a meeting, workshop, or conference talk in pictures to enhance everyone's understanding and engagement. For this, you will need a large, stable surface[11] in a prominent area and nice thick pens so that everyone can read what you're drawing from a distance.

EXERCISES

EASY Exercise 4-1: Treat yo'self

Give yourself permission to go out and buy a decent sketchbook and a couple of different markers to use for all the other exercises in this book. Ask the nice people in the shops for advice; you'll probably make their day.

EASY Exercise 4-2: Break in those new materials

Now, it's easy to think that everything inside a sketchbook has to look PERFECT, as if it just came from the desk of Monet, or Leonardo da Vinci. No, it doesn't. It's not only okay to make lots of futzy mistakes, you *should* make lots of mistakes. No one else is going to see inside this sketchbook.

So, open your nice new sketchbook, take up one of your nice new pens, and practice some sketching drills like those shown in Figure 4-9. Do them over and over. Fill a page with each type of swirl and pattern, to help forge a stronger bond between your brain and your hand.

---

10 Otherwise known as live scribing or graphic recording. There's more about this in Chapter 10.

11 I've learned from experience on this one. I remember live scribing at a Google breakfast meetup on a super wobbly squeaky whiteboard: needless to say, it was a bit distracting for the audience!

 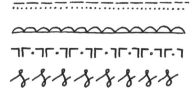

FIGURE 4-9
Sketching drills to try: Try copying these patterns with your new sketching materials.

EASY Exercise 4-3: Doodle some pixels

Now's a great time to try doodling in pixels! If you have a smartphone or tablet, open an app that allows you to doodle with your finger (like the native note-taking or messaging apps) and try sketching the drills in Figure 4-9.

Download a sketching app (try the apps mentioned in this chapter, or search for "sketching" in the App Store, Google Play, or Windows Store), and try the sketching experience in that app, as well.

SOME QUESTIONS FOR YOU

How do you compare the pair?
Get your hands on at least two different kinds of pencils, like a harder type (H, 2H) and a softer type (B, 2B). Try sketching some shapes, like in Exercise 4-2. Which do you prefer? Why is that?

Pixels and/or paper?
As I mentioned, I like the idea of sketching on both paper and screens rather than picking one mode over another. After doing Exercise 4-3, do you find doodling in pixels easier or more difficult? What do you like (or not like) about the experience?

How are whiteboards used at your work?
Do you have any whiteboards where you work? How do people use them? How do you think you might use them more effectively?

Interview with Justin Cheong

Justin is only just getting started in his graphic facilitation and sketch-noting career, but already he has been an amazing inspiration and example to others.

JC: I've been sketchnoting for a while, and I've just started my own freelance business in graphic facilitation. I attend events and work-shops to visualize the flow of a conversation as it unfolds, using a giant scroll of paper and tons of paint markers. It's been great fun, and I'm still learning lots along the way.

I really enjoy the live aspect of graphic facilitation. There's something powerful for the people in the room who see that the large piece of paper starts blank, and it's their conversation that is going to fill it. Rather than it being prefilled. They feel more connected to it, because the image emerges as they speak (Figure 4-10).

FIGURE 4-10

Justin in full flight as a graphic facilitator: "There's something powerful for the people in the room...They feel more connected to it, and to each other, if the image emerges as they speak."

Preparation is very important for these sessions. I prepare by reading any materials sent to me beforehand, and then I'll do some thumb-nailing to test out different layouts for the graphic. Thumbnailing is scribbling down about 10 ideas (according to what I know about the event), and then selecting one or two of the strongest compositions. Thumbnailing gives me some solid ideas for how I can draw the image during the event.

Buffering is another important part of my scribing method. Often at the start of a talk or conversation, I'm not really sure what topics are going to emerge. So if a speaker says something and I'm unsure whether it's relevant, I'll write it down on an index card as a buffer. Once the talk gets to a few minutes in, I usually get a clearer sense of what the key themes are, and I can start to transfer some of the mes-sages from the cards to the canvas. From there, it becomes much eas-ier for me to scribe directly onto the canvas. I just have to keep track of time, and make sure I don't run out of white space to capture informa-tion during the duration of the event.

I've developed quite a distinct style now. I mostly use black Posca paint markers because they produce dense, vivid colors. Shaking the pen adds to the theatrics and showman factor. I also use an Arm-adillo, which straps to my wrist and keeps my markers handy.

For smaller-format sketchnotes, I like to use the Procreate app on my iPad Pro. Procreate automatically records the sequence of my sketches, which helps me to look back and review my own process.

When it comes to finishing a graphic, I like to decorate content with frames, shadows and color. They give the content visual hierarchy and help to make important bits pop. I prefer to add frames towards the end of a session, so that during the session, new ideas have room to con-nect to each other. When people see the graphic and it doesn't have the frames yet, it doesn't look as complete, but it does save up the really nice bit—the magic—until the end, when I join it all up.

I still remember my first job out of university, before I knew anything about sketchnoting. On my first day, my manager set aside the whole day to explain to me how our company worked and where I fit in. He drew everything on flipchart paper as a diagram. Thanks to that one diagram, I could see exactly how the company worked. It was bril-liant. I also noticed that everywhere my manager went, he carried a sketchbook. He's not an illustrator—he's trained in finance—but he brought his sketchbook to all of his meetings. From then on, following his lead, I brought one too.

Now I see that effect continuing. A high school teacher friend happened to see my sketchnotes on Twitter, so he gave it a try himself at a teachers' conference, and got similar engagement and interest. He decided to then teach sketchnoting to his high school students, and now they're doing it. He shows their work on Twitter as well. Now he is going to the same conferences to teach *other* teachers how to teach *their* students how to sketchnote. That feels really nice. Imagine if they taught visual literacy during your schooling, imagine where you would be now? This is what inspires me to keep going, doing sketchnotes, sharing them with others, and keeping that ripple effect going.

Imagine if they taught visual literacy during your schooling, imagine where you would be now?

Part 2

Presto Sketching Techniques

I HOPE YOUR MIND is buzzing just thinking about new ways of approaching sketching, and I hope you've picked up some new markers and a sketchbook to try out.

We're about to head into the section with most of the techniques you'll find in Presto Sketching. First we'll nail down the basics, and then we'll move on to sketching more complex objects. We'll also tackle sketching using visual metaphor, and sketching abstract concepts.

This set of techniques will help you to extract what's in your head and move it onto paper (or a whiteboard) in a much more satisfying way. You'll also be putting these techniques to good use in Part 3.

[5]

Mastering the Basics

LIKE ANY LANGUAGE, VISUAL communication has its equivalent of letters, words, and phrases to learn, before you can combine them in lots of interesting ways. That's what this chapter is all about: showing you some letters, words, and phrases to try first.

I should emphasize again that there's nothing stunningly new here; whether you're new to sketching like this or a seasoned veteran, it's nice to establish the individual parts of this visual language first so that you can combine and extend them in any way you see fit.

Here's what we'll cover in this chapter:

- Basic mark making

- Sketching figures and faces

- Characterful lettering

- Sketching lots of basic objects

- Sketching frames and separators

Warming Up with Basic Lines

It's time to warm up and get some basic lines and shapes happening. As you go through this book, and as you advance in your own sketching proficiency, you'll come to realize that there's really just a fairly small set of different marks that you make, over and over again.

Figure 5-1 shows an array of different marks and patterns that you can use to get warmed up.[1] Go ahead, grab something to draw with and something to draw on, and fill a few pages with these lines, loops, and shapes.

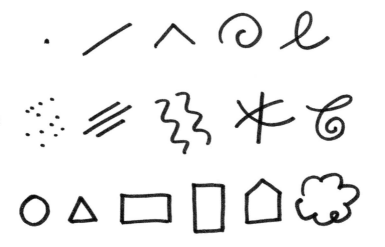

FIGURE 5-1

The basic set of lines and shapes that will make up pretty much everything in this book: The top row is the pure set of marks. The middle row shows variations of those marks. The bottom row shows a range of shapes.

Now, you might be thinking: "Hmmf! Drawing dots and lines is one thing, Ben, but drawing complex things like a car, or Gavin my little goldfish, is quite another." And you'd be right. But don't worry, I'm not going to ask you to leap up a cliff in one go; most of this book is devoted to taking you up to that level step by step.

---

1   The set you see here is derived from a mix of Dave Gray's Visual Alphabet, popularized by Sunni Brown in her book *The Doodle Revolution*, and Austin Kleon's array of five simple elements.

The more you practice, the more your hand will understand what your brain is trying to say, and the more natural it will feel.

Sketching at Different Scales

It's important to practice your sketching at different scales (Figure 5-2). I've worked with several designers who have incredible ability when sketching interfaces on paper, but lose all confidence when it comes to drawing on the smooth, unforgiving surface of a whiteboard. So, try sketching these basic practice lines and shapes at a range of sizes, from itty-bitty on a Post-It Note all the way up to nearly as big as you, on a whiteboard, if you can.

FIGURE 5-2
Get used to sketching at different scales: Smaller motions from the wrist (left), larger motions from the elbow (middle), and largest motions from the shoulder (right).

This is really useful because it gets you used to drawing from the wrist, from the elbow, and from the shoulder. When your body loosens up, your mind and confidence will loosen up, too.

EXERCISES

The following exercises will help continue building that important bond between your brain and your hand. The more you work on your accuracy with exercises like this, the more your hand will understand what your brain is trying to say to it!

EASY **Exercise 5-1: Parallel lines**

Draw some parallel lines. Begin with sets of shorter lines and then work up to sets that cover the full width of your page. Be aware of the pressure you're putting on the paper; you want to keep it light. Imagine the pencil (or whatever you're sketching with) is actually you holding the end of a thread, and you're pulling the thread evenly along the page. Take your time, and take care of the ends of your lines; keep them neat and avoid any little hooks.

`EASY` Exercise 5-2: Get to the point

Draw some lines at various angles, and try to make them all meet at one point in the middle. Don't beat yourself up if at first you can't seem to make three lines cross at the same point, and avoid curving the lines to make them cross. Give it a few goes.

`EASY` Exercise 5-3: That's the shape of it

Draw a few simple shapes, like squares, rectangles, and triangles. Try drawing some ovals and circles, too, but make sure that you enclose each shape (i.e., bring the pencil back to where you first started each shape). Then, fill each shape with parallel lines close together, as shown in Figure 5-3. Try drawing the lines at a variety of angles. Be aware of how your wrist and elbow are moving. If necessary, turn the paper around to make it easier; there's nothing wrong with doing that.

FIGURE 5-3
More shapes and lines: Practice precision and uniformity with these shapes and lines.

Sketching Figures and Action

Figures add vitality, interest, and scale to any sketch, as any architect will tell you. They also help us to understand and relate to whatever the object or concept is that's being illustrated because figures help us to empathize and put ourselves "in the picture."

SAY GOODBYE TO THE STICK FIGURE

We'll get more into conveying story as the book goes on, but for now I have some news for you. When it comes to drawing figures, you can do a lot better than stick figures. I'm serious, unless you're drawing

Actors in UML,[2] you'll experience far more satisfaction—and gain much more respect from others—if you put aside the sad old way of drawing stick figures and embrace the better way of drawing figures *with actual bodies*.

Now, in case you're smiling nervously and backing away slowly from this page, let me explain. As you probably know, more than half of our communication is through body language,[3] which means if our little figures don't have bodies, we're missing out on a whole lot of potential for communication. Plus, they just look better. And drawing figures with bodies really is easy.

Take a look at the very simple examples in Figure 5-4. It's amazing how much life, character, and action you can pack into a figure when it has a body.

FIGURE 5-4

A range of simple figures to try: Note that including a body makes it easier to hang arms and legs off a figure, which makes it seem a little more realistic and a little more alive.

---

2   That's Unified Modeling Language, which was all the rage in the 1990s for visualizing software systems. The official notation for Actors in these systems is—you guessed it—a stick figure. Sigh. Kills me.

3   A lot of people throw around the claim that up to 90% of our communication is nonverbal, which includes body language and tone of voice; the remainder (some say only 7%!) is up to the actual words. Do take this with a grain of salt, though. Those numbers stem from research by Professor Albert Mehrabian, who emphasized in his book *Nonverbal Communication* (Aldine Transaction) that it was about when the words didn't match the body language: "When there are inconsistencies between attitudes communicated verbally and posturally, the postural component should dominate in determining the total attitude that is inferred." So, yeah. Wheel that one out at your next dinner party.

Don't forget that we spend a lot of our time sitting, running, slouching, lying down—moving our arms and bodies in all manner of ways, rather than just standing bolt upright all the time. So, it's appropriate that our figure sketches reflect this, too, *n'est-ce pas?* Figure 5-5 shows some more simple figure sketch examples in different poses.[4] Look at them go!

FIGURE 5-5

A range of simple figure sketches in different poses: Make sure that you try sketching some figures that are sitting, lying down, and leaning on things, both individually and in groups.

---

4   You can also download more figures to copy and use to practice your simple figure sketching from *prestosketching.com/downloads.*

Now, as I've stressed from the beginning, Presto Sketching is about exploring, explaining, and envisioning. This isn't about rendering anatomically realistic people; it's just about capturing the *essence* of a figure.

This basic way of showing figures is all you'll really need, but if you do want to take the style up a notch, try rendering your figure sketches as silhouettes, like those in Figure 5-6.

FIGURE 5-6
A range of silhouette figures: A simple outline has a nice style on its own, but coloring in your figure sketch or adding parallel shading lines can add visual interest and attention.

Sometimes, we need to be a little more specific about what type of figure we're sketching, with indications such as gender, role, culture, and so on. Figures 5-7 and 5-8 show you some ideas for simple additions to figures to help your audiences understand those different aspects.

FIGURE 5-7
Simple ways of showing different gender and age: Try adding details such as hair and figure shape to indicate gender, and using head/body proportion to indicate age.

FIGURE 5-8

A simple way to show roles for figures: Try putting different hats on your figures to show different roles; for example, chef, police officer, construction worker, teacher, and monarch. Adding other details like hoods and caps also enhances visual interest and character.

Presto Tip: Dial Up the Drama

Use a trick from our cartoonist cousins, and try exaggerating the poses of your figures.

This is especially effective when the pose implies some urgency and action, like all those times when you need to sketch someone running from a bear!

EXERCISES

EASY Exercise 5-4: Basic figures

Sketch a range of basic figures, using the ones in this chapter as inspiration. Go ahead and fill a page. Make some smaller and some larger. Try some different styles of figures to see which ones appeal to you more.

EASY **Exercise 5-5: Figures in action**

This time, sketch some figures in different poses according to the suggestions in the list that follows, again using the range of basic figures in this chapter as inspiration:

- She went that way!
- Has anyone seen my glasses?
- I'm running from that bear!
- I'm dancing like no one's watching...

EASY **Exercise 5-6: Silhouette figures**

Sketch some figures as you did before, but this time try some silhouette techniques, as shown in Figure 5-6.

Sketching Faces and Expressions

Faces, of course, convey expression, making it possible for us as viewers to empathize and identify with figures in sketches even more. Figures and faces together convey more about the story, intention, and relationships, rather than just capturing an abstract clinical moment in time.

The rise and rise of emojis has made it easier to enhance whatever we write (typically in instant messaging and emails) with how we're feeling. They're a great shorthand that people tend to recognize, and they're a great place from which to draw inspiration.

Just like we've improved on stick figures, we can also do better at expressions than just the basic smiley and frowny faces. After all, think about the huge range of emotions that people have as they go about their daily lives. Indeed, we have 35 individual muscles in our faces,[5] capable of pulling an amazing number of expressions! As Presto Sketchers, we can sketch expressions that go beyond the basic "happy" and "sad" and cover so much more of the expression spectrum, like frustration, incredulity, and boredom. Or, what about surprise, disgust, or nostalgia?

---

5   This is straight from *Gray's Anatomy* (sigh, the original book, not the show on TV), although the Internet would tell us it's 43 muscles. I'm not sure where that number is from, maybe researchers have discovered more muscles. Either way, the point is that we have a lot!

The more nuanced the expressions are in your sketches, the more character your figures will have, and the more they'll resonate with your audience.

Take a look at the first set of faces in Figure 5-9. Notice the variations of eyebrows and mouths; even though they're just simple lines, they really bring the faces to life.

FIGURE 5-9

Faces, eyebrows, and mouths: Here's a set of faces showing variation in eyebrows and mouths.

Now take a look at this next set of faces, in Figure 5-10. This set demonstrates how changing the position of the eyes can convey the direction of gaze as well as the mood and expression.

FIGURE 5-10

Faces and position of the eyes: Another set of faces, this time showing variation in the position of the eyes as well as different mouths, eyes, and eyebrows to show where the face is gazing.

I've drawn all these faces as circles to emphasize the expressions, but of course faces don't need to be circles; it's worth experimenting with different shapes (as in Figure 5-11) to find what you like best.

FIGURE 5-11

Variation of face shapes: Here's another set of faces, with more variation in expressions and using different shapes for the heads.

It's also worth playing around with different shapes of hair, to add further interest and character (Figure 5-12). And that's not all! We can draw on[6] the visual language used in comics to bring even more expression to faces in our sketches, using elements like surprise lines, sweat droplets, and so on.

FIGURE 5-12
Yet another set of faces: This set shows various hair shapes and embellishments, from the visual language of comics.

---

6   C'mon...you *knew* this pun would happen in this book sooner or later.

Presto Tip: Put a Face on It!

It turns out that putting a face on anything in your sketches is an amazing way of creating interest, empathy, and story. Plus, it's far more likely people will remember your sketches.

It has a bit to do with how we humans tend to like anything with a face. Observe: by adding simple faces on these inanimate buildings, you can make them not only come to life, but suddenly imbue them with emotion and a story. Who knew you'd ever have feelings for a building?

EXERCISES

EASY **Exercise 5-7: Play with faces**

Draw a set of nine circles, which will become a set of faces. Experiment with different expressions by adding different sorts of eyes, eyebrows, and mouths. Play with the position of the eyes, noses, and mouths, too.

INTERMEDIATE **Exercise 5-8: Copy some emojis**

Open your nearest and dearest instant messaging app and take a look at the menu of emojis. Choose some of your favorites and copy them. As you sketch them, think about what each of the elements is doing; what is it about the eyes, mouth, and so on that conveys that particular emotion?

INTERMEDIATE **Exercise 5-9: Sketch these emotions**

Draw another set of nine circles, and try to capture the emotions suggested in the list that follows. Feel free to sit in front of a mirror (don't worry, no one's watching), act out the emotion, and try to copy what your eyes, eyebrows, and mouth are doing.

1. Pleasantly surprised

2. Really angry

3. Dreamy

4. Guilty

5. Smug

6. Skeptical

7. "I think I'm going to be sick…"

8. Exasperation

9. "Turn that music down!"

Lettering

Visual communication still involves words, and if your sketching is going to be viewed by others, it's good to pay attention to the way you write whatever it is that you're writing.

Your handwriting shows a lot of your character, and you can use this to good effect in your sketching. Your lettering can command attention and add another flavor of magic to your sketching. Let's look at neatening up your lettering first, and then we'll get into characterful lettering.

TREAT YOUR HANDWRITING AS A SET OF FONTS

There's probably a variety of ways in which you currently write. The way you write a shopping list might be scrappier than the way you write in your mum's birthday card, which might be different again to the way you write on a whiteboard at work (see Figure 5-13).

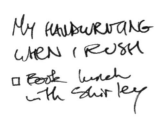

FIGURE 5-13

Messy writing versus neat writing: My normal handwriting (on the left) is shocking, but the writing on the right shows the two "fonts" that I've come to use regularly if I write neatly. Notice the lowercase e's in my capitals? I found that writing lowercase e's was faster than uppercase E's, and the habit has stuck over time.

Treat these styles as a set of fonts that you carry around with you, and focus on one or two styles with which you want to get better and more consistent. Practice them, be neater and more intentional about how you write, and your sketches will look much better for it.

Watch out for problem letters! Pay attention to any letters that you can't seem to get right, and practice them individually until you're confident with them.

PUMPING MORE MEANING INTO LETTERING

Now that you've smartened up your regular writing, we can get into more characterful lettering styles. As someone famous once said, fonts are the clothes that words wear; thus, there is so much character and meaning you can pack into each and every word by "dressing them in different clothes," and paying attention to how you graphically sketch those words.

Figure 5-14 shows some fun examples of different types of lettering to try. The range is as endless as your imagination.

FIGURE 5-14
Examples of expressive and characterful lettering: Note how different styles convey different mood and tone, depending on style (capitals, script), height, spacing, contrast, and texture.

Presto Tip: Sketch Open Letters

Text with "open" letters adds a lot of visual interest and energy to your notes, presentations, or just on the whiteboard, as demonstrated in the illustration that follows. It might be difficult to get going with sketching open lettering—that is, just the outlines—so here's a trick: sketch the basic shape of each letter, but leave a little bit of room at the top and bottom and either side. Go back over each letter and draw a "halo" around it. It can be difficult at first, but practice a bit and you'll be sketching outlined letters like a pro in no time.

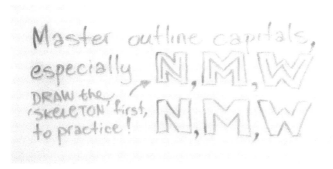

EXERCISES

EASY Exercise 5-10: What are your fonts?

Imagine that your handwriting is a font. Practice writing "Pack my box with five dozen liquor jugs"[7] a few times on paper. Now practice the same sentence on a whiteboard. Are there differences? What makes your "fonts" distinctive?

EASY Exercise 5-11: Graphic word hunt

Take a look at ads, billboards, movie posters, comics, and album (or, more accurately today, playlist) covers around you and try to spot some interesting ways in which someone else has "dressed" words in different clothes, to bring out different types of meaning and character. Copy them in your own sketchbook. As you do, think about how you just know what the meaning is that's meant to be conveyed. You might also want to think about how you could sketch the same words with even *more* of that meaning.

INTERMEDIATE Exercise 5-12: Words as pictures

Figure 5-15 shows some examples of how adding graphic style to words can express more character and meaning. Using these as inspiration, try sketching the following phrases:

- This is taking too long

- It's so foggy

- She's so in love with him

FIGURE 5-15

Examples of "words as pictures" for inspiration: As you sketch words, experiment with each word's shape, texture, and direction.

---

7   Or, if you like: "Sixty zippers were quickly picked from the woven jute bag." These two pangrams are a bit more interesting than "The quick brown fox jumps over the lazy dog."

INTERMEDIATE **Exercise 5-13: Try different markers**

The type of marker you use imparts a lot of character into whatever you write or sketch, too (Figure 5-16). Mix up your markers a bit and try variations like chisel-tips (rather than bullet-tips), alcohol-based tint markers, and so on.

FIGURE 5-16
Examples of words written with different types of markers: From left to right: Sharpie, Copic gray tint marker, Staedtler Calligraphy Duo Tip Marker (3.5 mm end).

Sketching Simple Objects

It's very useful to be able to sketch a wide variety of simple objects as a way to illustrate product designs and experiences. This will stand you in good stead when it comes to sketching more complex images, and then sketching visual metaphors in Chapter 7.

A WORD ABOUT FIDELITY

You might be wondering, "Why is a book about sketching suddenly swerving into marriage counseling territory?" No, it's not that *that* kind of fidelity. I mean *visual fidelity*, or how accurately we represent real-world objects and places in our sketches.

When we sketch real-world objects, *how* we sketch them is measured on a scale of visual fidelity (shown in Figure 5-17), with *literal* representation at one end, and *symbolic* representation at the other end.[8] At the literal representation end, you'll find photorealistic images. At the symbolic representation end, you'll find symbols and icons. In a sense, the closer you get to the symbolic end of the scale, the less "realistic"

---

8   The best exploration of this concept is by Scott McCloud in his book *Understanding Comics.* The spectrum actually extends further when we want to sketch ideas and concepts that *don't* exist in the real world. I get into this in Chapter 8.

and more abstracted the image becomes. But get this: an image can lose realism yet retain all of its meaning, if not more. Indeed, as Scott McCloud says in *Understanding Comics*:

> When we *abstract* an image…we're not so much *eliminating* details as we are *focusing* on *specific details*. By *stripping down* an image to its essential 'meaning', an artist can *amplify* that meaning in a way that realistic art *can't*.

NICE — FOR ART SKETCHING   SKETCHING WITH SOME DETAIL   SKETCHING THE ESSENCE   TOO ABSTRACT

FIGURE 5-17

Sketching at different levels of fidelity: From higher fidelity (more photorealistic) on the left, to low fidelity on the right. We'd be here all day if we always sketched things like the coffee cup on the left, but if the sketch is too simple (far right), we miss some important details and a little bit of character. Aim for the fidelity level of the second cup from the right.

This is another very important part of Presto Sketching: sketching the *essence*, and amplifying meaning. As Presto Sketchers, we need to sketch *just enough* to communicate our message quickly and clearly.

Photorealism is impractical for our purposes, but you might be surprised to learn that sometimes the other end of the spectrum isn't practical either. There are some pictograms that might make sense to you, but won't make sense to others, whether because they're from a different business or a different country and culture. The other thing to remember is, as the revered philosopher and media theorist Marshall McLuhan taught us, the medium is the message.[9] In other words, the

---

9   This famous quote of his is from his book *Understanding Media: The Extensions of Man* (MIT Press). If you want to dig into theories of how we communicate, Marshall McLuhan is your man. He also basically predicted the internet, when in his book *The Gutenberg Galaxy: The Making of Typographic Man* (University of Toronto Press) he wrote, "The next medium…will include television as its content, not as its environment, and will transform television into an art form. A computer as a research and communication instrument could enhance retrieval, obsolesce mass library organization, retrieve the individual's encyclopedic function and flip it into a private line to speedily tailored data of a saleable kind." Impressive, eh?

way the message comes to us *is* part of the message. So, it can actually be quite effective if you invest just a little bit of time, a little bit of skill, and a little bit of panache in your sketches. This is actually what makes Presto Sketching a bit different.

SKETCHING SIMPLE OBJECTS BASED ON SIMPLE SHAPES

Now, why have I included this fireside chat about fidelity, symbols, and capturing the essence? Because nowhere else do you see this so much at play than in sketching basic objects and icons. Thanks to the incredible spread and ubiquity of our symbol-oriented culture, everyone is carrying around a truly gargantuan load of images in their heads, with lots and lots of meaning attached to those images. This is why I can draw a rectangle with three lines in it, and you will probably recognize that as an icon that represents "page."

What do I mean by capturing the *essence* of the object? It means to look for what makes the object unique and meaningful and then ensure that your sketch shows that. This is going to mean different things for different objects.

I won't lie: this is going to take practice. You must not only work on your *confidence and ability with sketching*, but your *confidence and ability with synthesis*, which is distilling the essence from what you see and hear.

Consider the coffee cup in Figure 5-17. The handle on the cup and some wavy lines above it show enough visual information to communicate to us that it's a hot liquid in a cup and therefore probably coffee. Or consider objects like vases, bottles, and wine glasses (Figure 5-18). A lot of their essence is to do with the fact that they're *symmetrical*. Sketches of glasses and bottles look *wrong* when they're not symmetrical.

PHOTO   RECOGNIZABLE   BETTER   BEST   TOO MUCH

FIGURE 5-18
Sketch the essence #1: This shows a photo of a wine bottle and glass, with a progression of sketched equivalents. The first sketch is clearly of a wine bottle and glass, but the sketching technique lacks precision and confidence. The second sketch displays more confidence, but the essence—the symmetrical quality of their shapes—isn't quite there. The third sketch isn't perfect, but it's confident, crisp, clean, and includes the minimum amount of detail. The last sketch (right) has some finessing to display the liquid, but that detail probably isn't needed. (Photo credit: Guillermo Nolasco, via *unsplash.com*)

Or consider cats (Figure 5-19). A lot of their essence is to do with the two pointy ears, and the nose. The sketches here show how you can actually vary a lot of aspects of a drawing of a cat, but as long as the ears and nose connect with our mental image of a cat's ears and nose, each sketch "works" as a cat.

FIGURE 5-19
Sketch the essence #2: To the left is a fairly simple sketch of my cat, Albert. The rest of the sketches are very basic, but they all share the "essence of cat"—the pointy ears and the nose—and so no matter how simple the shape is, you still recognize each one as a cat.

So, with that, let's sketch some objects that we find around us every day that are easy to draw. The objects in Figure 5-20 are all based on a single rectangle. Begin by drawing a set of rectangles on a page, and then see how you go with drawing these objects over the top of your rectangles. Remember, there is no shame in copying. This is how you can train your hand to know what it's doing.

FIGURE 5-20

Some basic objects based on a rectangle: Watch those lines! Neatness pays off.

Figure 5-21 shows some more objects that are all based on a circle. If nothing else, these sorts of exercises help train your hand in drawing shapes like rectangles, circles, and triangles more consistently and more confidently.

FIGURE 5-21

Some basic objects based on a circle: They don't need to be perfect; I mean, that middle one is a bit wonky.

INTERMEDIATE **Exercise 5-14: The essence of laptop**

Take a good 10 minutes and sketch a laptop computer, with as much detail as you can cram in. Now, sketch the same laptop, but this time take only five minutes. Next, sketch the laptop again, but give yourself only one minute. Finally, draw the laptop in five seconds.

Take a look at your different sketches of the same object. What detail did you remove in each version? What would you say is the "essence of laptop," that you can record in five seconds?

EASY **Exercise 5-15: All squared away**

Sketch a row of four squares, and then, using your imagination and rapidly improving sketching skills, turn each square into a simple recognizable object.

Sketch another row of squares, but this time sketch them tilted at different angles. Again, turn each square into a simple recognizable object. Did looking at tilted squares rather than flat squares give you different ideas?[10]

INTERMEDIATE **Exercise 5-16: Sketch your skyline**

Wherever you are, go outside and sketch the silhouette of the skyline. If it's a city line, notice the geometric shapes and outlines of the buildings. If it's in the suburbs or country, notice the contrasts between angles and shapes of buildings and the angles and shapes of trees.[11]

Sketching Frames and Separators

The last basic sketching technique we'll tackle is sketching frames and separators. Frames and separators are the unsung heroes of visual communication,[12] and after you practice the different ways of using them, you'll come up with more ways yourself in no time.

---

10 That's a bit of a loaded question, isn't it? But honestly, I hope you *did* have different ideas, simply by looking at the same thing at a different angle.

11 And if you're feeling brave, put your skyline sketch on social media and tag it #prestosketching; it would be brilliant to see a growing community of skyline Presto Sketchers online!

12 Except maybe for arrows, but don't worry! They'll have their moment in the sun later on in the book. Several moments, even.

FRAMES

Frames (Figure 5-22) are a fantastic, economical way of grouping and drawing attention to certain objects in your sketches or written notes, quietly telling the viewer that whatever is inside the frame is different from what surrounds it.

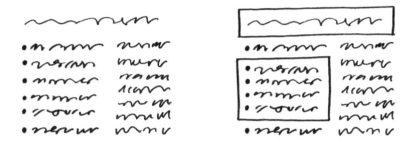

FIGURE 5-22

The power of being framed: The first set of content elements (left) all have the same level of importance; adding a frame around some of them (right) makes the ones within the frames look more important. The elements within the lower frame also look like they somehow belong together as a subgroup.

The frame can be as basic as a single line or as complex as a multifiligreed box with three-dimensional shading, and everything in between. Many visual conventions you've seen before are just frames, dressed up in different ways. The visual language of comics, for example, uses a variety of frames (Figure 5-23). Each frame of a comic is like a window cut through the paper or screen into another world that you're viewing, and the speech balloons and thought balloons inside those frames are frames, as well.[13]

---

13 Like comics? Stay tuned, because in Chapter 11 we're going to look at how to sketch storyboards.

FIGURE 5-23

Some examples of frames used in comics: The visual language of comics uses frame devices in different ways.

Your frames can take on the appearance of objects, too, like paper, signs, people, animals...anything! Consider the variations sketched in Figure 5-24 and the shades of meaning that they add to what's within each frame.

FIGURE 5-24

Some examples of frames made to look like various objects: Sketching frames to look like different objects in themselves adds a lot of meaning and interest.

Banners and ribbons (Figure 5-25) make really popular and interesting frames for titles, quotes, and just about anything that you want to hold up as the most interesting thing on the page for your viewer to look at.

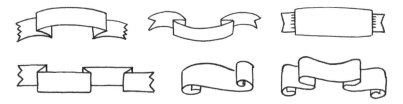

FIGURE 5-25
Examples of banners and ribbons: Experiment with banners and ribbons folding and flowing in different directions.

SEPARATORS

Just like frames can help visually prioritize different elements in an image or text, we can use separators to both visually and meaningfully separate content (Figure 5-26). White space, in a way, is an invisible separator, visually showing us different sections of content that are distinct from one another yet part of a whole.

FIGURE 5-26
Gotta keep 'em separated: The first set of elements (left) looks cluttered and noisy, whereas the second set has some separators, which group the elements and guide the eye.

You can also embellish separators with different visual effects (as seen in Exercise 5-19), to help emphasize certain aspects of meaning in your sketches or just to have some good clean fun.

EXERCISES

EASY **Exercise 5-17: Sketch a banner**
Write any word you like and then follow the step-by-step sketches in Figure 5-27 to sketch a banner.

Start with a rectangle around the word, and then add a zigzag line in each bottom corner. Fill in a top line, and try to keep the heights the same either side. Finish off by sketching a chevron at either end, and sketching the third side of the little triangle under each bottom corner.

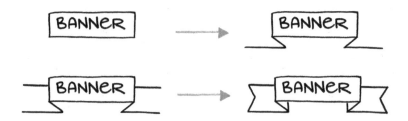

FIGURE 5-27

How to sketch a simple banner: Start with a rectangle (upper left), and then add a zigzag line in each bottom corner (upper right). Fill in a top line (lower left), and finish off by sketching a chevron at either end and the third side of the little triangle under each bottom corner (lower right).

INTERMEDIATE **Exercise 5-18: Sketch a ribbon**

This time, sketch a flowing ribbon by following the step-by-step sketches in Figure 5-28. Start by sketching a nice flowy line, but be careful not to have the line cross itself! Sketch lines of equal height straight up from each point where the line curves around. Copy each curve of the bottom line along the top, keeping the heights the same. Finish it off by sketching a chevron at either end, and some little lines straight up from the other edges of the bottom curves.

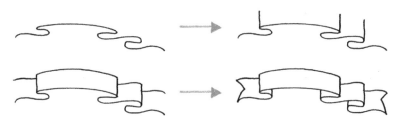

FIGURE 5-28

How to sketch a simple ribbon: Sketch a nice flowy line (upper left), then add lines of equal height straight up from each point where the first line curves around (upper right). Copy each curve of the bottom line along the top (lower left). Sketch a chevron at either end and then some little lines straight up from the other edges of the bottom curves (lower right).

Exercise 5-19: Sketch some separators

Try copying the styled separators in Figure 5-29. You might like to try copying them as straight lines first, and then try the curved versions (it helps to sketch a light single curved line first).

Feel free to come up with some of your own creative patterns and visual effects, too.

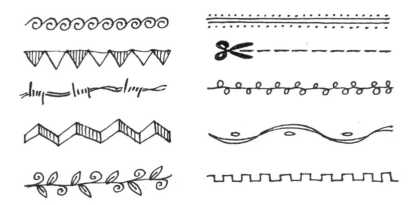

FIGURE 5-29

Styling your separators: Have fun with adding different visual effects to separators.

SOME QUESTIONS FOR YOU

What if your last presentation was in pictures?

Take a look through the last presentation you gave at work. What could you possibly show as pictures rather than words? What would you be brave enough to sketch yourself?

How could you improve on clip art?

Do you (or someone you work with) use clip art of some sort? Odds are, the images you (or someone else) use don't *quite* nail the meaning you're after. How might you sketch them differently, to more accurately show what you mean?

What if your annual report was in pictures?

Go through a few pages of your company's latest annual report (or a similar business document), and circle all the nouns. Try drawing each of those nouns.

How easy or tricky was that? Are there many real-world objects there (e.g., cars, customer, or buildings), or are they mostly abstract concepts (e.g., markets, leverage, or growth)? How might representing them visually affect readers' comprehension of what they're reading, do you think?

Interview with Matthew Magain

Creativity can spark in the most unexpected places. What began for Matthew in a Tokyo schoolroom has since flourished into Sketch Group, a thriving visual consulting business with a glorious vision.

MM: I always drew as a kid, but I had an affinity for computers, as well, which led me to an early career as a software developer. After three years of having my soul crushed by a toxic boys' club, I ran away to Asia and taught English in schools and businesses in Tokyo, Japan.

It was in these classes that I rediscovered sketching. I realized that I could create much more interesting ways to help students learn English by sketching things like conversation sheets, vocabulary activities, and board games. That's what sparked my creativity. Every lesson was a new opportunity to present something in a different way. It got me thinking: "What are we trying to achieve with this lesson?" I'd start there, and work back from the needs of the students.

Back in Melbourne, I started working at SitePoint, doing illustrations for SitePoint books and managing the design team there. We would get together, make a big mess on the wall with user flows, have stakeholders contribute, and I thought: "I need to capture and share this." Around then, I was inspired by those whiteboard videos by RSA Animate and Cognitive. I decided to distill what we learned about user experience [UX] design into a video like that.

My next door neighbor Simon is a videographer who shoots for TV, especially the cricket and football. We partnered up, borrowed a client's boardroom for an hour, and shot the "What the F*ck is UX?" video. It's now at over 600,000 views on YouTube. Around then I was also sketch-noting a lot, and getting more and more gigs for graphic facilitation.

Never underestimate the value of a sketch! I once had a client who was hoping to get funding for a new initiative to be launched in every country they were operating in. I had a brain-dump conversation with them and produced a sketch, just a simple A4 drawing. From that sketch, the initiative got 50 million dollars in funding. There's real value in this sort of sketching. That's the most valuable thing I can do with this skill that I have.

At the moment, I feel very energized and challenged about growing my business, which now has nine illustrators, and has actually tripled in size in the past year.

I engaged a business coach to learn more about working on the business rather than being *in* the business all the time. I've learned that being excellent at this craft doesn't necessarily mean being excellent at technical draftsmanship: it means being reliable as someone to partner with, responsible, and giving clients more than they expect.

FIGURE 5-30

Matthew showing his skill at sketching ideas: "The great joy and privilege in this industry is that we get to be the fly on the wall in so many industries. Most of my clients have never heard of graphic recording/facilitation; it's a skill people don't realize they need yet. When they see it, then they realize it could be a way to do things better."

I get asked all the time: "Isn't that hand-drawn style a fad?" The answer is no: people will always find it magical watching someone draw. Film directors work hard building suspense in a movie, and we get that for free, it's baked into the medium. Sure, there are a lot of effects we can add to animate a sketch, like stop motion, color, and so on. But the fact is that someone creating something with their hands in front of you is always going to be alluring.

There are so many industries and so many companies where most aren't utilizing that creativity, still stuck in business buzzwords and PowerPoint decks that spew forth those buzzwords. The great joy and privilege in this industry is that we get to be the fly on the wall in so many industries. Most of my clients have never heard of graphic recording/facilitation; it's a skill people don't realize they need yet. When they see it, then they realize it could be a way to do things better. So, there are infinite possibilities for someone who's prepared to package themselves in the right way in terms of skill set and the way they deal with clients, to help someone visually. The world is your oyster!

> The fact is that someone creating something with their hands in front of you is always going to be alluring.

[6]

Tackling More Complex Objects

BY NOW, YOU'RE GETTING to know your way around a marker or two. Give yourself a congratulatory fist bump on the shoulder—well done! You can start to bring figures and faces into your presentations now, and I'll bet that anything you draw on the whiteboard in meetings will already be improving, even with just a few frames and separators.

It's time to take it up a gear and tackle some more complex—and more interesting—objects. For this, we'll look at drawing "inside out," not "outside in" like you might already have been doing, and then applying that technique to objects that come up in the world of products and services.

In particular, we'll focus on sketching hands, in various positions and holding products (such as mobile phones).

Let's Go Inside Out

Want some good news? If you can draw the objects in the previous chapter, based on one shape (like a rectangle or circle), you can draw just about any object you want. It's all a matter of seeing those basic shapes within whatever it is that you want to draw and then drawing those shapes as *foundation lines* to help you sketch the entire thing.

Let's break it down. Figure 6-1 shows a picture of a pair of headphones on the left. On the right is another picture for which I've turned on my mental X-ray machine, showing the simple shapes that I see. Do you see the two semicircles for the speaker bits? Do you see how the soft parts that go against the ears are sort of like rectangles?

FIGURE 6-1

See the shapes within the object: A pair of headphones (left), and my foundation lines over the top (right), picking out simple shapes in the form of the headphones. (Photo credit: Alvimann, from *morguefile.com*).

I then sketch those shapes in pencil or a light color (such as the blue I used here), because, as you'll see, I'm going to then sketch over the top of the foundation lines.

In Figure 6-2, the image on the left shows the foundation lines by themselves, just like I would have drawn them on a piece of paper. The foundation lines are quite rough, but they won't really be seen much in the final picture.

Now I can grab my black marker and draw over the top of those foundation lines, using them as a guide (Figure 6-2, right). As you can see, as soon as black is added over the top of the blue color (or light gray if you're using pencil), the foundation lines visually recede to the background, and the black jumps forward. Nice, eh? It gives drawings a bit of architectural panache, too.

FIGURE 6-2
Draw the shapes within the object: Foundation lines of the headphones by themselves (left), and then my black marker drawing over the top of the foundation lines.

The foundation lines technique is a really forgiving way of sketching something, and having the "guidelines" underneath is good for building up your confidence when it comes to sketching the final version. In this way, you're sketching "inside out."

When most people try to sketch something, they tend to sketch "outside in"; they look at the perimeter of the object—the overall shape—and try to sketch that first. That's the difficult way. You'll find you get much more satisfying results if you sketch inside out, by looking for those internal shapes and then drawing them as foundation lines.

Let's go through it again, this time with two other objects that are a little more visually complex (Figure 6-3). Here are the steps again:

1. **Look.** Look at what it is you're sketching.

2. **See the shapes.** Look "into" the object and break it into several simple shapes.

3. **Sketch the shapes.** You can do a rough sketch; it doesn't matter.

4. **Sketch over the top.** Sketch the object using your foundation lines as a guide.

FIGURE 6-3
Can you see the shapes in Albert and Floyd? Sketching objects from
observation using the foundation lines technique.

Notice with the flamingo example in Figure 6-3 that you can use foundation lines to describe just certain parts of the object, like the S-shaped neck. I really like this technique. It makes sketching so much more fun, and in the end, I always end up with something nicer than if I hadn't use foundation lines. Rest assured, though, we're still doing Presto Sketching here; we're still aiming to sketch the *essence* of each object, not all of it.

This technique has a second and more powerful benefit, that's going to become more important later on in this book: seeing simple shapes inside objects helps us to tap into our natural pattern-seeking behavior and hones our observation skills. Right now, it's helping us *look at things better*; later, it's going to help us *listen and synthesize better*, too. Excited much?

Let's try the foundation lines technique again. This time, we'll use the technique to help us sketch objects from memory (Figure 6-4). Here's how we'll proceed:

1. **Think.** See the object in your mind's eye and break it into several shapes.

2. **Sketch the shapes.** Sketch those shapes. You can do a rough sketch; it doesn't matter.

3. **Sketch over the top.** Sketch the object using your foundation lines as a guide.

4. **Finish up.** Add a bit of detail if you think it will help bring out the essence.

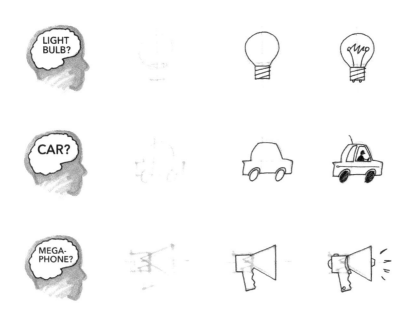

FIGURE 6-4
Exercising the mind's eye: Sketching objects from memory using the foundation lines technique.

Over time, you'll see those foundation lines with your mind's eye already on the paper, tablet, or whiteboard, and you'll be more confident in drawing the object without needing to draw the foundation lines first. Magic!

Some Object Libraries for You to Sketch

Let's get into some other objects that are fun and rewarding to sketch. I've grouped these into various domains, and each domain has a variety of shapes to try. Some are easier than others, but it's a good idea to try sketching all of them; it will increase the number of objects in your own visual library, and as we'll find out, the more you have the more you can combine them to make new meaning.

Take a look at the collections of objects in the following groups:

- Figure 6-5: Business and work objects

- Figure 6-6: Home objects

- Figure 6-7: Nature objects

- Figure 6-8: Hipster objects

FIGURE 6-5

Business and work objects: A set of business and work objects, and things going places.

FIGURE 6-6
Home objects: A set of household objects, and things you might find around the house.

FIGURE 6-7

Nature objects: A set of nature objects, with a variety of animal and vegetable, and a bit of mineral.

FIGURE 6-8
Hipster objects: A set of hipster objects—but I bet you were sketching these things before they became cool, right?

EXERCISES

`EASY` Exercise 6-1: Find the shapes in an image near you

Grab an existing picture of something you like, perhaps from a photo (printed) or a magazine. Try seeing "into" the picture; break it into simple shapes, and draw those shapes over the top of it. But make sure that you don't draw over the top of your uncle's super rare and expensive first edition copy of something. He probably won't appreciate your simple shapes over the top of that.

INTERMEDIATE **Exercise 6-2: Draw that image using foundation lines**

Use that same existing picture of something you like, but this time reproduce the shapes you drew onto a fresh sheet of paper or in your sketchbook as foundation lines. Make sure that you use something light, like a pencil or a tint marker. Now, grab your black marker and complete your sketch of the object using your foundation lines as a guide. Go ahead and show it off to anyone around; I'll bet it looks pretty ace.

INTERMEDIATE **Exercise 6-3: Sketch your favorite objects**

Look back over the examples of objects in Figures 6-5 through 6-8, and have a go at drawing 10 of your favorites. Use shapes and foundation lines as your guide, and fill a page. Remember, please don't be hard on yourself if your sketches don't look like mine. What's important is that you practice, and that you think about capturing the *essence* of the object.

INTERMEDIATE **Exercise 6-4: Treasure hunt**

Take a look around you, and have a go at sketching some objects you find. This is as much about practicing observation as it is about developing sketching dexterity. Go easy on yourself and pick an object based on a basic shape first (like a rectangle or circle), before you pick a more complex object. Remember: *essence.*

INTERMEDIATE **Exercise 6-5: Sketch how to make a pizza again**

Just like you did for Exercise 1-1 in Chapter 1, draw how you make a pizza, except this time, take a little longer and pay more attention to how you render each part of your sketch. Use the foundation lines technique, and go for something a little more ambitious. How does your sketching now compare to your first sketch of how to make a pizza?

Sketching Hands and Products

Just as figures and faces are important for conveying scale, interest, and empathy in our sketching, hands are also important for conveying scale, interest, and context. For example, as Figure 6-9 so ably demonstrates, we could sketch a mobile interface by itself, but sketching it within a mobile phone being held and used brings it to life and lets us provide a lot more context.

FIGURE 6-9
Sketch hands to show your products in context: Rather than just sketching the user interface (left), include the device around it as well (middle). Or better yet, include a hand holding the phone (right), for even more interest and context.

Now, when it comes to sketching hands, what we *don't* want is to do a quick curly thing that looks like broccoli. This says, "I'm not really in command here, and I'm not really that confident about my idea." And just like before, we don't need to go overboard with adding too much detail either. So, go for something like the third hand from the left in Figure 6-10.

UMMM...   GOOD! ESSENCE   GREAT! CAPTURES   NICE - FOR ART
BROCCOLI?   OF HAND   THE POSE   SKETCHING

FIGURE 6-10
Remember to sketch the essence of "hand": Broccoli, anyone? We can do better than the head of broccoli on the far left, without going overboard. The hand second from the left is OK, but the hand third from the left is better.

Let's use the foundation lines technique to draw hands. Take a look at the foundation lines in Figure 6-11, how the basic hand shape is broken into a rough square, a triangle for the thumb area, and a "garden gate" shape for the fingers. Begin by drawing the basic shapes in your lighter color (I'm using a tint marker again here) and then follow up with your dark marker, using the foundation lines as a guide. The trickiest part is the thumb; think of it as two long backward "S" shapes.

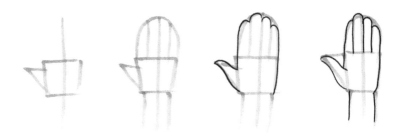

FIGURE 6-11
Foundation lines of a hand: To draw a basic hand, begin with a (sort of) square with a line through the middle, and a triangle for the thumb. Follow that up with a "garden gate" shape for the fingers. Now trace around your foundation lines in black to show the hand.

Now that we've conquered that basic hand shape, let's get into some more natural positions that hands tend to use. After all, it's pretty rare to find people going around with their hands held rigid in the shape shown in Figure 6-11. Except maybe for people doing karate. Best not to make fun of them.

For drawing a "thumbs-up" hand, imagine the triangle lifting up and the "garden gate" shape of the fingers folding forward, as shown in Figure 6-12.

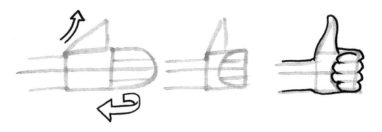

FIGURE 6-12
Foundation lines for "thumbs-up": When you can see the triangle of the thumb lifting upward, and the garden gate of the fingers folding forward, it's easier to draw a convincing thumbs-up hand.

Now try a similar hand, but with the triangle of the thumb and the garden gate folding inward, for a fist shape (Figure 6-13). This shape also works well for drawing hands holding things.

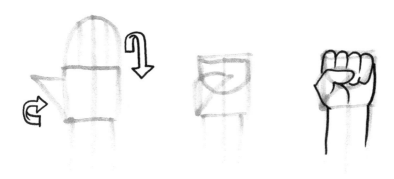

FIGURE 6-13
Foundation lines for "fist": This is similar to the "thumbs-up" hand shape, but with the triangle shape of the thumb folded in, in front of the garden gate.

Not all hand shapes we need to sketch quickly are with hands front-on; we also need to tackle hands side-on, as if pointing. To do this, think of that basic square of the palm as a thin box. Take a look at your own hand, and visualize the thin box that's living just underneath the skin. See it? Now, look at your hand side-on, and you'll see a thin side of that box now at the front. That's what we'll draw next (Figure 6-14).

FIGURE 6-14
Foundation lines for "pointing": Turning the "box" of the palm shape side-on, makes it easier to see the box, garden gate, and triangle shapes working together to make a pointing hand.

Drawing a pointing hand from the front is pretty tricky, but if we can see that box of the palm and the garden gate and triangle shapes folded in, it makes it a bit easier (Figure 6-15). It's also worth drawing the pointing finger a little bit in front of the rest of the fingers, to help with the illusion.

FIGURE 6-15

Foundation lines for "rock salute": Let's see that rock salute! A pointing hand from the front is probably the trickiest hand shape to draw, but seeing the garden gate and triangle shapes folded in will help a bit.

It's worth combining the hand shape with other shapes, to practice poses in which the hand is holding something in different ways. Figures 6-16 and 6-17 show my take on hands holding mobile phones. Try using your X-ray vision to see the shapes in the hand behind the object, moving around it, and the garden gate shape curling around it.

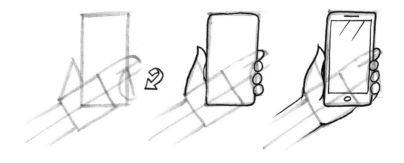

FIGURE 6-16

Foundation lines for holding a phone: Take your time in drawing the shapes that you see in a hand holding an object, like this hand holding a mobile phone.

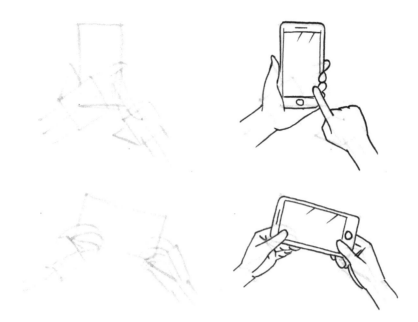

FIGURE 6-17
Foundation lines for more hands holding phones: Here are two poses with a phone and two hands. The first has the right hand pointing and tapping the screen, whereas the second has two hands holding the phone in a landscape position. Keep thinking about what the triangle of the thumb and the garden gate of the fingers are doing, as they curl around the rectangular shape of the phone.

Hands holding other hands get pretty tricky too, like the hands shaking in Figure 6-18. Remember that we don't have to be anatomically accurate in our sketches, just convincing enough to make them recognizable. Use your X-ray vision again, and think about how the fingers curl under each box shape of the palms.

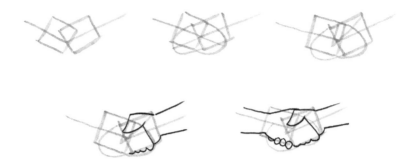

FIGURE 6-18
Foundation lines for shaking hands: The foundation lines get pretty messy in this one, but use these to help your X-ray vision in seeing the fingers of one hand curl under and grip the other palm.

Granted, none of these hands will ever win any art prizes, but after all we're capturing the essence of the position of the hand, enough to signify what it's doing, and enough to instill confidence in our audience.

As with all foundation lines, over time you'll be able to see these lines in your mind's eye and use them as a convenient shorthand to sketch the hands that you want. With practice, you can simplify your hand sketches to become more like those shown in Figure 6-19.

FIGURE 6-19
Sketching simple hands comes with practice: With practice, you will see the shapes and foundation lines in your mind's eye, and be able to use them as convenient shortcuts to produce nicer-looking hands.

EXERCISES

INTERMEDIATE **Exercise 6-6: Give yourself a hand #1**
Use your own hand as a model and practice some basic hand shapes using foundation lines and ink-over. Try an open hand with fingers spread, then pointing, and then a thumbs-up.

Again using your own hand as a model, sketch some hands holding objects, like a phone, a piece of paper, and something round like a ball. Think about what the box shape of your palm, the triangle of your thumb, and the garden gate of your fingers are doing in each pose.

SOME QUESTIONS FOR YOU

What does your product look like being used?

If you work at a company that makes products or provides services, sometimes it's easy to forget what those products and services are like when they're actually used by customers. What might it look like if you sketched your product in the hands of your customers? Does that give you a fresh perspective?

What other products do your customers use?

It's always useful to remember the contexts in which your customers use your product or service, and especially what other products they use to get their jobs done. What other products can you sketch, that you know your customers use? Does that help you to communicate different contexts to others?

Interview with Andrew On Yi Lai

From the conference to the classroom, Andrew has used sketchnoting to improve the experiences of teachers and students alike. And he's only just getting started.

AL: I'm a teacher at Northern Beaches Secondary College (Sydney, Australia), Freshwater Senior Campus, and I'm currently teaching Industrial Technology Multimedia and Visual Arts. I also teach part time at Bradfield College, a senior high school specializing in the creative industries.

I first got into sketchnoting—or visual note-taking—when I saw a close friend post a batch of sketches on Twitter, so I thought I'd give it a try too at a GAFE (Google Apps For Education) Summit in Melbourne. I had so many attendees fascinated by what I was doing and taking photos of my sketches, that I thought: "This has some serious value!"

That was about a year and a half ago. Initially, I sketchnoted for my own learning purposes as a visual summary of presentations, but that has transformed significantly over time. My sketchnoting began to become more structured, and rather than trying to capture every detail, I started to focus on the key ideas.

I started sketching visual summaries of all sorts of things. One time, I sketchnoted the key ideas from a 50-page document on the NSW Quality Teaching Framework, as part of my preparation for an interview. I was offered the job, and when I showed my colleagues the sketchnote, they printed a large-scale version which now sits in the front of the staff room! The staff were very curious about what it was, and it opened opportunities for discussion about education and visual thinking. Witnessing colleagues appreciating my visual notes inspired me to continue to improve my craft.

I've also incorporated sketchnoting into my teaching practice. Initially I run one or two sessions to take the students through the different elements of sketchnoting (typography, symbols, layouts, and so on). That equips them with the individual elements, and then I show them how those elements can be combined to create a sketchnote for learning. Lately in my multimedia class, I've utilized sketchnoting to engage students with the "industry study" part of the course, as it is commonly viewed by students as lengthy and difficult to digest. Those topics have now been transformed into one-page sketchnotes with interactive links to related YouTube videos, which appears to be much more learner-friendly.

I also get my students to create their own version. This provides an opportunity for their own creative input into visualizing the content as we discuss collaboratively what is required to create an effective one-page summary of the topic so that they can later recall what they have learned.

Sketchnoting is a creative and engaging method of note-taking which I feel has definitely improved my teaching practice and the learning process for my students. I'm very confident with what my students have achieved and what they will achieve down the track; I've received positive feedback from my students, like: "Thank you for teaching me how to sketchnote Sir. This is how I feel like I learn best." The most awesome thing to see is when my colleagues show me sketchnotes from students who I haven't even taught, yet are sketchnoting in their class because they saw another student sketchnote and thought they'd give it a try, too!

FIGURE 6-20
Andrew on the power of visual thinking and communication in teaching: "My hope is to bring more value to public education and improve the teaching and learning experience of educators and students alike through visual thinking."

Sharing my sketchnotes on Twitter and Instagram has brought up many inconceivable opportunities: from famous podcasters resharing my content, working with best-selling authors to collaborating with other sketchnoters on educational masterclasses. Sketchnoting has taken me to places I never thought I'd reach. My hope is to bring more value to public education and improve the teaching and learning experience of educators and students alike through visual thinking. That's my vision.

I get great feedback from students, like: "Thank you for teaching me this, Sir. This is how I feel like I learn best."

[7]

Harnessing Visual Metaphor

IN OUR METAPHORICAL WORLD of sketching, we've just explored the Timberland of Technique, and we're in a good place to rest up a bit, rehydrate, and gaze up the Mountains of Metaphor that we're about to tackle. It's time to elevate how you think about your sketching—and what you want *others* to think about when they look at your sketches. It's time to harness the power of what your sketches *mean*, not just what they look like, to help you explore and explain problems, and to explain your ideas and plans to others. Together, we'll look at how to do the following:

- Illustrate concepts using visual metaphor.

- Solve problems using visual metaphor.

- Mix metaphors in new and interesting ways, for greater meaning.

There's also a library of 101 visual metaphors for you to use. Ready? Let's go.

Enter the Metaphor

A metaphor is a comparison between two normally unrelated things to convey a concept, based on the meanings of those two unrelated things. Metaphors help us to make sense of our world and are a powerful way of explaining and communicating because they help to convey ideas based on concepts we already know (and might hold very strongly). They tap into that bank of concepts we all have in our heads to accelerate comprehension and conviction.[1]

The easiest way to understand metaphors is to see some examples, so let's look at a few from one of my favorite books of all time, *To Kill a Mockingbird*, by Harper Lee:

- *I tried to climb into Jem's skin and walk around in it.*

- *Summer was everything good to eat; it was a thousand colors in a parched landscape.*

- *The Governor was eager to scrape a few barnacles off the ship of state.*

Indeed, the mockingbird itself is used in the story as a metaphor for childhood innocence. Powerful stuff, eh?

MAKING IT VISUAL

Visual metaphors are metaphors brought to life with pictures rather than with words; they still rely on some associated meaning that we have learned at some point and remembered. And being visual, of course, they're easier to remember.

Consider the two examples of visual metaphors in Figure 7-1.

---

1 If you want to really get into this metaphor stuff, look no further than the book *Metaphors We Live By*, by George Lakoff and Mark Johnson (University of Chicago Press). It explores the power of metaphors to help create meaning and therefore shape and shift our reality. Yeah.

Getting through to talk to a real person was like trying to get past a huge wall.

She had a way of planting seeds in people that bore fruit later on.

FIGURE 7-1
Two examples of visual metaphors: A huge wall and planting seeds.

MAKING IT WORK

There are two main things we need to pay attention to when using visual metaphors, for them to "work"; that is, to do their job of communicating the unfamiliar in terms of the familiar. First, we need to ensure that the metaphor itself resonates with our viewers. So, you must be careful to use metaphors that are either universal (e.g., a light bulb representing the concept of "idea"[2]) or something that particularly resonates with your specific audience.

Some visual metaphors can be confusing for others, especially if they are either of the following:

Ethnocentric

Treating your own culture as universal and dominant, and just assuming that everyone understands you and what you're trying to convey

Anachronistic

Using an outdated metaphor that has lost its meaning over time, as is demonstrated in Figure 7-2

---

2   Trivia time: the first recorded use of the light bulb to signify "idea" was in a *Felix the Cat* animated film, in the mid-1920s. This begs the question: what did people use to signify this concept before light bulbs were invented? A hurricane lamp, maybe?

If you're not sure about any visual metaphor you're using, check if it works by testing it out on a few people.

Second, we need to ensure that the viewer comprehends the image itself to catch the meaning. So, sketch just enough detail to convey what it is that you're trying to convey (which, after all, is what Presto Sketching is all about).

In Figure 7-3, the metaphorical meaning of the soldiers on the left and center is clouded by the viewer having to take in all the unneeded detail in each of the soldiers.

FIGURE 7-3
Sketch the essence of the visual metaphor: Compare these three sketches that visually explain the nature of our bodies' immune response. The one on the left has a lot of unnecessary detail. The one in the middle is better, but the unneeded details still distract from the meaning. The one on the right is the best choice.

Sometimes, exaggeration helps. Note from the examples in Figure 7-1 that visual metaphors often exaggerate the connection to be made. In other words, the visual metaphors wouldn't work as well if the wall wasn't enormous, or if we didn't get to see the light bulb "fruit" grow from the seed.

ICONS: VISUAL METAPHORS IN ACTION

Nowhere else are visual metaphors used as often, or understood as well, as with icons. Each icon you see is a visual metaphor that, through regular, constant use, has come to have its meaning more and more deeply entrenched in our collective consciousness.

Most icons are simple images known as *pictograms* (Figure 7-4); they are nonliteral signifiers of something. In other words, if you see a button on a website or in a software application with a simple image of a magnifying glass on it, you know what it's going to do. Clicking it isn't going to make a magnifying glass suddenly appear. Through constant repetition and reinforcement, you know that a simple image of a magnifying glass probably means "search."[3]

FIGURE 7-4

Examples of pictograms: Their meanings have been entrenched with use over time, and have become conventional.

Some images, known as *ideograms*, are purely symbolic. Examples (Figure 7-5) include the peace symbol, male and female symbols, and a checkmark (meaning: correct). Pictograms tend to be real-world objects (e.g., a magnifying glass is an actual thing), but ideograms don't have real-world counterparts.

---

3   Which is sort of weird, if you think about it: you'd think that an icon of a magnifying glass would mean magnify or zoom, which it does in many applications. The original Mosaic Netscape web browser used a binoculars icon for search (actually, it was called Find). Later, Netscape Navigator used a flashlight, and the Dogpile search website used...um...a dog. Since 1993, Apple products have used the magnifying glass as their search/find icon (starting with the Apple Newton), and it's basically just stuck around since then. The visual metaphor owes its roots to the way detective characters have often been shown looking for clues using a magnifying glass.

FIGURE 7-5

Examples of ideograms: Even though some ideograms have indeed been derived from real-world objects, many of those connections have been visually lost.

Metaphors are especially powerful when we purposefully communicate concepts that will resonate with our particular audience more, because we choose metaphors that are more meaningful to them, or more strongly held by them. This is where we can apply many of the tools in our Presto Sketching toolkit to use visual metaphor in powerful ways.

How to Illustrate Concepts by Using Visual Metaphor

After you "see" visual metaphor in action around you, it's difficult to un-see it. But how do you apply visual metaphor to your own communication?

Remember that metaphor is all about explaining one thing by using another thing. The biggest area where I see people become stuck is when they try to communicate too much in one image. It's best to break whatever it is you're wanting to think about or communicate into specific chunks of specific meaning.

Try this step-by-step process:

1. **Identify the essence of the concept that you want to communicate.** What are you *really* trying to say? Write it out as a sentence and separate it into several objects by underlining the main nouns and verbs. What are the two or three main words that carry the most meaning for you?

2. **Play with the key words.** Write a list of some other words and phrases for each of the key words you underlined. Go beyond being a human thesaurus, and think of other ways to say what the concept behind the word is. Think about your own experiences, or, better yet, the experiences of those to whom you're explaining.

3. **Think of various images that reflect the list of words, and sketch them.** As you doodle different things, you might get more ideas to sketch about the concept, as well. You can be as rough as you like; no one is going to see these sketches.

4. **Refine and combine the best sketches.** Look at your various sketches of the each word and phrase. Select the strongest one, and refine that as another sketch. You might end up combining a couple of those sketches together into one, to bring the essence of that concept to life.

This is where trying to *sketch what you're thinking* can actually *hone your thinking skills* as well as your communication skills. Think of all the PowerPoint slides you've sat through that could have been axed, if only the presenters had really thought about the concepts that they were actually trying to communicate!

Let's try it out in a simple step-by-step example:

1. Identify the essence of the concept that you want to communicate. For example, "Last quarter, our company goal was to increase our customer satisfaction score by *20* points. We increased it by eight points, so we still have a way to go."

I'd change the statement, and underline the following key words and phrases: "Last quarter, our company <u>goal</u> was to increase our <u>customer satisfaction score</u> by 20 points. We increased it by eight points, so <u>we still have a way to go</u>."

2. Play with the key words and phrases:

GOAL	CUSTOMER SATISFACTION SCORE	WE STILL HAVE A WAY TO GO
(makes me think of...)	*(makes me think of...)*	*(makes me think of...)*
Target	Happy customers	We're not there yet but we're on our way
That speech the CEO gave last quarter	Score card	It's a journey
Win	Games and competition	Not even half way
Team	Judges holding up score cards	It might take more than one quarter
Help customers		

3. Think of various images that reflect the list of words:

GOAL	CUSTOMER SATISFACTION SCORE	WE STILL HAVE A WAY TO GO
(makes me think of...)	*(makes me think of...)*	*(makes me think of...)*

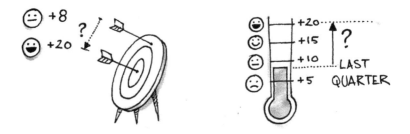

4. Refine and combine the best sketches.

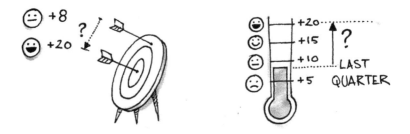

In the preceding example, I refined and combined my various sketches into two separate ideas, that represent two different ways of representing this problem. I'd probably use the second one. Note that there's no right or wrong answer; there are many ways to bring this message out using visual metaphors, depending on your perspective, your experience, and the experiences of your audience.

There are two things that I really like about doing this example. First, it shows me how I can bring out different nuances in the meaning of "goal," depending on what I might want to emphasize the most. It might be a team goal, in which case images of a touchdown or a flag on a hill might be better—signifying how something can be achieved as a team—or it might be more of an individual goal, for which a target is more apt.

Second, sketching this out as a concept actually makes me think of the conceptual *next step*. I begin asking myself questions like: Why did we not even get halfway? Is +20 the highest (capped) goal there is, or will "the journey go on and on" past +20? And how might we increase that score from +8 to +20? This indeed is the magic you conjure when your brain and hand work together.

How to Solve Problems by Using Visual Metaphor

As we've now seen, presenting concepts in visual ways helps people to understand them more rapidly and more deeply. When we bring visual metaphor into the picture,[4] we encourage ourselves to see problems in new ways, and we encourage others to see problems in new ways, too. When we do this, new solutions emerge.

WE HAVE A PROBLEM WITH PROBLEMS

But, before we go any further, we have a problem with problems. Especially in today's "be happy at all costs" culture, we like to avoid them—really avoid them. We trivialize them, we defer them, we disguise them, we hide from them behind chocolate and other vices, we punt them to others...*anything* to avoid actually dealing with them.

---

4   I promise, that's the last bad visual pun I make in this book, honest.

And when it does come to dealing with problems, we tend to have this kooky default behavior of trying to solve them silently by ourselves, don't we? Think about it: that thing that you're worrying about, that's taking up so much of your brain-space? It's amorphous, thick, spongy, constantly changing shape inside of your head, and always just outside of your mental grasp. You lie awake at night thinking about it, without actually *really* thinking about it.

In other words: we tend to keep problems invisible, when the best thing is to make them visible.

When a problem is visible, we can see the true scope and nature of it. When it's visible, we can better see the assumptions baked into it. When it's visible, an entire group can see different perspectives on it, and gain a shared, richer understanding of it.

Believe me, real magic happens when you visualize your problems. Sketching out problems helps you to quantify them and see them for what they really are. It exposes assumptions, and articulates different perspectives. And when a problem is made visible, you are best able to see a lot more solutions to it.

Now, of course problems can be understood better and solved better through writing and talking about them. The wise thing to do with problems is often to discuss them with trusted friends, family members, colleagues, and professionals. Counselors, facilitators, and psychologists are skilled in using language and questioning to help us pull problems apart.

But visualizing has two things going for it that can work really well alongside talking for articulating and solving problems:

- Images are instantaneous. They get the point across a lot faster than written or spoken words.

- Images can pack in a lot more meaning, which is where visual metaphor comes in.

This is why visual metaphor is so important when it comes to visualizing and solving problems. This technique is all about creating simple sketches to look at problems in new ways. And when we do that, new solutions emerge.

You can use visual metaphor to visualize and solve problems using a similar step-by-step process to the one outlined before:

1. **Identify the essence of the problem.** Even just asking yourself, "So, what's really going on here? Why is this problem happening?" can be really insightful. Remember: you might need to separate the problem into several parts.

2. **Play with the key words.** Write a list of some other words and phrases for each of the key words you picked out. Use this step to test any assumptions that are baked into the way the problem is written. Think about your own experiences, or, better yet, the experiences of those to whom you're explaining the problem.

3. **Think of various images and situations in life that reflect that problem, and sketch them.** Think about your own experiences, or the experiences of your audience; that might give you more ideas to sketch the problem, as well. You can be as rough as you like with your sketching; this is "thinking out of a pen" rather than "thinking out loud."

4. **Try sketching out how you would solve the problem, as displayed in the sketches.** Note: at this point you might be solving the problem *in the world of your metaphor* rather than the *real* world, but it's still a stimulus for how to solve the real problem.

5. **Write or sketch any new ideas you have**, based on how you solved the metaphorical problem. Solving the problem in the world of your sketches might give you an insight into the real problem.

Let's try it out in a step-by-step example:

1. Identify the essence of the problem: "Our telephone IVR support system is outdated and broken. Customers are not getting through, and getting frustrated."

2. Play with the key words:

SYSTEM IS BROKEN	FRUSTRATED CUSTOMERS	NOT GETTING THROUGH
(makes me think of...)	*(makes me think of...)*	*(makes me think of...)*
Wires, phones, switches	Clients, mums and dads, businesses, busy people	Lost, in the dark, can't find a way through the maze
Too many inward calls that can't be handled	Bewildered, impatient, angry, fed up	Walls, tunnels, trapped in cages
Outdated, complicated, a total mess	Expectations not met — this should be simple!	Hard ground
Broken pottery, can't be put back together		

3. Think of various images and situations in life that reflect the problem, and sketch them:

SYSTEM IS BROKEN	FRUSTRATED CUSTOMERS	NOT GETTING THROUGH

Looking at the various images I sketched above, the maze resonates with me the most.

4. Try sketching out how you would solve the problem, as displayed in the sketches.

The strongest sketch for me was the maze metaphor. Customers should just have a straight open path through that maze.

5. Write or sketch any new ideas you have.

This made me think that getting lost happens because there are too many options at the beginning for where to go. If I take away options, there's only one way through. So, it's actually reducing choice that's important.

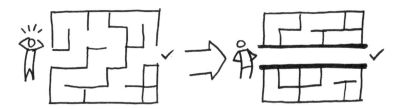

Mixing Metaphors

Now that you're getting the hang of the idea that one simple sketch can convey a lot of meaning, I hope you can see that visual metaphors really are a language unto themselves.

Now, this is where things become super exciting. All languages are about constructing smaller pieces (words, hand movements, notes) into larger pieces (sentences, sign language, music), and you can do the same thing with visual metaphors. You can add them together, and mix them up to really bring your ideas to life!

Take a look at Figure 7-6 and consider the metaphors of the cloud and the light bulb that we used before.

FIGURE 7-6
Two common visual metaphors: A cloud and a light bulb.

By combining them visually, we can create new meanings, as illustrated in Figure 7-7. And each different way we combine them generates a different meaning.

FIGURE 7-7

New meanings by mixing metaphors: Experiment with mixing visual metaphors in different ways to see what new ideas and connections spring forth. Don't forget: they don't all need to make sense, but they could lead to other ideas that do.

Let's try another couple. What if we combined a jigsaw puzzle and a light bulb (Figure 7-8)?

FIGURE 7-8

More new meanings by mixing other metaphors: Another example of different ideas from mixing metaphors.

Fun, isn't it? This is a great creative sketching technique in and of itself. And remember: each idea doesn't need to make sense. Park that inner critic and just draw whatever combinations and permutations come to mind.

EXERCISES

EASY **Exercise 7-1: Easy visual metaphors**

Copy the images in Figure 7-9. Each of these is a visual metaphor for something; write what you think the metaphorical meaning is for each one, under each of your sketches.

FIGURE 7-9

Three visual metaphors: Sketch these images yourself, and then write something about the metaphorical meaning of each one.

`CREATIVE` Exercise 7-2: More visual metaphors

Sketch some images that represent the common concepts presented in the following list (see if you can sketch more than one thing for each concept):

- Goal
- Process
- Decision

`CREATIVE` Exercise 7-3: Mix your metaphors

Combine each of the following pairs of metaphorical objects in new and random ways, to play with combined meanings. For example, what might a light bulb and a shield look like together? Remember: try to silence your inner critic; it doesn't need to make sense first before you sketch it.

- Light bulb and shield
- Light bulb and tree
- Road sign and fruit

`CREATIVE` Exercise 7-4: The lame boss cliché

Take a look at the following list of clichés that your boss might say. Try thinking about each of these as a visual metaphor, and bring them to life by sketching them:

- Time is money.
- That's a half-baked idea.
- Think outside the box.
- We'll stitch the communications throughout our project plan.

- We need to be in the driver's seat.

- This plan is rock solid.

- Anger was bottled up inside her.

- Unfortunately, this CTO is a dinosaur.

- The journey is more important than the destination.

Visual Metaphor Library

The easiest way to get better at using visual metaphor to explore problems, explain concepts, and generate ideas is to take a look at lots of them to see how they work, how they resonate with you, and how you might use them in your own sketches.

The catalog that follows is by no means comprehensive—the number and variety of visual metaphors is growing all the time—but it's a nice start.[5] Browse through the catalog, sketch some of the examples yourself, and practice "seeing" problems and concepts in terms of these visual metaphors. Note that items in bold refer to other metaphors elsewhere in the catalog.

VISUAL METAPHORS FROM NATURE

Cliff

Cliffs are dangerous! That's why they're useful for indicating danger and risk, whether it's anticipated or being experienced right now.

You also can use cliffs to illustrate an insurmountable problem, or something that just can't be reached.

Be sure to include a figure, or something to give it scale; otherwise your cliff could be perceived as just a step.

---

5   I'm sure you'll think of more! If you do, sketch them in this book for reference, and while you're at it, why not add them to your favorite social media stream? Be sure to tag them with #prestosketching!

Cloud

The simple cloud shape can mean some-thing that is purely conceptual (formless, like thought), or it can have a more literal meaning to do with **weather** or indicate mood (down-cast, grumpy, sad). In the IT world, a cloud these days means virtual computing and file storage that's available anywhere.

The cloud typically has curved lines, convey-ing its organic, soft nature.

Cobwebs

Cobwebs are a great way to show something that's really old, or something that just hasn't moved in a long time. They come in really handy for showing slow work colleagues, or parts of a process that are holding up the entire show.

Dams

It takes something incredibly strong to hold back the might of a river, and dams are just such struc-tures—unless, of course, there are cracks and holes in them! Dams represent a tension of great force held back, and that great force can be any-thing, from water, to emails, to feature requests... you name it.

Dinosaurs

If you grew up with dinosaurs in books or toys, you'll know the fear/fascination factor that dino-saurs have. A dinosaur can be terrifying! Or it can also mean something that's really old, outdated, or extinct.

Eggs

Eggs are a rich symbol of new life, rebirth, and fertility across many cultures around the world.

Because of its thin, pale shell, the egg is also a metaphor for fragility. Just the thing to represent anything new, or renewed in some way, that you must treat delicately.

Fire

Fire *can* mean warm, welcoming, and reflective, like the lovely flames in a fireplace or a campfire, but fire generally means danger and threat. Sketching anything on fire is a fast way to show that it's in danger, or failing in some way.

Four-leaf clover

The four-leaf clover is famous in Irish tradition as a symbol of good luck. There's something delightful and magical about finding one, so it's good for representing the element of surprise in some ways.

What you might not know is that the four leaves also represent faith, hope, love, and luck. So, it's like five little metaphors in one!

Gem

Whether it's a diamond or any other precious stone, an image of a cut gemstone like this represents value, something very precious and/or something very rare.

I use this image a lot as a simple shorthand to represent value in a product or service.

Horizon

The horizon is a powerful metaphor for anything to do with vision, a journey, distance, perspective, and direction.

It's really good for evoking the contrast between having a long-term view versus being "in the weeds" with a short-term view.

Iceberg

The iceberg has to be one of the most commonly used visual metaphors, seen in everything from strategic models to stock photography to motivational posters—and with good
reason. Icebergs are majestic and mysterious;
they combine their metaphorical power of
solidity and strength with the metaphor of the
waterline (see **ripples** and **waves**), and remind
us to not always rely on only what is seen.

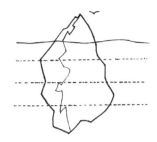

The thought of icebergs melting brings in yet another layer of
meaning: even something as strong as an iceberg can actually be
quite fragile.

Icebergs help us to understand how the complete picture is made
up of not only the visible and tangible parts (symptoms), but the
invisible, intangible parts as well (causes).

Freud used the metaphor of the iceberg to distinguish between
an individual's consciousness (top of the iceberg) and the sub-
conscious (below the water line) and suggested that an individual needs to "lower their waterline" to resolve their psychological
issues. Jung applied the metaphor to groups, suggesting that when
two or more people gather there is a conscious part of the group
(e.g., the meeting agenda and people's job titles) and an unconscious part of the group (hidden agendas, the gossip before the
meeting, the emotional state of the people involved in the meeting,
and issues seen as taboo).

Here are a few tips for taking icebergs beyond the cliché:

Add something to give them scale, like a bird or a boat.

Think about how those other objects can be part of the metaphor: is
there something about the freedom of flying or floating, rather than
being submerged, that would help add meaning?

Use the iceberg as a way to help a group articulate what's really going
on as a group for them. As you sketch, you can ask: "What are we here
to do? Now, what do you think is going on 'below the waterline' for
us?"

Think about separating elements of what's going on "below the waterline" into deeper and deeper layers.

Island

The island represents anything that is alone and unconnected, or disconnected. This can be a good thing, meaning solitude, peace, paradise, holidays (imagine two figures on the island pictured here), and tranquility, or it can mean less-delightful things like loneliness (imagine if there were only one figure sitting on that island) or being left behind.

Islands are really useful for illustrating networks and systems of nodes and connections, where some nodes are well connected whereas others aren't.

Peter Drucker's *The Theory of the Business* (Harvard Business Review) uses the visual metaphor of an island to show the *core competency* of a business (or how a business does what it does), with a **bridge**—representing its *products and services*—going to the mainland, where the customers are. This opens up a wealth of conversation and activity using this as a map, to discuss questions like "Does the 'island' need to be bigger (i.e., more competencies)?" and "Is the 'bridge' landing at the right place on the 'mainland'?

Layers

From strata in rock to layers in a cake, layers are really useful to graphically represent different elements of a system laid on top of one another, with the oldest layer at the bottom and the youngest at the top.

You can use layers to represent all sorts of things that related metaphors like the "onion rings" and "tree rings" can't (because they're round and enclosed), like different types of data collected, different parts of a customer service system, or periods of time at a company.

Lightning

The lightning bolt has a literal meaning of "storm" in **weather** icons, but there's a lot more to this guy. Lightning represents power: energy, electricity, light, strength, zeal, and enthusiasm. Lightning bolts are typically sketched with dangerous-looking jagged lines.

Lightning is unexpected, so it also represents surprise, shock, speed, and action. My own pet theory is that exclamation marks came about because people wanted something in writing to represent lightning! Pow!

Mountains

Mountains certainly share the **limelight** with **roads** and **icebergs** for most-often-used visual metaphors. Their height inspires wonder and a feeling of closeness to the heavens, and their sheer size, mass, timelessness, and spectacle serve as visual reminders of eternity and dependability, and help us keep a healthy perspective on our own situations.

You can use this in a sketch either way: you can use a mountain to represent grandeur or to represent a really stubborn person!

The main way that mountains are used as metaphors, though, is to represent a challenge. Whether it's to do with a personal goal or a team project, mountains work well because they imply that the journey will be challenging but also achievable and rewarding. So, it's good to combine the mountain with a road to represent the path, as well as **milestones** along the way and a **flag** at the top to represent the ultimate destination.

Onions rings

Onion rings, which are related to **ripples** and **tree rings**, are exceedingly useful in visual communication, to show concentric layers of a system. A set of onion rings implies that each ring is somehow dependent on its internal sibling. (Dang, now I have a hankering for tasty onion rings.)

This is definitely a case where speaking in clichés (e.g., "peeling the onion") is tedious, but sketching in clichés is really effective. Please just don't ever say "peel the onion."

Orbit

There's something in the gentle curves of the orbit shape that I find really soothing. The orbit represents an eternal movement of one thing dependent on another: planets around a sun, electrons around a nucleus, a community around a shopping center, and so on.

Ripples

Related to **onion rings** and **tree rings**, ripples convey a sense of outward movement and influence from a single event in time or a central catalyst of some sort.

When you sketch each ring, think about the character of the line. Is it a strong thick line? Or a fragile wavy line? Is it important that it actually looks like water to convey movement rather than the solidity of tree rings?

River

I find the visual metaphor of the river really intriguing. A river carries you along with an energy of its own, taking you from the present to the inevitable future. If it didn't do this, you might as well just sketch a road.

Think about how much energy your metaphorical river has; the more energy it has, the more difficult it is to go where you want to go (as opposed to how far and fast the river will take you). Is it a calm, wide, gentle flow? Or fast and furious?

Are there obstacles that you have to negotiate, like rapids and rocks? Are there forks and turns, and how difficult is it to navigate those changes?

Or maybe you're not even in the river, but on the banks? What is upstream or downstream from you? What is the river washing toward you?

Seeds

From Jesus's parable of the mustard seed to great Australian singer Paul Kelly's 1991 song "From Little Things Big Things Grow," the concept of a tiny seed sprouting and flourishing into something huge is really powerful and resonant with people. A seed can represent an idea, a person, a team, a company... anything that you can sketch to show how it grows and grows.

Tree

The tree is rich in metaphorical meaning to harness in sketching, and indeed if you sketch trees you'll be in good company; the tree may be the oldest visual metaphor we have.

Trees have guided the very way we *think* more than most of us realize. Back in 270 AD, Neoplatonic philosopher Porphyry of Tyre wrote about knowledge, building on Aristotle's work, and articulated it as a tree, with a set of branches of relationships. That way of arranging information was to be so seminal that it spread through the middle ages and onward to influence naturalists like Carl von Linneaus, Jean-Baptiste de Lamarck, and Charles Darwin in how they thought about evolution, and how they classified different living things based on one form of life deriving (branching) from another.

The branching of a tree is a great way to represent a timeline of growth in which "younger" child elements have "grown" from "older" parent elements (like family tree diagrams).

You might also want to think about using the roots of your metaphorical tree; where does the concept you're sketching draw strength and nutrients from? What is it grounded in?

Likewise, how might you use the leaves and fruit of the tree? As any keen gardener knows, many trees will yield more fruit if you prune them well and at the right time; is there metaphorical pruning going on in your sketch, and is there more fruit as a result?

Showing growth of trees in sketches is also a great way of evoking growth in size and strength, from a seed all the way up to an enormous tree.

Lastly, just like with arrows, faces, and figures, think about the physical character of the tree that you sketch. Is it tall, upright, and slender, evoking healthy growth? Is it stooped and gnarly, implying age or pain? Seriously, isn't sketching trees just fascinating?

Tree rings

I'm amazed we don't use tree rings more in visual communication; they're a really evocative way of showing a shared experience over time, or a personal/corporate history. The cross-section of a tree can show us different seasons and tribulations in its life; here there was a bushfire, scarring the outside of the tree; here is where it wept sap to heal after a cut; there was a long, healthy rainy season.

Vine

The vine wanders over anything it can and keeps on growing in any direction, unlike a tree. And no matter how large or sprawling it grows, everything still stays connected. This is handy if you want to show that something or someone can do its own thing, provided it "stays on the vine" when it comes to certain constraints.

Intranets and websites can be thought of as vines, growing in lots of directions, flourishing in some areas, atrophying in others. And like any vines, they need a good trellis to give them structure and encourage them to grow in the right ways.

Waterfall

The waterfall is related to the **river**, and represents situations in which something is passing from upstream to downstream in either multiple stages (like a cascading series of steps) or just one almighty big drop.

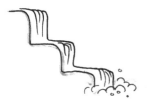

If you're sketching a waterfall to indicate several cascading steps, think about the height and length of each step. If you're sketching a true waterfall of one big drop, make sure you include something to give it (huge) scale, like a tiny fish or a tiny figure.

Waves

Waves are another really effective visual metaphor that's related to any of the water metaphors, like the **river** and the **waterfall**. You can use soft undulating lines to indicate a peaceful rhythm and flow, or more choppy lines to indicate turbulence and trouble.

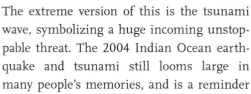

The extreme version of this is the tsunami wave, symbolizing a huge incoming unstoppable threat. The 2004 Indian Ocean earthquake and tsunami still looms large in many people's memories, and is a reminder

to always be mindful of local context and people's feelings when using powerful metaphors like this.

Weather

These icons are pretty ubiquitous descriptors of weather, but they can serve us as visual symbols of other things, as well. They're a great shorthand for mood (like a storm cloud over a figure's head to indicate a bad mood), as well as intensifying actions and feelings in a situation: think of a large sun in a desert scene, baking everything beneath it, or "raining cats and dogs," or being "left out in the cold."

The world of customer experience design uses these icons to indicate a spectrum of how a customer is feeling when experiencing a product or service: this can range from a "sunny day" great experience to a "stormy" hassle-filled experience. Sometimes, an experience is so great it can be like a rainbow.

Wings

There's a certain energy drink that uses the metaphorical power of wings to convey that sense of being lifted out of the ordinary, that sense of freedom. But for me it would have to be the myth of Icarus, who made himself a set of wings out of feathers and wax to escape the island of Crete, that has immortalized the power of wings.

I love wings as a visual shorthand for giving anything freedom and life. Ideas "take flight," one concept can go higher than another, and packages are delivered faster. On the other hand, we can tap into the mythology of Icarus and draw a flying pig, to show the irony of a situation.

VISUAL METAPHORS FROM US

Bones

Sketching a few bones can indicate danger and impending doom. The skull and crossbones of the Jolly Roger flag is great for conveying rebellion (and just about anything to do with pirates, generally), or you can use it to indicate something is poisonous or dangerous. As with the tsunami **wave**, however, be aware of any different cultural implications that skulls and bones in your sketches might have.

Fingerprint

The fingerprint is a nice shorthand meaning identity, personalization, and increasingly biometric security.

Footprints

Footprints are a great way to show a journey and the space that the path takes up, like footprints along a beach, or through a desert. Footprints also show the effect we have on a place and the imprint we leave. In the case of an "environmental footprint," someone who doesn't have much effect on the environment would have a visibly smaller footprint than someone who does.

We can also represent someone doing what has done before by showing them "following the footprints of others."

Handshake

A handshake is an international symbol for agreement and friendship. It doesn't need to be two humans shaking hands, either; in these days of digital security, the "digital handshake" means two sides of a system following a protocol, exchanging the right credentials, and establishing a secure, trusted connection. This is definitely a case in which a lot of technical information can be distilled into a simple and meaningful sketch.

Head

The head is often used to show think-ing (especially if it has a sketch of a brain inside it), and what's going on "inside the head," as opposed to feelings (in which case the **heart** is featured). Younger heads are a little smaller, of course, with the nose lower down in the profile.

Heart

The heart—usually in its stylized rather than anatomically correct form—is a really quick and valuable shorthand for love, kindness ("heart of gold"), cour-age ("heart of a lion"), zeal (to "set our

heart on something"), and infatuation. On the other hand, sketch-ing a heart made of stone would indicate a total absence of pity or empathy.

Sometimes it's handy to sketch a heart and a **head** at different sizes, to show whether the *rational* or the *emotional* is in control of a situation.

Holding hands

Two people—or any two objects, really—hold-ing hands is a great way to signify companion-ship, support, togetherness, and friendship.

This metaphor of togetherness and friendship can extend to include more and more people, which evokes the peaceful symbol of people linking hands around the world in harmony.

Muscles

Muscles, especially flexed like this arm here, are a useful shorthand to convey strength and vitality. On the other hand, the *absence* of muscles indicates impotence and weakness, which usually looks pretty comical.

Just like you can put a face on just about any-thing to give it personality, you may consider putting arms on it, too, flexed to show the guns, as a way of indi-cating strength.

VISUAL METAPHORS FROM OBJECTS AND SYSTEMS

Anchor

Seen with or without a boat of some sort, an anchor can indicate stability and safety. It's a handy metaphor to use in group situations when discussing what values or principles hold people firm.

You also can use it as a pictorial version of "weaknesses" in a SWOT[6] analysis, where several anchors can be sketched attached to a boat, holding it back. If you do this, think about sketching anchors at different sizes, to indicate that some weaknesses are holding things back more than others.

Arrows

The arrow is a bit like a **tree** or **river**, in that it has several layers of meaning. It can act as a representational metaphor, like an arrow hitting a target exactly where it's supposed to (or not), or an arrow that is broken and therefore unusable.

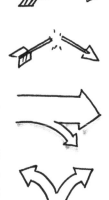

Or, you can use the arrow more as a conceptual metaphor to indicate a process, where it acts as a connector from one place to another.

Think about sketching your arrows like we thought about sketching figures, with mass, personality, and character. That way, you can pack a lot more meaning into your sketches.

Take a look at the different arrows shown here. The first one simply indicates progression from one state to another, and nothing more. The other arrows all have a different treatment that brings in a lot more meaning, such as a complicated path, or several sequential steps.

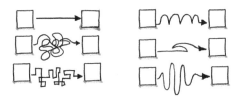

---

6 Strengths, weaknesses, opportunities, and threats. You can see this used to good effect in the SWAM Canvas in Chapter 10.

Balloons

Balloons are like **wings**; there's something to them that speaks of freedom, and being lifted up out of the ordinary. The difference with balloons is that they can't really control where they go; they're at the whim of the winds.

You could also sketch a hot air balloon, with someone or something in the basket beneath it being lifted and transported on some adventure somewhere.

Battery

Just like phones and other electronics can run low on energy, so can we. The visual metaphor of a battery—especially if it's running flat—combined with a figure (as shown here) is a powerful image that conveys exhaustion, and everyone who sees it will identify with it. This combines well with the power point metaphor, for recharging.

Belt

You can use a belt to symbolically "wrap around" and unite several other elements, to convey a sense of collective unity and sometimes safety. Or, you can use it to convey a tightening (as shown here).

Think about the form and material of the belt itself. Is it thin and fragile, or wide and solid? Is it made of silk, or leather, or iron?

Box

With one box, we can symbolize lots of things, like a product, a delivery, a gift, or something being hidden or stored away. We can show the box being opened, either in expected ways (like opening a gift) or unexpected ways (like a jack-in-the-box).

The delightful thing about boxes is that they stack. This means we can use boxes to represent several products combining to form a larger product (think a Rubik's Cube), or several people bringing their skills and ideas together and combining them to create something bigger and better.

Boxing gloves

Boxing gloves symbolize grit and determination, and thanks to the symbol of the boxing kangaroo (first immortalized in posters in the 1890s, believe it or not), you can sketch boxing gloves on anything to evoke that spirit of fight and determination.

Bridge

A bridge connects two places, such as where you are now compared to where you want to be, or a company to its customers (as we saw in the **island** sketch).

The bridge can be shown in profile (as shown here), or from overhead. This example shows just one simple line, but you can enrich it with more meaning like we did with the figures and arrows. Is it strong and solid, like a box-girder bridge? Is it fragile, like a rope bridge? Does it cover a really deep, precipitous ravine? What dangers are there below if our figure falls off?

The sketch here illustrates a classic and very effective personal coaching metaphor: what is your ultimate goal (depicted by the **flag**) that you want to reach by going over the bridge? What are the different **milestones** to reach as you go across that bridge?

Cogs and gears

Cogs and gears symbolize technical systems and settings. It's nice to show the teeth of the gears interlocking, which reinforces that the system is working. Or, you can show a system that isn't working well by showing the gears crunching and crashing together, or free-wheeling without moving each other.

Compass

This is a nice, simple metaphor to symbolize the importance of navigating to something important, of having focus and direction. You can sketch a compass as a way of showing that a direction has been set, or perhaps you can sketch a compass going all awry to show that there *is* no direction.

Crown

The crown is a potent symbol of royalty, power, and authority. In some cases, it can represent outdated or antiquated authority, or it can represent a struggle for power (who is wearing the crown, or multiple crowns?). Sometimes it can look like an unwelcome burden, too, especially if the crown you sketch is obviously way too big for its wearer.

Dice/die

Dice are a neat symbol for luck, or for trying out one's luck ("rolling the dice"). They can imply leaving an outcome to chance rather than deliberate choice.

You can also play with what's on the actual faces of the dice: instead of dots it can be company values, people's faces, or any other set of possible outcomes.

Dominoes

Sketching dominoes is a neat way to convey cause and effect—especially a sequence of events that, once started, can't be stopped.

Elephant

I think we've definitely reached Peak Elephant when it comes to using the "elephant in the room" cliché, but that doesn't mean we can't sketch elephants. If you're sketching with a group of people who are

aware of an issue but can't bear to mention it, then to me that's giving you permission to sketch an elephant as a light-hearted way to bring the issue to light.

And as any Presto Sketcher knows, to see a problem is to solve it.

Engines

For most of us, engines are magical. We know what they do, we know the basics of how they work, and we can throw around words like "carburetor" and "gasket." But honestly, there are so many bits and pieces going on in there that if we opened one up and found little Oompa Loompas inside, we wouldn't be that surprised. Magic.

That's why engines work well as a metaphor. We metaphorically refer to the crucial part of any system or organization as the engine, so sketching a simple engine works well to represent these crucial parts.

Factory

A factory can be a positive metaphor meaning productivity, or it can be a negative metaphor meaning depersonalization, generic mass production, subservience, and robotic standardization.

You can accentuate different parts of a factory to bring these nuances out. For instance, it doesn't have to have smokestacks, or maybe the smokestacks are enormous and belching black smoke.

Faucet

A faucet represents anything "on tap"; i.e., available whenever you want it. Think about what you could attach that faucet to, to render anything available anytime and anywhere.

The second image shown here actually combines three metaphors in one—a **tree**, some books, and a faucet—to show "knowledge on tap."

Filter

The filter (often confused with the **funnel**) reduces the amount of material going through to the other side, where that material could be anything: information, emails, search results, and so on.

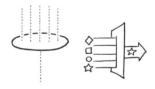

Flag

The flag is a common shorthand for an end goal or a series of goals (like **milestones**) along a journey.

Think about the shape of the flag and whether you can combine it with other metaphors to enrich its meaning. The image shown here shows a flag on top of a **mountain** (signifying a challenging journey ahead to reach it), but you could also try adding an image to the flag shape itself.

Funnel

The funnel *can* represent channeling material into a small opening, but it's usually used to represent a reduction of material as that material descends (think "sales funnel"). Oddly enough, it's the de facto icon for representing filtered material, like search results on websites and filtered data in Microsoft Excel.

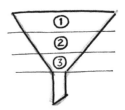

Gauges

Gauges are really familiar to people, and you can adapt them in lots of different ways as a metaphor. Anything you're dealing with that exists on a scale you can turn into a gauge: temperature, energy, pressure, risk, or any other factor to which you want to draw attention.

Gift

The gift is similar to the **box**, but with a ribbon. Consider how different sizes and shapes of the gift you sketch can emphasize the meaning that you're after.

Gravestone

Here lies the floppy disk, the rotary-dial phone, that terrible campaign idea that the marketing team had, or whatever object or concept you need to emphasize that is no longer with us. May it rest in peace.

Hammer (and nail)

Clichés abound with hammers ("He's a hammer looking for a nail," "When you've got a hammer, everything looks like a nail," and so on), but hammers and nails can still be effective to sketch as visual metaphors.

Try to take it further by playing with the size and material of the hammer, or the result of what happens when the hammer hits the nail.

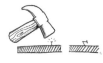

Hats

There are a lot of different types of hats around that represent different jobs and characters (e.g., wizard, royalty, cowboy) or attitudes (e.g., relaxed like a baseball cap, officious and formal like a top hat). Try emphasizing a role or attitude you're representing by adding its "hat" equivalent as part of the sketch.

Another idea is to draw multiple hats on a head, to indicate having to shoulder multiple (maybe too many) responsibilities. It can look quite comical, but very effective.

Hook

If you need to metaphorically "catch" something (like an idea, a customer, or a manager), you need a metaphorical hook to catch it with. Bonus points if you sketch the right metaphorical bait on that hook.

I remember a while ago there was a really effective anti-smoking television campaign that showed a hook emerging from the back of a cigarette as the smoker took a puff. The hook lodged itself in the smoker's mouth. Icky, but potent.

Jigsaw puzzle

Ah, the jigsaw puzzle. The internet is tipping over with the weight of bad stock photography featuring puzzle pieces, but I think there's still life in this metaphor. Try combining it with other metaphors, and play with the ideas of interlocking parts, missing pieces, or what's printed on the puzzle pieces.

Key and lock

It's fun playing with the idea of keys and locks, especially when they don't match. We're used to seeing locks on padlocks, doors, and maybe even piggy banks, but try adding locks to other objects to symbolize them being inaccessible.

Knot

The knot is an ancient symbol that—apart from being well known to sailors and truckers down the ages—signifies bindings, vows, and fidelity.

It also symbolizes difficulty ("a knotty problem"). To "tie yourself in knots" is to let anxiety or frustration affect the way you're trying to get something done.

Ladder

The ladder represents a way we can get from where we are to somewhere higher, maybe somewhere better. Ladders abound in images to do with career progression, but see if you can pull the concept apart a little bit more. What does each rung represent? How far can the ladder really go? What if it branched? And in the current business climate in which diversity is

receiving a lot of attention, imagine if that "corporate ladder" had rungs missing, so that a sketched figure can't even *begin* to climb it?

Lens

We all view each other, situations, life, problems, and so on through one or more lenses. So much of visual thinking is looking at things in new ways, through new lenses.

Lenses can focus, or magnify, or, through the magic of sketching, show us new things we'd never see at all if it weren't for those lenses!

Lightbulb

Just like **jigsaw puzzle** pieces, you it's hard to a more common visual metaphor than the light bulb. Challenge yourself to change it up a little. Would a face make it better? Or changing the shape and size?

Lighthouse

The lighthouse symbolizes safe harbor (a bit like the **welcome mat**), and a warning of rocky dangers nearby. It's often confused with (and used in the same way as) a *beacon*, which is a symbol of leadership, best-practice example, and direction.

Limelight

Limelight was a type of stage lighting used in theaters in the olden days, so called because it involved calcium oxide, or *quicklime*. The term lives on to mean "spotlight" and "being in the public eye." Is there a figure in your sketch who could do with a spotlight?

Maps

Maps are a visual language unto themselves. We'll look at them again in Chapters 10, 11, and 12, but as a visual metaphor they're good for signifying navigation, orientation, wayfinding, and journeys. The map as an object can signify "travel" and seeing objects arrayed on a grid implies wayfinding, especially if there are map markers there, too.

Matryoshka dolls

Matryoshka dolls—otherwise known as Babushka dolls or Russian dolls— are sets of crafted wooden dolls which open to reveal another doll inside. Such visual metaphorical goodness!

Try sketching a smaller doll popping out of a larger one to imply a "nested" concept, or (similar to **onion rings**) show several circular layers nested inside one another.

Maze

The ancient Greek myth of the Minotaur and the Labyrinth is an absolute cracker, and has given us the lasting metaphor of the maze. To be in a maze is to be on a journey yet lost, to be bewildered, to be looking for the way out. It's interesting seeing the different effects of sketching a figure at the beginning of a maze, as opposed to in the middle, as opposed to nearly making it out the other side.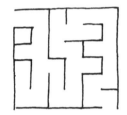

Meat cut chart

Meat-cut charts are those butcher's charts of cows and pigs and so on. It's a total nightmare for any vegetarians present, but I think it's an interesting visual trick to sketch, if you want to convey something being cut up (or something being sized up for being cut up).

Milestone

The word "milestone" is used so broadly now to indicate a general progress marker that most of us forget that milestones were actually once used (and in a lot of countries, still are) to mark out distances along main roads.

So, milestones are a friend of Presto Sketchers, and you should incorporate them often, and in intriguing ways. Just be careful that you don't make them look like **gravestones**, instead.

Padlock

Similar to **keys and locks**, padlocks represent security, privacy, and protection. Consider adding padlocks in unexpected places to generate more nuance in your sketches, like halfway up a **ladder**, in a **light bulb**, in a **factory**, and so on.

Parachute

If there are risks in your project, sketch those risks, and then sketch parachutes on top of them. Those parachutes represent how you're going to *mitigate* those risks. The parachute represents safety, and a magical way of cheating gravity. Anything with a parachute in your sketches is going to be okay.

Prize ribbon

Sketch a prize ribbon on something in your sketches to show that it's best practice, first prize, number one, worthy of recognition. Also, think about its size relative to the recipient (too big and it looks effusive and false; too small and it looks trivial), and think about what's on the round bit, to give it more meaning.

Reflection

A sketched figure looking at its own reflection invokes contemplation, study, maybe melancholy, or maybe just narcissism. For Presto Sketchers, (like with **lenses**) it's actually more effective showing the reflection to be something *other* than what is before it. Something more heroic, perhaps?

Road

The road, or path, is a simple but very powerful visual metaphor to use to invoke a sense
of journey and purpose. Junctions in the road
represent *choice*, **milestones** represent achieve-
ments to be made along the way, **signs** can indicate progress or warnings, and obstructions on
the road represent challenges.

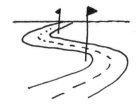

Think of the road as having a character all its own. How wide or
narrow is it? What is its texture? Is it smooth and straightforward?
Bumpy or overgrown? Can we see the **horizon** so that at least we
know the way ahead? Or is the way ahead hidden in some way?

Rocket

Rockets are everywhere these days, metaphorically
speaking. Rockets are a symbol of adventure and innovation, and it feels like everyone is out there building their
own rocket to their own metaphorical Mars. Sketching
rockets is cool, especially if you can show a bit of savvy
with extra jets, windows, and nose cones.

Rollercoaster

Any journey, project, or family can be viewed
as a rollercoaster, with exhilarating peaks and
white-knuckle drops. If you sketch a rollercoaster, make it work hard for its space on the
page: think about the angles of peak and dip
you use, and any surprises, tunnels, and characters along the way.

Ruler

Any time you add a ruler to your sketch, you imply that
something can be measured or is being measured. This is
particularly effective if you pair a ruler with something that
is normally difficult to quantify, like love, customer satisfaction, or anything politicians say. Indicate *benchmarks*, or
known measurements, on the ruler to help people understand what the thing being measured is being compared
against.

Scales (or balance)

Any line that isn't horizontal strikes a tension that we can't help but want to resolve in some way. Scales are great to sketch if you're showing a comparison of the weight or value of two things, especially if you're showing how or why one thing is "heavier" and therefore preventing a sense of balance.

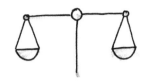

Shield

You can sketch shields as physical objects (in various shapes and sizes) or as conceptual barriers. Either way, they imply protection and stability. Think about how you might use multiple shields together (like an immune system), or add cracks in a shield to signify flaws in a protective system.

Sign (and signpost)

Signs are definitely your friends in Presto Sketching. Use them often, and use them creatively. Use them whenever you're communicating plans and journeys, risks and warnings, advice and recommendations, and basically whenever an inanimate object needs to "say" something.

Think about the shape of the sign that you're sketching, and whether it's just words on the sign or another visual metaphor of some sort.

Silos

Silos are up there with "change management," "reaching out," and "moving forward" in business parlance, and they all make me see red. However, because this is such a well-worn metaphor, it's worth bringing into our Presto Sketching visual library.

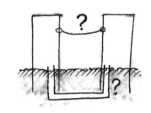

That said, like with all of these well-worn clichés, consider how you might breathe fresh life into it. Most organizations want to "de-silo," so think about what that might look like. Are there rope ladders between tall towers? Tunnels? People jumping from top to top on trampolines or jetpacks?

Spring

Speaking of trampolines and jetpacks, springs are another simple but powerful visual metaphor for magical jumping. Adding springs to anything gives it an advantage because it can bounce higher and faster, perhaps bouncing over the competition and so on.

Steps

Steps are related to **waterfalls**, but go up instead of down. Borrowing from the visual language of charting, the higher each step is, the more difficult it will appear to climb (like the **cliff**). The longer a step is, the more relaxed the pace is.

Steps are really popular in graphically showing maturity models of all sorts, and curved steps can represent multiple **horizons** of activity in an organization's plan.

Stopwatch

The stopwatch represents time—either being timed, or time running out. Consider how you might sketch a stopwatch ticking down to the last seconds (if something is due), or something being timed (like processes).

Tandem

The tandem bike represents team effort, whether it's 2 people on the bike or 20; everyone has a job to do, and everyone is contributing to the motion of the bike. Or, perhaps it's important to sketch two people working hard on the bike, but the third person not doing anything!

Target

The target is a real workhorse of a visual metaphor. It's regularly used to signify a goal, and there are always more ways it can be modified slightly to enhance its meaning.

One trick I've done recently is to show two arrows on the target; one is in the center (the desired goal), and the other is lodged partway out (where we actually got to). This stimulates a great discussion about how to close that gap and get the next arrow back "on target."

Note: **flags** on **roads** and **mountains** can be targets, too, as can soccer goals, finishing lines, and football goal posts. But for my Presto Sketching dollar, nothing gives more value than the concentric **onion rings** of an archery target.

Thermometer

A thermometer doesn't need to indicate just temperature; it can indicate lots of other things, like the amount of funds raised compared to a target figure, the level of customer satisfaction, or the number of votes compared to a total needed to win an election.

Thermometers don't need to be vertical, either; that status bar that we spend so much of our time looking at on websites and in software applications is just a thermometer on its side, inching toward that target.

Toilet

The toilet represents where we put things that we never want to see again. I could've chosen "drain" for this, but drains just look too plain and simple and lack that visceral impact that toilets have on us!

Traps

Traps can take many forms. They can be pits in the ground for hapless figures to fall into, or rope snares and **hooks**. But my favorite trap for Presto Sketching is the big, angry-looking metal bear trap.

You can enhance traps by adding other visual metaphors as bait to lure your metaphorical prey.

Treadmill

Despite being a well-worn metaphor, there's something so viscerally powerful about showing a figure on a treadmill, especially if it has some extra details that make it much more contextually meaningful to your audience. A treadmill just spells misery for anyone! Except maybe for Marvin, my friend's gerbil. Marvin loves his treadmill.

Trophy

The trophy is akin to the **prize ribbon**, only with more prizy-ness and glory. And, of course, the bigger the trophy the better. This is definitely a case in which you can dial up the drama and add a few extra levels if you want to.

Wall

The wall is a very underrated visual metaphor. You're probably familiar enough with its basic use—to represent a problem—but actually visualizing it lets us play with different ways we might tackle that problem.

What might we sketch to get through that wall? Or over it, or under it, or around it?

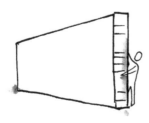

Wand

One of my favorite questions to ask in research interviews about customers' experiences with a product is, "If you had a magic wand and could change anything about this project, what would it be?"

Wands give us permission to think without constraints, which is why they come in handy in sketching problem and solution situations.

Welcome mat

Including a welcome mat in whatever you're sketching might be a nice short-hand way to show that ideas are wel-come here, or collaboration is welcome here, and so on.

It can also be handy to include where a figure has to make choices; for example, one **road** has the welcome mat, and the other has a big gate with bars and a **padlock**.

Windows

Windows give us the metaphorical glimpse through a **wall** to the other side, whether inward (like into a situation, or into our own mind) or outward (to the future, to a competitor). Consider the size and shape of the window you sketch, too, to indicate how easy or difficult it might be to look through.

SOME QUESTIONS FOR YOU

What metaphors live at your work?

Every workplace has various themes, values, or concepts that are on high rotation. It could be a company value of "transparency," or it could be a current product focus area, like "simplification."

What concepts are on high rotation at your work? How might you sketch them as visual metaphors to help people understand and remember them?

What metaphors are living in your presentations?

Take a look through some presentations you've done. Is there some bullet-pointed text that you could illustrate as a visual metaphor?

How might you reframe problems using visual metaphor?

What tough, long-standing problems or issues do you have at your work? How might you express them as visual metaphors to try to see them—and solve them—in a different way?

[8]

Visualizing Abstract Concepts

BEFORE WE LET THE entire metaphorical representation thing go, let's take a metaphorical look over our shoulder at the ground we've covered so far. I hope you can see that the variety of figures, faces, and objects that you are sketching has increased, and I hope you can see where you're becoming more confident. And there's that cool "happy accident" you drew with which you were delightfully surprised! I hope you took a selfie at that point: it was worth it. And by now you're taking visual metaphor in your stride, too.

We now stand at the rugged steppes of *conceptual representation*. In this chapter, you'll learn how to sketch the *intangible*—as opposed to the tangible. You'll also learn how to synthesize meaning and sketch visual models to communicate that meaning to others.

Conceptual Representation

It's worth briefly recapping the types of visualizing that we've being doing so far (Figure 8-1). First, we looked at how to sketch actual real things, like figures, hands, headphones, and so on. That's *literal representation*. Sketching things like this is very useful for telling the story of the problem or solution that we're thinking about, and helping others identify with that problem or solution by mentally putting themselves in the picture.

Then we tackled visual metaphor, for which we sketched *concepts* (like walls, targets, and ladders) based on real things and other concepts. That's *metaphorical representation*. Sketching with visual metaphor is tremendously useful for engaging people's hearts as well as their heads, and helping people to understand new concepts (or complex concepts) based on what they already know.

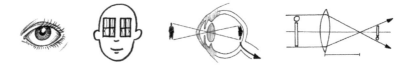

FIGURE 8-1
The visual communication spectrum: At the left end is literal representation. The spectrum then moves right toward metaphorical representation, then diagrammatic representation, then conceptual representation.

There's also *diagrammatic representation*. Diagrammatic representation is useful for showing how something works. It can be a blend of what is seen (tangible) and what is unseen or conceptual (intangible). Diagrammatic representation is also essential for showing things and processes that are real but invisible to the naked eye, like how rays of light work (see Figure 8-1) or how cellular and atomic processes work.

Now we come to the right side of the visual communication spectrum (again referring to Figure 8-1). This is where we visualize things that we can take in and understand, even though they don't actually exist in the real world. This is *conceptual representation*.

It's easier to explain conceptual representation by showing you examples. Take a look at Figure 8-2, and you'll be surprised to see that you're probably already quite familiar with conceptual representation.

Conceptual representation visualizes and explains *invisible, intangible concepts*. The trick is to not only understand *how* this conceptual visual language does what it does, but know how to wield it yourself.

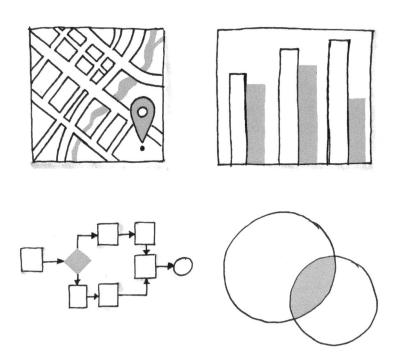

FIGURE 8-2

Some familiar examples of conceptual representation: Map, chart (in this case a column chart), flowchart, and Venn diagram.

I hope that by looking at these examples, you can see how important it is to have these different visual languages to explain and represent concepts that literal representation just can't handle.

Conceptual representation is also really important for helping us to synthesize. You know that feeling when you have so much going on in your head that you can't think straight? Or when a problem seems so huge, vague, and complicated that it's almost too difficult to know where to begin solving it? What you're suffering from, as I mentioned in Chapter 2, is too much information and not enough synthesis.

In this chapter, we're going to do that special magic of making invisible problems visible and synthesizing big, foggy, muddled messes into crisp, clear, visual models and communications. To do this, we'll first look at how to *think* about problems, ideas, and plans in a better way as well as how to *sketch what we're thinking*. By adding just a little bit of structure to your thinking and sketching, you'll witness more of that beautiful chemistry of your brain and hand working together more effectively.

The Three Elements of Conceptual Thinking and Sketching

Sometimes, all we need is a little bit of structure to help us on our way to unmuddling and visualizing. With that in mind, here's a way to pair thinking and sketching to help you *synthesize*, to distill meaning from muddledness and signal from noise. Try to think of any problem, situation, idea, or plan in terms of these three things:

- The *entities* involved in the problem, idea, or plan
- The *relationships* within and/or between those entities
- The *spaces* involved in the entities and relationships

Entities, relationships, and spaces are like three different lenses that you can use to look at the same situation. These three lenses work together to help you think, synthesize, and communicate. Let's look at each one in turn, and then some examples of them in action.

ENTITIES

Entities are the separate objects and things (or nouns) involved in whatever the problem, idea, or plan is that you're thinking about. Entities include objects, people (or groups of people), roles, products, services, and processes. You also can think of entities as separate pieces that make up a product, service, or system, and consider whether they're visible.

Looking at a set of entities helps you to understand simple comparisons between them (e.g., size) or different attributes worth noting about the entities (e.g., locked/unlocked, active/inactive). Examples include all the parts that make up a hammer drill, or all the parts of a support service.

To explore a problem, idea, or plan in terms of its entities, ask questions that begin with "Who" or "What," and sketch what you're thinking about. By immediately sketching what you're thinking, you are *thinking visually*. You are pulling the problem apart, putting it onto paper (or a tablet or whiteboard), and making all the parts of it real and tangible.

It's super important to note that you don't need to sketch a fully formed problem, solution, or whatever, in one go. Your sketching is a process; it represents mental stepping stones toward a fully realized outcome of some sort. Figure 8-3 shows some examples of how entities can be visualized even just as letters or words in frames.

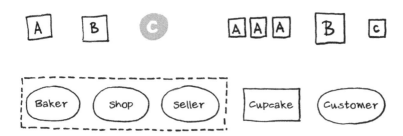

FIGURE 8-3

Three examples of simple sketches of entities: These capture what is present (and not present) in a set. The different coloring of C indicates a different type of entity compared to A and B (top left). Some entities (A) might belong to homogenous groups (top right). Some entities might belong to a collection that is thematically different from the other entities, like a Baker, Shop, and Seller versus a Cupcake and Customer (bottom).

As you can see, you don't need to sketch the actual entities to represent them visually. After all, some of those entities might not exist as *real things*. But if you *do* want to sketch them as real things, go right ahead (Figure 8-4).

FIGURE 8-4

A collection of real-world entities that you can sketch as images: Customer, mother and two children, crowd, and assistant.

Example: Cane toads

Let's apply this entities lens to a situation that's certainly well known to people in Australia (where I'm from): the introduction of cane toads. If you've been to Queensland (a state in Australia), you might well have seen these stocky, poisonous, and highly smug-looking amphibians. And you also might know that unique creepy feeling of opening up the back door at night, turning on the outdoor light, and seeing your back yard *seething with cane toads*, as they scuttle around doing all their smug little cane toad activities.

Cane toads were introduced to Queensland from Hawaii in 1935. They were meant to put an end to the beetles that were eating all the sugar cane crops (by eating them), but instead have spread, multiplied, and wrought devastation on Australia's northern flora and fauna as a feral pest ever since. They eat just about everything, they spread disease, and they also kill anything that eats *them*, because of their poison. I mean, they might as well bleed acid and take all our jobs, too.

Let's take a look at that last paragraph again, and then sketch the entities we can find (we can probably ignore the entities of acid and jobs: those might not be 100 percent accurate...). We can visualize them simply as words in circles, as depicted in Figure 8-5.

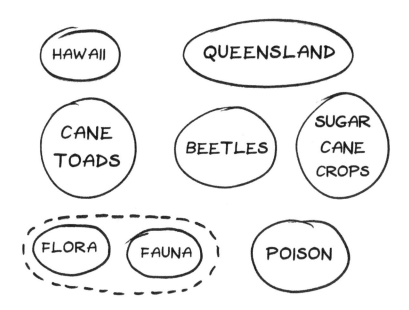

FIGURE 8-5
Simple schematic sketch of the entities from our example situation: Note that using words in bubbles is just fine.

We can also visualize the entities as real-world objects if we want to (Figure 8-6). This certainly helps us (and others) to clarify what each entity means, but it isn't always necessary.

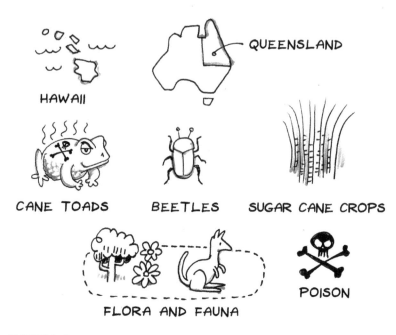

HAWAII

QUEENSLAND

CANE TOADS   BEETLES   SUGAR CANE CROPS

FLORA AND FAUNA

POISON

FIGURE 8-6

Literal representations of the same entities: Note that sketching literal representations of entities doesn't always add extra meaning.

For example, sketching flowers and an animal might make it clearer to people what you mean by "flora and fauna," but sketching an icon version of the term "poison" is probably a bit redundant.

Some common gotchas

Here are some things to keep in mind when you think about the entities in your problems, ideas, and plans:

Using vague terms and clichés

Keep your entities specific and meaningful. For example, avoid picking words like "collaboration" or "outcomes." If this happens, ask yourself: "What do I really *mean* by 'collaboration'?"

Using noun-verbs

Using a noun that's actually a verb (like "transformation") can hide a lot of important information that's worth thinking about. In the case of "transformation," *what* is being transformed? *How* is it being transformed?

Scoping your situation too widely or too narrowly

Sometimes it can be tricky to know the boundaries of the situation that you're thinking about. If the scope is too small, you can limit the effectiveness of any solution you come up with. If it's too large, it will be too difficult to tackle.

If this happens, add sizing words to your "Who" and "What" questions, like these: "*Who* is experiencing this problem the *most*?"; "*Who* has the *most* to gain from this idea?"; "*What* is the *most* significant part of this situation?"

EXERCISES

EASY **Exercise 8-1: Write down the entities**

Just like we did with the cane toads situation, take a look at these problem statements and write down what you think are the entities involved:

- My kids become bored waiting in the car while I'm filling it up at the service station, but I don't want them just playing on screens all the time.

- There's this fantastic group of local volunteers who really want to help the community around them, but they're all chasing after their own individual ideas rather than putting their energies behind just a few integrated ideas.

- The Department of Transport is going to sell the rail network to three separate private companies. One of the companies is going to put in a new rail line to connect two previously unconnected cities, but this will break a lot of existing train trips into three separate train trips, and commuters aren't happy.

EASY **Exercise 8-2: Sketch the entities**

Take a look at the sets of entities you've written for each problem statement in the preceding list and sketch each set. First, try sketching each entity as an abstract concept (just the word in a circle). Does this raise any questions about each entity for you?

Next, try sketching each entity as more of a real-world object. Which type of representation works best? Why is that?

RELATIONSHIPS

Sketching entities might help you to clarify, classify, and compare all the parts of the idea, problem, or situation that you're thinking about, but they're not that useful by themselves. As Donella H. Meadows said in her wonderful book *Thinking in Systems* (Chelsea Green Publishing): "The behavior of a system cannot be known just by knowing the elements of which the system is made."

You often need to think about—and sketch—the relationships going on between the entities. Relationships describe the ways in which the entities are connected, or the ways that the entities regard, behave, and contribute toward one another. To explore a problem, idea, or plan in terms of its relationships, ask questions that begin with "When," "How," and "Why," and sketch what you're thinking about.

As usual, let me show you what I mean with some helpful examples of patterns that you can use:

Process relationships

Process relationships describe how one element leads to another, and another.

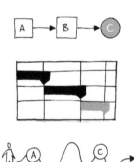

Examples:

- Flowcharts

- Gantt charts

- Customer journey maps

- Swimlanes

- Circuit diagrams

- Timelines

Dependency relationships

Dependency relationships are related to process relationships, and describe situations in which one entity or step can't happen before another finishes.

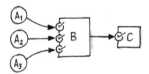

Examples:

- Flowcharts

- Herringbone diagrams

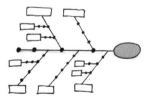

Hierarchy relationships

Hierarchy relationships
Hierarchy relationships describe situations in which one entity has one or more entities related and subordinate to it. Examples:

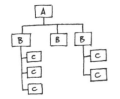

· Genograms

· Decision trees

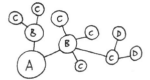

· Information architecture schemas

· Mind maps

Value relationships
Value relationships indicate what value one element gives to another. This can be one-way or reciprocal. Examples:

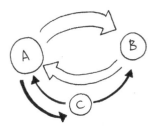

· Money

· Support

· Goods and services

· Saving time

Causal relationships
Causal relationships describe how one or more elements (lower-level causes) contribute to one or more outcomes (higher-level effects). Example:

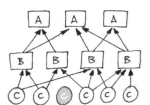

· Outcomes hierarchies

Proximity relationships
Proximity relationships describe how close a connected set of entities are to one another. Example:

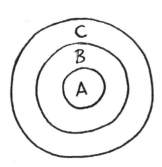

· Brand onions

It's pretty rare that any one thing exists in isolation, which is why looking at the relationships *between* entities can be really insightful. One example of this is in root-cause analysis, wherein causes can be mapped according to symptoms (using a causal relationship map of boxes and arrows).

Another important example is mapping systems that store and move resources around, and the flows and dynamics between entities in systems.[1] Visualizing what the relationships are doing can yield a lot of insight, whether the system is as simple as a thermostat-regulated heater or as complex as the economic and social effects of closing factories and moving labor offshore.

Example: Cane toads

Let's take the same cane toads situation as before, but this time apply an entities *and* relationships lens. Here is the same paragraph, for convenience:

> Cane toads were introduced to Queensland from Hawaii in 1935. They were meant to put an end to the beetles that were eating all the sugar cane crops (by eating them), but instead have spread, multiplied, and wrought devastation on Australia's northern flora and fauna as a feral pest ever since. They eat just about everything, they spread disease, and they also kill anything that eats *them*, because of their poison.

As soon as we apply relationships thinking and sketching to this situation, an interesting thing happens. Remember the UST model back in Chapter 3? We have to begin making lots of little decisions about what relationships to show (*synthesis*), and then *how* to show those relationships, using the library of visual patterns we have at our disposal (*translation*).

There tend to be several ways to synthesize and translate a situation, problem, or idea. It's also important to note that we don't have to cram the *entire situation* into each synthesized sketch. Figure 8-7 shows a few from the cane toad situation.

---

1   Again, I can't recommend *Thinking in Systems* by Donella Meadows highly enough; she codified—and visualized—some really neat ways of breaking complex systems into simpler components to help understanding and problem solving.

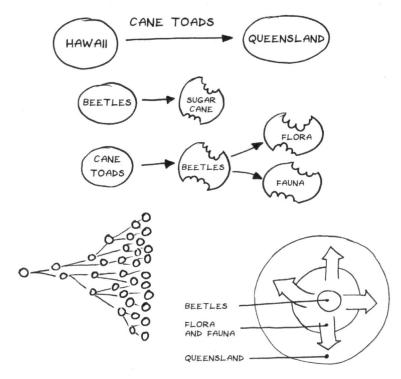

FIGURE 8-7
Some different sketches showing the entities and relationships from our example situation: Note that there can be several ways to show the situation, and you don't have to represent all of the situation in each sketch.

It's up to you and the context of the situation to decide which variation and angle to pursue. It's important to remember to try to go broad and *generate several visualizations of the situation first* (just like here) and then decide which direction is most relevant. This is a key part of visual thinking and synthesis.

EXERCISES

INTERMEDIATE **Exercise 8-3: Write down the relationships**

Take a look at these problem statements, and write down what you think are the relationships involved:

- My kids become bored waiting in the car while I'm filling it up at the service station, but I don't want them just playing on screens all the time. (Examples: parent/child relationship, child/device relationship)

- There's this fantastic group of local volunteers who really want to help the community around them, but they're all chasing after their own individual ideas rather than putting their energies behind just a few integrated ideas.

- The Department of Transport is going to sell the rail network to three separate private companies. One of the companies is going to put in a new rail line to connect two previously unconnected cities, but this will break a lot of existing train trips into three separate train trips, and commuters aren't happy.

INTERMEDIATE **Exercise 8-4: Sketch the relationships**

Take a look at the sets of relationships you've written for each problem statement, and try to sketch several ways you might visualize the entities and relationships together. Remember, each visualization doesn't have to show the entire problem statement.

For each problem statement, which sketch of entities and relationships is most relevant? Why is that? Is this making you "see" each problem in a different way?

SPACES

Spaces describe the *locations* and *proportion* of the entities and relationships involved in your problem, idea, or plan. This includes aspects like area, position, distance, and boundaries. Depending on your situation, it might also include movement (and velocity) of elements into, out of, and within those spaces. Again, let's explore this with some pictures:

Comparison of areas as parts of a whole
These patterns help people instantly see the proportion and position of one or more parts of a whole, compared to other parts. Examples:

- Pie charts

- Donut charts

- Stacked triangle diagrams

- Tree maps

- Heat maps

- Sunburst charts

Comparison of areas representing different amounts

The different amounts can be different sub-groups of the same entity (e.g., sales figures for different sales teams) or the same entity over time (e.g., profit over four financial quarters). Examples:

- Column, bar, and stacked bar charts

- Line charts

- Venn diagrams

- Sankey diagrams

- Mosaic (Mekko) charts

- Area charts

Distribution across an area

Plotting instances of an entity on two axes can reveal distribution trends and aggregations. Examples:

- Scattergrams

- Bubble charts

- Radar charts

Maps

Maps describe the layout and locations of various features (physical or virtual), usually using an *x*/*y* coordinate system. Examples:

- Road maps

- Building blueprints

- MRI charts

- Heat maps

 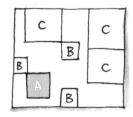

To explore a problem, idea, or plan in terms of its spaces, ask questions that begin with "Where" and "How much,"[2] and then sketch what you're thinking about.

Example: Yep, you guessed it—cane toads

In the last example, we combined the entities and relationships lenses in visualizing the cane toad's situation. We could apply all three lenses, but for clarity, let's focus on the spaces involved. Again, here is the same paragraph, for convenience:

> Cane toads were introduced to Queensland from Hawaii in 1935. They were meant to put an end to the beetles that were eating all the sugar cane crops (by eating them), but instead have spread, multiplied, and wrought devastation on Australia's northern flora and fauna as a feral pest ever since. They eat just about everything, they spread disease, and they also kill anything that eats *them*, because of their poison...

There are two insights that stick out from this situation that could be visualized using spaces. The first is the distance from which the cane toads were imported. The second is based on the keyword *spread*, so it's worth visualizing the spread of cane toads across Queensland (Figure 8-8).

Applying these lenses as thinking devices and visualization devices might also prompt questions that can help you to explore problems, situations, and ideas more. In this case, I was prompted to wonder how far cane toads have spread across Queensland, at what rate, and indeed how far they will go.

Visualizing the folly of introducing alien species to fragile ecosystems is one thing, but how does this apply to product management, research, and design? Never fear, there are plenty of examples coming up in Chapters 10, 11, and 12 that show this form of conceptual illustration in action.

---

2 A grateful hat-tip to Dan Roam for the "How much" question. You can read more about his treatment of analyzing problems in *Unfolding the Napkin* (Portfolio).

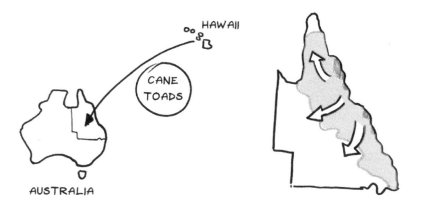

FIGURE 8-8
Two different sketches showing some entities and spaces involved in our example situation: It's good to emphasize scale and movement when sketching spaces.

EXERCISES

TRICKY **Exercise 8-5: Sketch the entities, relationships, and spaces**

Take a look at these problem statements one more time, and sketch the sets of entities, relationships, and spaces involved:

- My kids become bored waiting in the car while I'm filling it up at the service station, but I don't want them just playing on screens all the time.

- There's this fantastic group of local volunteers who really want to help the community around them, but they're all chasing after their own individual ideas rather than putting their energies behind just a few integrated ideas.

- The Department of Transport is going to sell the rail network to three separate private companies. One of the companies is going to put in a new rail line to connect two previously unconnected cities, but this will break a lot of existing train trips into three separate train trips, and commuters aren't happy.

See if you can sketch combinations of the entities, relationships, and spaces in different ways. Remember to refer to the sets of patterns for relationships and spaces to give you ideas for how to visualize all three lenses.

SOME QUESTIONS FOR YOU

How might you reframe work-related problems using conceptual representation?

Think of an issue at your work, about your company, team, or product. Try writing out the entities, relationships, and spaces involved in it, and then try sketching visual equivalents for each entity, relationship, and space involved.

Does this help you to see the issue in a different way? Does it give you some ideas about how to solve it? Remember, this method certainly isn't a silver bullet, but it should open up other avenues to thinking about the problem.

How might you communicate a work-related issue using conceptual representation?

This method isn't just for pulling apart issues; it's for communicating them more accurately and compellingly, as well. What issue has your team or management been trying to communicate at your work that's getting a little lost in translation?

Try visualizing the entities, relationships, and spaces in that issue. Can you find ways to visually communicate that issue better?

[*Part 3*]

Presto Sketching in Action

Up until now, we've been looking at sketching techniques in isolation. It's time to move out of the classroom and take a look at applying your new sketching skills in various ways at work.

The next three chapters contain sets of visual patterns and techniques for you to use in your own product strategy, direction, and design work. They use a mix of literal, metaphorical, and conceptual representation techniques that we've looked at earlier as well as some storyboarding techniques.[1]

This section also gives you some handy information about sharing your work with others and developing your sketching skills further.

---

1 There are links to downloadable templates for each of these patterns to get you started at *http://prestosketching.com/downloads.*

[9]

Bringing Out Your Style

Pᴀᴛs ᴏɴ ᴛʜᴇ ʙᴀᴄᴋ ᴀʟʟ ʀᴏᴜɴᴅ, you made it past the theory part of conceptual illustration! Honestly, the more you apply conceptual illustration in your work, the more uses you will find for it.

If you've been sketching along as you read this book and doing the exercises at the end of each chapter, by now you might be beginning to notice patterns in the way you sketch. Your own style is emerging!

This chapter is about giving you ways to put more vitality into your sketches, and to be more intentional about finding and enhancing your own style. This includes the following:

- Different ways to emphasize different parts of your sketches
- Adding texture and shadows
- Using color for emphasis

Would the Real Style Please Step Forward?

Suppose that you and I introduced ourselves to each other at a cocktail party,[1] and I said to you "Hey, I really like your work. I dig your style." How would you describe your style?

For some professions, like music and fashion, it's much easier to articulate a particular style.[2] But for most of us, it can be pretty difficult to think about even *having* a style, let alone describing it.

When it comes to sketching and visual communication, I reckon most of us would like a definite *look* to our work. But what is that look? And how do we know if it's distinctive or attractive enough? And is it really us, or is the *real* style still waiting to come out?

I think "style" is more about *consistent confidence* than anything else. Your confidence will drive your work to have a more cohesive and focused look about it. And don't forget that "style" isn't the same as "perfection." It's important, as Kit White says in *101 Things to Learn in Art School* (MIT Press), to cultivate your idiosyncrasies:

> Every hand, every eye, every brain comes with its own built-in distortions. These distortions represent your signature, your personal slant on the world. When they manifest themselves in your work, do not be afraid to embrace them.

In a way, I think your style is actually just the best version of yourself.

If you've done any sketching at all so far, you already *have* a style; it may just be difficult for you to see it. And who knows, others might already be admiring your style! Back in Chapter 3, I mentioned that sketching is an extension of your voice and your character; the sketches you leave on the whiteboard and the sketches you include in your presentations will speak of you and for you, no matter what.

---

1   Or a game of football, pub, local school fair, or cage-fight den. You get the idea.
2   Although some music genres these days are totally beyond me.

Having said that, here are seven ways to find and refine your own style:

Learn from work that you admire
Take the time to find others' work that inspires you in some way. It could be old masters' paintings and sketches, or a particular cartoonist, or a favorite graphic novel artist. Pick at least three different people's work, and then analyze *why* you like it. Is it something about the line work? The colors used? A particular technique? The subject matter? Try to be as specific as possible, because this will help you lock into details that you then can try yourself.

Copy to learn
Many artists know the benefits of copying from others' work they like, not as a shortcut to success, but to learn. The action of creating your own version of someone else's work teaches your mind and hand about the little decisions the other artist made. This is far more effective than gramming, saving stuff on Pinterest, and downloading oodles of images to collect is ever going to be.

Try using different materials
I've had lots of "happy accidents" when trying an unfamiliar type of brush, or pen, or paper, just to see what I can do with it. You might stumble across a way of sketching that feels better for you based on how a particular new marker works in your hand.

Play to your strengths
What shapes and ways of sketching are you most comfortable and confident with? What do you enjoy? What looks and works best about your sketching to your eye? Focus on that, and then incorporate that into every sketch that you do.

Be patient with yourself
Despite what some people might say, it does take time and practice to develop that consistent confidence. So, go easy on yourself, celebrate the small wins, and reward yourself when you turn out a sketch that you're really happy with.

Find a community

Sing the Michael Jackson song "You Are Not Alone" to yourself, and find others who are into sketching, too.[3] Put your work in front of others more experienced than you, and ask them for advice on refining the way you sketch.

Weed out bad habits

Even top athletes and elite public speakers have little habits that they try to catch and get rid of.[4] One way to do this is to critique a sketch you've done that has those habits in it, and then redraw it, paying attention to avoiding those habits.

Thankfully, there are some great ways to help bring your existing sketches to life and add character to them in different ways, which we'll take a look at now. As you read these examples and sketch the exercises, think about how these tricks could amplify your own style.

Adding Visual Emphasis to Your Sketches

You'd be amazed at how much character, style, and vitality you can bring out quite quickly by trying these easy additions and embellishments to your sketching.

FORMATTING IMAGES

I'm sure you're used to changing the format of text, using features like **bold**, *italics*, and underlining. Each of these formatting changes implies a different sort of emphasis to the text. Using this principle, you can apply "formatting" to your images, too.

Consider the sketch of some figures in Figure 9-1. Which figure do you notice first? And why is that? Your eyes can't help but gravitate to the figure with a thicker line. This is applying a common design principle of **contrast**: our eyes can't help but lock on to areas of highest difference between light and dark. In this way, you can "bold" your images, for emphasis.

---

3 We'll come back to this point in more detail in Chapters 13 and 14.

4 My own little habits that I try to get rid of are not leaving enough white space between words and frames (my work can look a bit cluttered), and going back over some lines unnecessarily.

FIGURE 9-1

Bolding your sketches: Which of these figures did you notice first? Our eyes lock on to areas of higher contrast, like thicker lines.

FRAMING IMAGES

You can also emphasize images by adding visual framing elements around them, like boxes and banners, just like the ones we learned about in Chapter 5. Framing elements also work really well when placed "underneath" the object you've sketched, as demonstrated in Figure 9-2.

FIGURE 9-2

Some examples of adding frames in sketches: Frames can be around or under other elements in your sketches.

ADDING TEXTURE TO IMAGES

Another way to add visual interest and richer meaning is by using textural patterns, like the examples in Figure 9-3. Experiment with different effects, like a couple of light lines to convey shiny plastic, or stippling and cross-hatching to convey dirt and dust, or wear and tear.

FIGURE 9-3

Some examples of visual texture: Experiment with lines, dots, and cross-hatching to convey different surfaces and effects.

ADDING SHADOWS TO IMAGES

It's marvelous what adding a simple shadow to your sketch can do, whether it's to add emphasis or bring it to life. As soon as you add a shadow, a little bit of magic happens; the shadow acts as an illusion, tricking the eye to believe that the object is separated from the surface beneath it (Figure 9-4). Even if the object itself is rendered in two dimensions, a shadow will turn it into a three-dimensional object in space, before your very eyes.

FIGURE 9-4

Examples of shadows in action: The top row demonstrates objects with shadows sketched with a black marker. The bottom row shows some objects with shadows sketched in with gray tint marker. Black shadows are more dramatic.

Note that for the effect to work, it must obey the laws of how light falls on objects and shadows are cast. This is important especially if you have two or more objects together; their shadows must be "cast" from the same source of light.

My biggest tip with shadows is to be neat. Take that extra moment to make the shadow line run parallel to the object, and avoid the temptation to do hurried scribbly shading in (Figure 9-5).

FIGURE 9-5
Examples of shadows done wrong and right: Analyze with your eyes why two of these shadows look wrong and two look correct.

But don't let this put you off! Drawing in a shadow really is pretty easy. And as bang for your sketching buck goes, it's hard to beat. The simplest way to add a shadow is by adding a line directly under an object, like in Figure 9-6.

FIGURE 9-6
Examples of shadows as single lines under some objects: You don't need to put a line under parts that are in midair.

Another easy method that's similar to the first is to add a line to the side as well, join them up to the object, and color in the space that those lines now contain (Figure 9-7).

FIGURE 9-7

A simple way to add a shadow: The top row shows how you can add a shadow to a shape, step by step. The bottom row shows that it's OK to move the shadow around underneath the object, provided that the angles in the corners stay consistent. That last one is wonky; how do you think you would redraw that to fix it up?

HALOS AND OTHER VISUAL EFFECTS

Finally, there's a group of other "formatting" effects that you might like to try in your sketching (Figure 9-8) that involve borrowing a lot from the visual language of comics.

FIGURE 9-8

Some examples of other effects to try: A figure breaking out of a frame, shock lines around a face, flash lines and splat lines around anything, and—er—liquid lines.

EXERCISES

EASY **Exercise 9-1: Format some objects**

Draw a few objects like you did in Exercise 6-3. Now try a range of the formatting tricks on each object, like bolding, adding frames, and adding textures.

EASY **Exercise 9-2: Add shadow to some objects**

Practice some shadows by drawing some shapes and filling in the shadow line and shadow with your marker. Be bold and go for high contrast.

CREATIVE **Exercise 9-3: Shadow boxing**

Get a magazine and a marker. Go through and add shadows to objects and people. Pay attention to where you position the shadows and to the shadow line. Try to make the shadows look pretty convincing.

Color

"Finally, we get to use color!" I hear many of you gasp. There's so much you can do for visual thinking and communicating in just black and white and gray, but it would be a pretty dreary Presto World if we didn't have color, wouldn't it?

The main thing about color in Presto Sketching is that we can use it for emphasis and meaning, not just for realism. Obviously, there are going to be times where a dash of color will achieve all those things, but try to focus on using color to draw attention or inject more meaning rather than just trying to make the sketch more realistic.

THE MEANING OF COLOR

There's a lot of faux-science snake oil around explaining why certain colors seem to invoke certain things and why certain people prefer some colors to others. Suffice it to say, it's *not* like some people have bigger bunches of neurons in their brains that get super excited whenever orange comes into view, or anything like that.

Research shows[5] that there are a host of factors that influence our views of color, including our surroundings, experiences, cultural differences, the fact that my ex-girlfriend always wore purple, and so on. So be wary of the thinking that using orange in your sketches will make everyone run out and buy your product.

Having said that, colors can definitely mean different things in different cultures, and there are definitely trends in mood and character traits associated with various colors, largely because those associations are continually perpetuated by product marketing, branding, movies, and other places that use color.

Bottom line? Explore colors and color combinations that you enjoy, and that hold some contextual meaning for the material that you're sketching. If your sketches are going to be viewed by people from cultures different from yours, it's best to test your color combinations with them early on.

COMBINING DIFFERENT COLORS

It can be tempting to spray all sorts of colors all over your sketches, and there's definitely a place for riotous explosions of color in sketching. But in Presto Sketching, where you probably don't have a lot of time, it's best to stick to a few colors at a time.

So, which colors should you use? Obviously, it's up to you, your preferences, your situation, and what colors you actually have on hand, but there is in fact some theory that might help. Here's where we need to bring in our good friend, the color wheel.

The color wheel and color schemes

The basic color wheel comprises 12 colors; 6 of these are warm, 6 are cool. I've done one in Figure 9-9 using Copic art markers.

---

5   The most comprehensive review I could find on this is "*Color Psychology: A Critical Review,*" by T.W. Whitfield and T.J. Wiltshire (*Genetic, Social and General Psychology Monographs*, 1990 Nov; 116(4):385–411).

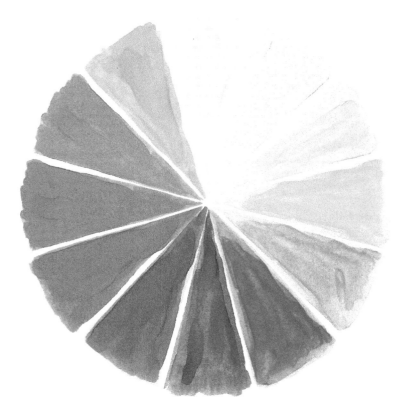

FIGURE 9-9

The color wheel: Your handy guide to navigating color harmony.

The spectrum of colors is made up of three types: primary colors, secondary colors, and tertiary colors. The primary colors are red, blue, and yellow; the secondary colors are the result of mixing the primaries with each other; and the tertiary colors are the result of mixing neighboring secondaries (Figure 9-10).

PRIMARY COLORS
Can't be formed by
mixing any other color

SECONDARY COLORS
Formed by mixing
primary colors with
each other

TERTIARY COLORS
Formed by mixing
adjoining primary and
secondary colors

FIGURE 9-10

Know your color types: A simple look at primary colors, secondary colors, and tertiary colors.

Now, why am I dredging this up from some distant memory of an art lesson in school? I'm glad you asked. It's because studies have shown[6] that people tend to like sets of colors with one contrasting color, rather than too many colors all over the place (when it comes to consumer behaviors such as reading content and selecting products).

Knowing different types of color schemes helps us understand different color harmonies, or what colors we can combine to stimulate different results (Figure 9-11).

---

6 You might like to check out "Aesthetic Response to Color Combinations: Preference, Harmony, and Similarity," by Karen Schloss and Stephen Palmer (*Attention, Perception and Psychophysics*, Feb 2011; 73(2):551–571) and "Consumer Preferences for Color Combinations: An Empirical Analysis of Similarity-Based Color Relationship," by Xiaoyan Deng, Sam K Hui, and J. Wesley Hutchinson (*Journal of Consumer Psychology*, 2010 Oct; 20(4):476–484).

COMPLEMENTARY COLORS
Opposites, for maximum
contrast

ANALOGOUS COLORS
Adjacent colors can
be soothing

TRIADIC COLORS
Dynamic equal spacing

SPLIT-COMPLEMENTARY
COLORS
High contrast, but not
as extreme

TETRADIC COLORS
Two complementary
pairs

SQUARE COLORS
Four colors, evenly
spaced

FIGURE 9-11

A variety of different color schemes: Try using different color combinations, and experiment with tint, shade, and saturation as well.

As a rule of thumb, it's good to feature one color with hints of other colors according to different schemes, like those shown in Figure 9-11.

Keep in mind, too, that you don't need to use colors at full intensity like the ones printed here; explore the nuances of *tint* (how much white is added to a color), *shade* (how much black is added to a color), and *saturation* (how pure or vivid the color is).

Figure 9-12 looks at this in action, with some colored examples of my friend, Stan the ukulele-playing pangolin.

FIGURE 9-12

Stan, the ukulele-playing pangolin, in different color schemes: Can you guess the color scheme types? Which one appeals to you the most?

APPLYING COLOR IN DIFFERENT WAYS

How you use color in your sketching will vary depending on the nature of the work and your level of confidence with color. Sometimes, it can be a trap: you may be tempted to apply too many colors at once when just one color would be perfect. The main thing is to experiment a bit. Try different types of color art markers, like the Copic art markers also earlier in this chapter or fine-line Stabilo markers. Try not using any black at all, but using two complementary colors instead. You'll be amazed at how playing with color can stimulate your own imagination and creativity.

Following are some different techniques for you to try out.

Spot color for emphasis and attention

Coloring specific elements adds immediate emphasis and attracts attention,[7] especially if there are multiples of those objects (Figure 9-13), or if there's visually a lot going on on the page. It's also an effective way of adding drama to a sketch.

---

7   This is known in psychology circles as the *isolation effect*, or the *Von Restorff effect*. German psychologist Hedwig Von Restorff showed in her 1933 research study how one different (isolated) item in a series of similar items was not only noticed the most, but *remembered* the most, as well.

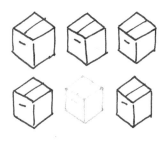 

FIGURE 9-13

Two examples of color used for emphasis: The colored box (left) implies importance, whereas the colored interface seen on the screen (right) draws the eye to it and focuses on its presence.

Different colors for different meanings

Figure 9-14 shows a few examples of how several colors can work together to communicate differences in the data or information you are presenting in your sketch. Whenever you use color to denote differences in information like this, always be mindful of how the colors appear to people who are colorblind.[8]

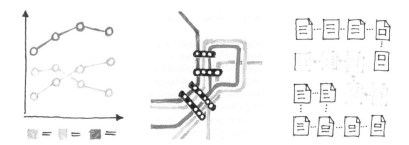

FIGURE 9-14

Examples of color used to denote different types of information: If you use color in this way, make sure the colors are of sufficient contrast to each other.

---

8   There are numerous online resources that you can use to check whether the colors you're using pass colorblindness and other accessibility tests. If hexadecimal color codes don't scare you off, a nice one is the Snook.ca Colour Contrast Check (*https://snook.ca/ technical/colour_contrast/colour.html*).

Background color for structure and interest

Adding background shapes is not only lots of fun but has the visual effect of lifting the subject off the page, and giving a sense of dimension to your sketch (Figure 9-15). Background shapes also help to unite several disparate elements among others.

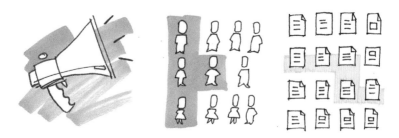

FIGURE 9-15

A few examples of color used for background: The orange Copic marker background behind the megaphone (left) adds energy. The orange background behind the four figures (middle) visually groups them and separates them from the others. The green Stabilo marker background behind the page icons (right) implies a pathway through those five pages.

Interface element color for interaction highlights

If you sketch user interfaces, sketching specific elements in color can really help people understand what is changing in your designs from screen to screen. You can use color to highlight specific parts of the interface that are changing state or appearing and disappearing. Those elements could be active navigation elements, buttons, or calls to action. This is particularly useful if you're sketching a sequence of screens representing a specific user pathway.

When using color in this way (Figure 9-16), I deliberately choose a color that isn't in the brand style color palette. This makes it really clear that colored areas represent *interactivity*, not visual design.

 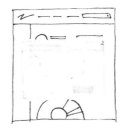 

FIGURE 9-16

Using color to show important differences in user interface sketches:
It's actually effective to use a color that's not associated with the brand of whatever it is you're designing. This minimizes any confusion about what the color means.

Color and other visual effects like line weight, frames, and shadows are fantastic elements to experiment with, so it's worth filling a few pages of your sketchbook with different ideas and combinations (Figure 9-17). Before you know it, you'll begin to see a visual style emerging that you can call your own.

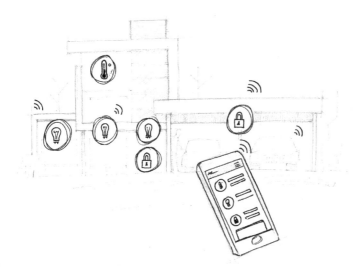

FIGURE 9-17

A figurative sketch of a mobile phone and a smart home: In this example, I've sketched the main elements of focus in black (the phone and the "smart" icons of temperature, power, and security), while rendering the house in blue Stabilo marker and blue Copic marker.

EXERCISES

EASY **Exercise 9-4: Practice sketching in color**

Take some color markers—preferably smaller ones, like Stabilo fine-liner markers or Copic tint markers—and practice applying color on the page by doing Exercise 4-2 (back in Chapter 4) again. Get a feel for different ways of using the markers, and notice how you can build up the intensity of the color.

Watch out for bleed! It depends on the paper you're using as well as the marker solvent (water-based or alcohol-based).

CREATIVE **Exercise 9-5: Dial up the drama by adding color**

Draw some figures as silhouettes, and some faces. Now, dial up the drama by adding different colors to them. Try jagged red around an angry face, or a curvy green swatch of color behind a walking figure.

TRICKY **Exercise 9-6: A colorful hand and phone sketch**

Use the foundation lines technique from Chapter 6 to draw a hand holding a phone. Ink it in with black. Then, grab your color markers and add some color accents to the user interface displayed on the screen of the phone.

SOME QUESTIONS FOR YOU

What do you want your style to be?

Do you have a better sense of what your style is now? Or, do you have an idea of what you'd like your style to be? How would you describe it?

Whose work do you admire?

Take some time to graze Pinterest, Amazon, and your local bookstore and art supplies store. Whose work do you admire that you'd like to emulate? Analyze why you like it (refer to page 195).

What are your sketching strengths?

What sort of sketching do you feel confident with? What subject matter do you enjoy? What looks and works best about your sketching to your eye?

[10]

Tackling the Problems

THE FIRST AREA WE'LL look at applying our Presto Sketching powers to is understanding products, services, systems, and the world around us. We can tackle problems a lot better when we can see them in different ways, analyze them in different ways, and communicate them to others in different ways.

Let's see how this approach applies to understanding the following:

- People with the Empathy Map
- Value exchange with the Value Relationship Map
- A product experience with the Journey Map
- An offering with the Value Proposition Canvas
- A system with Concept Modeling
- An organization with the SWAM Canvas
- An organization's place in the world with the PESTLE Canvas

Why All These Maps and Canvases?

It's much easier to mentally keep track of a lot of parts of a problem, situation, or solution by—surprise, surprise—visualizing them all together as some sort of map. That way, it's easier to see which part to focus on and which other parts are related to it.

These sorts of maps also give you and your team a *common method* to understand and solve whatever it is you're working on, a *common language* to use, and a *common reference* throughout the project (and after the project), as illustrated in Figure 10-1.

COMMON METHOD   COMMON LANGUAGE   COMMON REFERENCE

FIGURE 10-1

A common method, a common language, and a common reference: Maps and canvases are an efficient way to—as they say—keep everyone on the same page.

Some maps have already been worked out by others (based on regular patterns in things like products, services, and businesses), like the Empathy Map and Value Proposition Canvas. These have been working super well for countless organizations for a while now, so it makes sense to use them where you can.

Other maps can be made only by you and your team, because you're the ones who really know your domain, your business, and your customers best. This is where you can apply other methods (like journey mapping and storyboarding) as well as your powers of conceptual representation to produce your own visualizations.

Since we're looking at using visual thinking and visual communication to understand and tackle problems, let's begin with a map of the various parts we're going to look at. I hereby present to you: The Burger of Understanding (Figure 10-2).

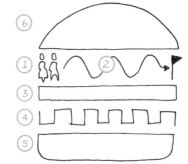

1. People and their goals
2. Product experience
3. Product or service
4. System
5. Organization
6. The world around

FIGURE 10-2

The Burger of Understanding: This is a simple map of the various parts that we're going to delve into. It shows at a high level how each part relates to the others.

I believe in keeping people at the heart of the solution that I'm working on, so I have put them and their goals in the middle. This is closely tied to the experience they have with a product or service (number 2 in Figure 10-2). The product that they are using (number 3) conceptually sits underneath them, and on top of the parts of the system that support that product (number 4). Under that part of the system sits the organization (number 5). Finally, the world "outside" the organization is conceptually above everything else, as number 6.

HOW TO USE THESE PATTERNS

The visual patterns in this chapter (as well as Chapters 11 and 12) use a variety of elements from Part 2. These patterns work well whether you're using them by yourself or as a team.

It's crucial that you use these as a catalyst for deeper thinking and better conversations, rather than just as "filling in the boxes" exercises. Remember that circle of synthesis we looked at in Chapter 3? The magic is in giving your brain and your hand the best opportunity to work together as you sketch, to uncover insight and to refine your thinking.

In the same way, there'll be more magic if you and your team talk and sketch together to frame problems and generate ideas rather than just passively talking around a table. Take time to consider what each person in the group has sketched and written, ask questions, and be prepared to "rinse and repeat" the activity (Figure 10-3) for better results. Use these patterns with an attitude of being ready to see problems and ideas in new ways.

FIGURE 10-3

Sketch together for deeper thinking and insight: The visual patterns in this section are made to be tried several times, either individually or together as a team; don't be discouraged if the first time isn't magical.

In other words, you can't box-check your way to breakthrough thinking!

Using them by yourself

You can use these visual patterns as a way of organizing your thoughts and ideas first, before putting them in front of anyone else. That way, you can develop your own thinking, and get a feel for what it'll be like for your entire team.

If you have a whiteboard near you, you can also "think in public"; you can work away at the whiteboard by yourself, and then grab people as they walk by for their thoughts and feedback.

Using them as a team

I know what you're thinking: facilitating something like this is best left to the experts, right? Believe it or not, you're probably a better facilitator than you give yourself credit for. With a bit of preparation and a clear objective, you'll definitely be on your way to cracking that long-standing product conundrum, or hatching a new set of feature ideas. What's more, each of these visual patterns has some facilitation baked in, as you'll see.

Here are some facilitation tips to help you get the most out of these patterns:

Help people to do their homework
> When everyone who's attending prepares well, by reading up on the area they're responsible for, everyone will be more invested in the session's success. Help them by gathering links to important information, or other shortcuts to save them time.

Be clear about the objective
> Make sure everyone knows ahead of time what will be covered, and what you're collectively meant to achieve by the end of the session.

Give people jobs to do
> You don't have to shoulder everything yourself! Increase everyone's engagement levels by giving people specific jobs to do, to help the session move along efficiently. Do you need a timekeeper? What about someone to take photos of what people are sketching and writing? And I'm sure someone can go and get coffee and snacks for everyone, too.

Start with a brain oiler
> Kick off the session by getting everyone to answer a simple but interesting question, to help get their minds in the right place for the session, like "What's one thing you personally want to get out of the session?" or "When was a time you were really frustrated with a product, and why?"[1]

---

1   This can eat up a bit of time, so if the group has more than eight people, consider organizing people into pairs and getting them to ask each other.

As a facilitator, it's often easier to keep a discussion on track, and to help everyone listen and analyze, by asking questions like "Is this the right conversation to have?" or "Is this moving us closer to the decision?" Asking "Why..." and "What if..." questions is always useful, too.

See the shapes in the conversation

In writing about how to use these visual patterns, I'm assuming that you're in the driver's seat when it comes to running each meeting. But what about when you're not? What about those times when you're sitting there in long, drawn-out discussions, going around and around with no outcome?

Those are the times when you can really bring out your powers of synthesis and sketching! Remember the UST model in Chapter 3, and how most people find it difficult to translate what they're synthesizing into anything else but words? You can use your growing mental library of visual patterns to help them.

"Whoa, that's a big ask Ben," you might be thinking. But remember in Chapter 6 how you used your mind's eye to break down complex objects into simple geometric shapes, to help you sketch them?

Guess what? Conversations are the same.

When you hear a complex conversation, try to "see" the separate "shapes" within the conversation. By recognizing a "shape" and adding just a little bit of structure by using a visual pattern, you will help everyone involved have a much more useful conversation.

Here is a list of conversation "shapes" (or things that people are actually after) that I have found come up regularly in meetings, workshops, offsites, and so on:

- Shared clarity
- Fresh thinking and discovery
- Actionable insights
- Invention
- Strategic perspective
- Prioritizing

- Direction and alignment

The patterns we're about to explore help bring more meaning and structure to conversations when these shapes emerge.

So, with all that in mind, let's dig into the patterns themselves. Each visual pattern includes the following:

- A description

- Advice as to when to use it (according to what you want to achieve)

- A tutorial on how to do it

The more you use them, the more you can adapt them to help explore different situations, problems, ideas, and plans that you have at your work.

Understanding People with the Empathy Map

When it comes to visually exploring and understanding people and their goals for product and service design, it's difficult to find a better tool than the Empathy Map. The version displayed in Figure 10-4 is a recently updated version created by Dave Gray (founder of XPLANE).[2] I've used the Empathy Map both individually and with others for years, and it's a really effective way to capture raw information from research results about a predetermined type of customer or prospect for your product.[3]

---

2 The Empathy Map is one of many hugely valuable activities described in the book *Gamestorming: A Playbook for Innovators, Rulebreakers, and Changemakers*, by Dave Gray, Sunni Brown, and James Macanufo (O'Reilly).

3 If you're new to the field of user research or want to up your skills, you might like to check out *UX Research: Practical Techniques for Designing Better Products*, by Brad Nunnally and David Farkas (O'Reilly), and *Just Enough Research* by Erika Hall (A Book Apart).

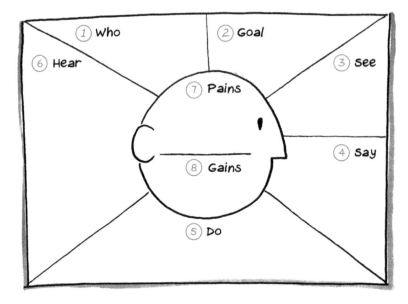

FIGURE 10-4
The Empathy Map: Capture everything about what's going on in the heads, hearts, and hands of your customers. This is a recently updated version that features an area for the customer goals.

This is the best visual tool for getting a team to "mentally sit with" customers themselves and deeply consider their hopes and dreams, their habits, and the factors that drive their behavior. That's what empathizing with customers is all about.[4]

And now that it has been updated with a Goals section, it's easier to use for *making design decisions for customers.* By that I mean that it structures research information in a way that the team can then pick up and apply to product planning, designing, and building more easily.

Use this pattern when you want to do the following:

- Get help in distilling customer research information into something actionable by a team.

---

4   Another avenue for synthesizing research results about what drives customer behavior is constructing their mental models. For a terrific reference all about researching and constructing mental models, look no further than *Mental Models: Aligning Design Strategy with Human Behavior,* by Indi Young (Rosenfeld Media).

- Clarify what you know about your customers, and separate facts from assumptions.

- Unearth gaps in your understanding about your customers.

- Help a team get a shared understanding for what is driving your customers.

Here's how do to it:

1. Draw up a canvas using the pattern shown in Figure 10-3 for each type of customer (external) or stakeholder (internal) that you want to map on paper or a whiteboard. Don't worry if you have a lot and can't decide which are most important; part of this activity is to help you see where you can refine and reduce.

2. Fill in all of the sections using the numbers as a guide. For each section, think about the questions included, write answers on as many sticky notes as you want, and stick them up in a separate area. Go through all of the sticky notes, look for patterns, and transfer a summarized version over to the Empathy Map itself.

3. After you've finished all of the sections, cross-check each section with the others for consistency. For example, sometimes there's information in the Pains and Gains sections that can help you articulate the Goals.

4. After doing Empathy Maps for all the various types of customers you think you have, analyze the entire set that you've drawn. Which ones have unique sets of goals? Which ones could be combined?

5. Don't throw them away! Refine them if need be, but stick each Empathy Map up in your team area to remind everyone who your product is there for.

This is what each section means:

1. **Who**

   Who are we empathizing with? Who is the person we want to understand, and what situation is she in? What's her role in that situation?

2. **Goal**

What are the customer's goals? *Why* is the customer doing what he's doing? Does he have emotional goals (e.g., "to feel in control of my future") as well as tactical goals ("to save enough money for my retirement")? If you're familiar with the "JTBD" way of thinking, this is where the jobs go.[5]

3. **See**

   What does the customer see? What does the customer see in her environment, marketplace, what others are saying around her, and the media she reads that affects her view and behavior?

4. **Say**

   What does the customer say? What have you heard this type of customer say, to others they work with, and/or other customers?

5. **Do**

   What does the customer do? What does the customer currently do to achieve his goals? What other products does he use that are similar to yours?

6. **Hear**

   What does the customer hear? What does the customer hear from her colleagues, friends, and family that affects her view and behavior?

7. **Pains**

   What are the customer's pains? What are the customer's pain points, fears, frustrations and worries? What is getting in the way of him accomplishing his goals?

8. **Gains**

   What are the customer's gains? What are the customer's wants, needs, hopes, and dreams? What would a perfect day for him be, if he did what he needed to do and achieved the goals you've included above?

---

5   JTBD stands for "jobs to be done." In other words, what job is your customer hiring your product to do for him? JTBD is a customer-centered rationale devised by scholar, consultant, and author Clayton Christensen. Thinking about your product in terms of a job to be done is a great way to focus on customer need, rather than product feature set. The "job" should begin with a verb and can be functional (e.g., "cut my grass") or emotional ("give me that feeling of satisfaction when I look at a nicely trimmed front lawn"). Hire your "give me more information on JTBD" job at *jobstobedone.org*.

Understanding Value Exchange by Using Value Relationship Mapping

No one person is an island, as they say, and products often depend on several types of customers using them at once to succeed. I mean, where would Tinder be if no one actually looked at the photos people posted of themselves?

Although the Empathy Map is great for understanding what tasks each type of customer needs to do and why, they're probably not doing those tasks in isolation. Value Relationship Maps are a way of visualizing the different sorts of value exchanges that exist between those various parts and roles. If you can visualize these exchanges, you can better understand how your product plays among them as a connected system.

Value exchanges can be simple and *explicit*, like a customer and a baker exchanging money for bread (Figure 10-5), or *implicit*, like a parent and child exchanging nourishment and teaching for feelings of fulfillment and purpose.

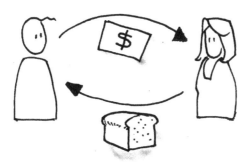

FIGURE 10-5

A simple value exchange: I pay money to my local baker, and she gives me a loaf of bread. My value to the baker is money. The baker's value to me is bread.

Sometimes Value Relationship Maps can reveal surprising insights, like a particular internal service being underused, or a specific role in a business providing all kinds of value to multiple parts of the business (visualized with many arrows radiating out from that role) but not getting much in return.

In the second example, shown in Figure 10-6, we can see that the Help Desk role is providing all sorts of value internally (to management, one another, IT, and the knowledgebase) *and* externally (to customers), outnumbering other roles' value relationships by four to one.

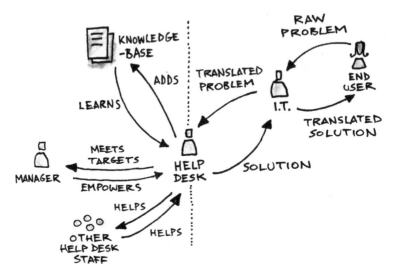

FIGURE 10-6

A more complex value exchange: Mapping more complex sets of value exchanges can reveal redundancies and risky dependencies in teams and systems.

It's widely accepted that customers should be at the center of a business. This might make sense in spirit, but Value Relationship Maps can show that it might not make sense from a system point of view. Looking at the example depicted in Figure 10-6, it's clear how crucial the Help Desk role is in order for the entire system to work smoothly.

Use this pattern when you want to do the following:

- Get a better understanding of the value chain in a product or service.

- Gain insights about unlocking new value in a system of people, products, and services.

Here's how to do it:

1. Draw all the roles involved in the problem or situation you need to understand (like the Manager, Help Desk, IT, and End User roles in Figure 10-6).[6]

2. Draw arrows from one role to another wherever there is a relationship; that is, some value given.

   It's okay if it gets messy, that's part of the fun! It's also okay if some value exchanges are only one-way. You will probably need to draw the map a few times as you rearrange and neaten up the organization of those entities and relationships.

3. Step back and visually analyze the map of value relationships you've created. Are there any entities with lots of "spokes" radiating from them? What might this indicate? Are there any entities to which you found it really difficult to attribute any value relationships? Does this point to any areas where you need to flesh out more information in order to understand the system better?

Understanding a Product Experience by Using Journey Mapping

Like Empathy Maps, Journey Maps can get your team and stakeholders closer to the hearts and minds of customers and move them in ways that data and metrics alone can't. Journey Maps, which you can see in Figure 10-7, are also a brilliant diagnostic tool; they let you take a bird's-eye view of an entire chain of events to see the important signals above the noise of detail.

---

6   For a refresher on this, check out page 82.

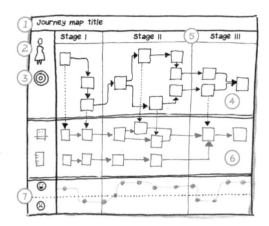

	Journey map title			
① TITLE	①			
② MAIN CUSTOMER TYPE		Stage I	Stage II ⑤	Stage III
③ GOAL	②			
④ ON-STAGE	③			④
⑤ JOURNEY STAGES				
⑥ OFF-STAGE				
⑦ SENTIMENT CHART				⑥
	⑦			

FIGURE 10-7

The anatomy of the Journey Map: Journey Maps can vary in content (and size), but they always show at least one main customer type and their on-stage actions toward a goal.

Different roles in your team will want to focus on different types of information in a Journey Map to solve different types of problems. Here are some examples:

Designers

Seeing the overall coherence of the flow (i.e., do all the steps being taken hang together properly as a whole, or are there disconnections or redundancies?); seeing where the pain points and mismatches in expectations are; and seeing potential areas to lift the experience in different ways

Product managers

Identifying opportunities to improve customers' evaluation customers' experience evaluating and using the product/service; spotting opportunities for upselling, cross-selling, and introducing new features; and checking if user stories (if they are writing user stories for planning and estimating work) align with tasks and goals that customers actually have

Content writers

Seeing how the language and location of interface copy and documentation is lining up with customers' questions and decisions

Researchers

Spotting assumptions the team might have as well as gaps in information and understanding that need further investigation

Journey Maps are also a brilliant way to plot what's going on for the customers "on stage" as they use the product, versus what's going on "off stage"; that is, the people, processes, and systems behind the scenes that are needed to provide that experience.

If you have your map of customers' tasks and goals, it's a very good idea to then visually map out how they do those tasks over time, using this journey mapping technique.

As with all of these visual patterns, your Journey Map doesn't need to be perfect the first time. Give one another permission to make mistakes, and expect to uncover more insights and assumptions as you try it several times. Aim for progress more than perfection!

Here's how to do it. This set of steps yields a Journey Map as a living thing that you and your team can continue to use and consult for reference:

1. Ensure that you have a clear and shared understanding of the main customer type that you're going to map and that customer's end goal. Gather your team and find a large wall or whiteboard. Begin by writing the customer type and the customer's goal on sticky notes. Then, stick them up at the upper left of your Journey Map area, as shown in Figure 10-8.

2. What is the last thing you think the customer is going to do? Write that on a sticky note and stick it up at the upper right of your Journey Map area (Figure 10-8).[7]

---

7 I like starting with the end in mind; it's amazing what clarity even this simple step can bring to your thinking and to the team's understanding.

FIGURE 10-8

Capture the boundaries first: Write sticky notes to show the customer type, the goal, and the last thing you think the customer will do to achieve that goal.

3. Think about how the customer achieves his goal, step by step, and write each step on a separate sticky note (Figure 10-9). What is the customer thinking, feeling, and doing along the way? Try to do this fairly rapidly, and fill the space between each end with as many sticky notes as you can. Messy is good! Try not to overthink it as you go.

FIGURE 10-9

Fill the space with the on-stage journey: Capture what the customer is thinking, feeling, and doing along the way toward the goal.

4. Go back over your sticky notes and groom them where you can. Are there any distinct stages that the journey goes through?[8] Are there any duplicates you can remove or steps on which you need to expand?

---

8 A common set of stages is called the Five E's: Entice, Enter, Engage, Exit, and Extend.

5. As a team, analyze the journey and write up more sticky notes, in a different color if need be. What pain points are worth paying attention to? What moments of truth are happening that really define or change the journey in some way? Are there any gaps that make the journey awkward for the customer?

6. You've just mapped out and analyzed what the customer experience is like "on stage." If it's important for your context, run the journey again, but this time capture what's going on "off stage," as demonstrated in Figure 10-10. What people, processes, and tools are involved behind the scenes that link up with what you've captured here?

FIGURE 10-10

Capture what's going on behind the scenes: If necessary, go through the journey again and capture what's going on "off stage."

As you capture various aspects of the journey like this, try to make at least some of the different sections line up vertically so that it's easy for everyone to link up the most significant moments in the journey with what's going on behind the scenes.

7. If you like, run a line underneath the Journey Map, and add a customer sentiment chart (Figure 10-11). For each moment in the journey, mark a circle to indicate the customer's sentiment on a vertical scale, with happy at the top and frustrated at the bottom.

This is definitely not a scientific exercise, and not very quantitative. Its main purpose is to visualize large dips in sentiment to which the team should pay attention.

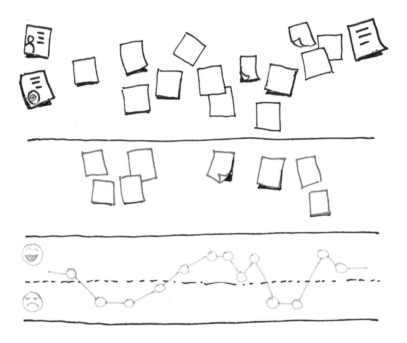

FIGURE 10-11
Add a customer sentiment chart: Plot circles showing approximately where the customer's feeling is at each significant moment in the journey.

8. The last step is to synthesize all those sticky notes that the group generated into a map that everyone can continue to refer to, along the lines of the template shown in Figure 10-7. By now I hope you can appreciate that building it first with sticky notes on a wall, rather than going straight to pixels using some sort of graphics software, lets you synthesize more rapidly and effectively. Once all the sticky notes are done, sketching the map allows you to have that conversation with your mind and hand about what to extract and give greater visual prominence, what to discard, and how to arrange it all.

This is only a very brief description of how to make a Journey Map with others, and it's well worth diving into other resources if you'd like to know more.[9]

It's really valuable getting a team to make a Journey Map like this together, because of the shared insights and revelations it generates. There's so much magic in the making as well as what is made.

Understanding an Offering with the Value Proposition Canvas

There are boatloads of books and articles out there to help you if you're creating a brand-new product or service. But my experience tells me that most people are engaged with *existing* products and services. What's more, they often inherit a product or service that has loads of legacy code and legacy thinking, loads of disparate systems and teams involved, and loads of competing long-term priorities to achieve, while still having to pay attention to a backlog of bugs and issues as long as their arm.

That's a lot to untangle and understand!

The first step is to make sure you and your team are crystal clear on the purpose and value of whatever the offering is, both to your customers and to the growth and sustainability of your own business. You need to be rock solid on what success means for your feature, product, or service (from both perspectives) and how you can measure that success.

I've always found doing a Value Proposition Canvas with a team is a great way to achieve this clarity and to galvanize a team for how to improve the offering. It's also a brilliant way to diagnose how well an offering is aligned with the needs of those customers you have analyzed earlier.

The Value Proposition Canvas shown in Figure 10-12 is my variation of the original Value Proposition Canvas created by Alexander Osterwalder.[10] I use a modified version, shown in Figure 10-12; my

---

9 Jeff Patton's *User Story Mapping: Discover the Whole Story, Build the Right Product* (O'Reilly) is a marvelous book, and includes really useful details about transforming such a map into a set of actionable user stories for designers, developers, QAs, and others to work on.

10 Osterwalder's Value Proposition Canvas is copyrighted and can only be published with credit to his firm, Strategyzer (*http://www.strategyzer.com*).

version places the customer on the left and the offering on the right, to emphasize focusing on the customer before the value proposition. It also includes *channels*; that is, how the value of the offering comes to the customer. To me, the *way* through which that value is given is often part of the value itself.

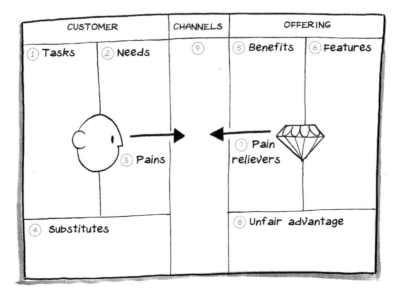

FIGURE 10-12
Value Proposition Canvas: This is my take on the Value Proposition Canvas; it includes a space to add channels (or how the offering reaches the customer), which to me is part of its value.

Use this pattern when you want to do the following:

- Move a discussion with a team about a product from being about features to being about value.

- Discuss and get alignment on the value of your product with a team.

- Clarify and prioritize any aspects (messages and benefits) of your product according to target customer types and whether they're "choosers" or "users."

Here's how to do it:

1. Draw up the canvas that you see in Figure 10-12 on a wall or whiteboard, and label the various sections as indicated.

2. Write the particular customer type to which this value is going to be offered. If you're not sure, try the empathy mapping technique to highlight which ones are most important for your offering.

3. Either by yourself or as a team, fill in the customer side first (Tasks, Needs, Pains, and Substitutes); if you've already done an Empathy Map for this particular customer, this should be a good reinforcing exercise.

4. Next, fill in the offering side (Features, Benefits, Pain relievers, Unfair advantage).

5. As a group, analyze what you've produced. Is the offering side actually relieving *that* pain and creating *that* gain for the customer, rather than just being a list of previously known but unconnected items? Is your offering as *relevant* and *resonant* for the customer as it could be?

As I mentioned earlier, don't be afraid to rinse and repeat; it's rare that you'll nail this in one go. Be prepared for some tough thinking and tough decisions; laying all these vital elements out visually is a great opportunity to sense-check that your product's fit for purpose, but it can raise more questions than it answers!

This is what each section means:

Tasks
> *What* does the customer want to do?

Needs
> This is synonymous with goals, or JTBD (as I described for the Empathy Map). *Why* does the customer want to do what she's doing? Just like with the Empathy Map, it's good to record emotional needs (e.g., "to feel in control of my future") as well as tactical needs ("to save enough money for my retirement").

Pains
> What are the customer's pain points about what she's experiencing now? What is getting in the way of her getting those tasks done and those needs fulfilled?

Substitutes

What products is she using instead of your product? What other behaviors, hacks, and workarounds does she employ instead of using your product?

Features

What are the features of your product that will get the customer's tasks done and her needs achieved?

Benefits

Why would this customer use those features? Why should she care?

Pain relievers

What are the things about your product that give immediate relief to the pains the customer is experiencing?

Unfair advantage

Considering what you've included in the sections for Benefits and Pain relievers, what does your product offer this customer that no other product can provide? This can be unbelievably difficult to articulate, but it's really *really* worth it.

Channels

How does this customer experience your product? Note: this isn't about advertising and attracting new customers; this is after they *are* customers. Is it through an app on her mobile phone first thing in the morning? Is it on her laptop at work?

Understanding a System with Concept Modeling

Just as we saw earlier in value relationship mapping, no one person is an island, and we need to see that each product or service or business unit or whatever we're dealing with is usually part of a connected system. As convenient as it would be to just focus on one thing, at some point we need to see that one thing as a connected part of a greater whole. We need to know what's going on in other parts that might have an effect on our part.

Conceptual representation is perfect for this. Conceptual representation visualizes and explains invisible, intangible concepts in terms of connected entities, relationships, and spaces (if you need a refresher on conceptual representation, go to Chapter 8).

Conceptual models themselves (or concept models, or concept maps) can be anything from light sketches on a whiteboard (such as the learning management system concept model I've sketched in Figure 10-13) to polished, full-color, three-dimensional illustrations, professionally printed as posters on the wall.

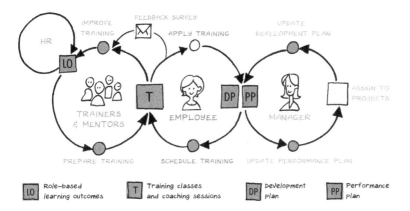

FIGURE 10-13

Conceptual model of a learning management system: This is a simple diagram of a system to coordinate learning and professional development. Note the mix of entities (e.g., staff, trainers), relationships (staff use the education resources), and spaces (the management area versus the delivery area).

They often use visual metaphor as well (Chapter 7), because metaphor is really good for explaining *unfamiliar* concepts using *familiar* concepts, or as a way to unify several separately understood concepts into one. Figure 10-14 shows two conceptual models of change management. We could just use plain boxes (left), but visualizing the three areas as a layer cake opens up avenues to add more meaning, interest, and memorability.

Conceptual models are an ideal companion to the more technical boxes-and-arrows sort of diagrams you might be used to seeing, like object models, entity relationship diagrams (ERDs), and process diagrams. These technical diagrams are vital, but there are probably a lot of people you need to communicate with who aren't technically minded and don't need to see that amount of detail.

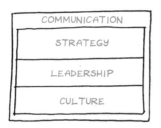 

FIGURE 10-14

A comparison of two ways to visualize a conceptual model of change management: The model on the left uses plain boxes, whereas the model on the right uses a layer cake visual metaphor. The three parts are discrete, but work together as a whole with communication (the icing). What might the candles represent? And if I drew a cherry on top, what might that be?

SYNTHESIZE THE ESSENCE OF THE SYSTEM

Most of the time when people want to visually think about or explain a system, they reach for boxes-and-arrows software like Visio, OmniGraffle, Lucidchart, and so on. There'll always be a place for boxes and arrows, and for software that generates those boxes and arrows, but there's a very important point to keep in mind.

Boxes and arrows are agnostic to the level of detail you need to show, and software tends to make it easier to create *more* boxes and arrows, not less. I suspect that you've seen system diagrams and other visual models that showed far too much detail, and you found it difficult to decipher what was really going on.

To paraphrase Albert Einstein: if you can't explain your system simply, you don't understand it well enough. The trick is to think, "What is the *essence* of my system?" What can you simplify in your visualization to make it really clear what it is, or what it does?

So, be careful with the level of detail! Decide at what level of detail you need to illustrate your system for each particular audience. Most of the time, people want to see a high-level view *first*, even just to get their bearings, before diving into any detail (Figure 10-15).

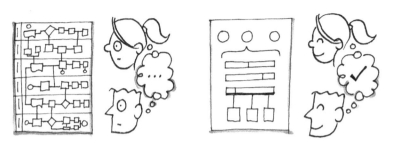

FIGURE 10-15

Decide on the level of detail to show your audience: Be careful not to bamboozle people when illustrating systems! Most people like simplicity and one main idea at a time (even though they might never tell you this).

USE A WELL-UNDERSTOOD METAPHOR

Sometimes, a great way to explain the essence of a system is to visualize it by using a metaphor, especially a metaphor that you know will resonate with your audience because of some shared understanding they have about the system, or the project, or whatever it is that you are visually describing.

If you can't think of a particular visual metaphor, you can always begin with food; everyone can relate to food!

For some reason things that look like food are just more fun, more interesting, more understandable, and more memorable. Figure 10-14 used a layer cake as the visual metaphor, and Figures 10-16 and 10-17 use a hot dog and a hamburger, respectively.[11]

---

11 I've actually really been wanting to come up with a concept model that sort of looks like a taco...but I haven't found such a system yet!

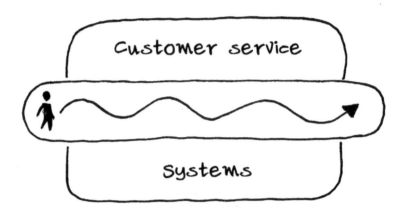

FIGURE 10-16
A "hot dog" conceptual model of customer service experience: The wavy
line represents the customer experience that conceptually sits "on top of" the
product, and looks like ketchup on a frankfurter. The entities of "customer
service" and "systems" conceptually "wrap around" the product and the
experience.

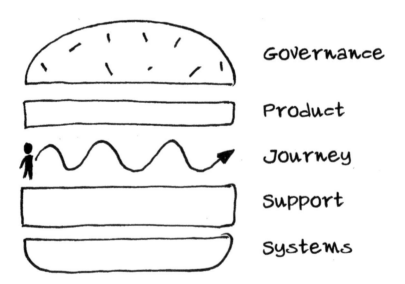

FIGURE 10-17
A "burger" conceptual model of customer experience: This model is a
variation of the preceding hot dog model. It includes a "governance" layer that
looks like the top of a burger bun.

Use this pattern when you want to do the following:

- Communicate an entire system in simple terms, before delving into detail.

- Communicate an unfamiliar concept that's made of several intangible entities, but framed in an approachable way.

- Get "up above" the level of screen designs and database schemas to show how several internal and external entities work together.

This visual pattern assumes that you have some sort of system in mind for which you want to create a conceptual model. We've seen a learning management system (Figure 10-13); other examples could be a product support system or a sales network. Here's how to do it:

1. Sketch the entities (or parts) involved in your system (you can use the examples described on pages 177 through 180 to help you). You can begin by sketching them as words in circles.

2. Next, think about how the entities sit together as a whole. Use the range of visual patterns described on pages 182 through 187 to think about how best to represent those relationships (maps, hierarchy relationships, and proximity relationships patterns tend to be good in these cases).

3. Are the parts "conceptually" stacked on top of one another? Or maybe most parts sit as a combined ring around one single part?

4. Now, try to think of a theme or metaphor that you could use to communicate the system that would resonate with your audience. If this system were a real thing in the world, what might it be like? A wall of many different-sized bricks? A river or lake? A spider's web? A building with different sorts of levels?

   You might like to check the library of visual metaphors in Chapter 7 or the reverse lookup table of concepts in Appendix A for inspiration.

5. Your sketches might look a bit crazy and complicated at this point, and that's totally fine. Remember our cane toads example in Chapter 8? There's no harm in actually producing several

illustrations of the same system, just like we did with the cane toads situation, and then asking yourself some synthesizing questions, such as these:

- What is the main point I'm trying to show here?
- What is important for each stakeholder to understand?
- What visual "landmarks" should I include so that each stakeholder can see where their "part" is?

6. It's always a good idea to put your sketched conceptual model in front of someone else (to see if it communicates what you want it to) and refine based on feedback. Iteration is great; it usually takes me a few rounds before a conceptual model makes some sense!

Understanding an Organization by Using the SWAM Canvas

As the 26th President of the United States (and owner of an epic mustache) Theodore Roosevelt said, "Keep your eyes on the stars, and your feet on the ground."

It's all too easy to stay in the weeds of features, traffic stats, and the latest nifty JavaScript framework, but it's oh-so important that we *also* keep a clear eye on *why* any of those things matter. It's important that someone in the organization is asking the right people (and reminding the right people) what the change that your organization wants to see in the world is, and how it is effecting that change.

That person will be well served with visual patterns to help others think about these high-falutin' conceptual things. Know anyone who would fit that bill? That's right: it's you! The rest of this chapter will help you to help others think about the value and purpose of your organization, and what it's putting out into the world to effect the desired change.

An effective way of gathering a lot of important strategic information— and highlighting gaps in understanding about that information— is the SWAM Canvas (Figure 10-18). SWAM stands for stars, wind, anchors, and mines, and is a fresh metaphorical take on the good old SWOT (strengths, weaknesses, opportunities, and threats) analysis. It also visually positions you, your team, and/or your organization as a boat in the middle. Because the boat itself is a metaphor, you can have a bit of visual fun with it; your organization might be more of a pirate ship, or a sleek yacht.[12]

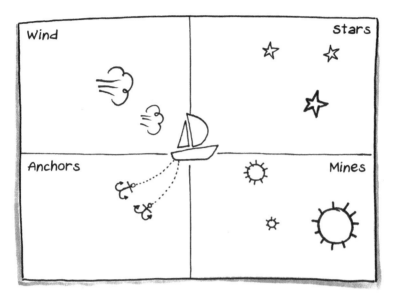

FIGURE 10-18
The SWAM Canvas: This canvas of stars, wind, anchors, and mines is a fresh metaphorical take on SWOT analysis.

Use this when you want to do the following:

- Analyze the strategic position of a team, product, or organization.
- Get a shared understanding of an organization's strategic position across a team (especially with new members).
- Clarify strategic direction and priorities for an organization.

Here's how to do it:

1. Gather the team (if you're doing it as a group) and draw up the SWAM Canvas, as shown in Figure 10-18. Remember to have a bit of visual fun sketching all of you in the boat.

---

12 But hopefully not something that looks like the *Titanic*!

2. Begin with the positive: ask everyone to write what they think the organization's strengths are on sticky notes (one strength per sticky note), and then stick them in the Wind quarter. This is what powers your boat.

3. Continue by asking everyone to list the opportunities they see and stick them in the Stars quarter. These are the stars by which you navigate your boat.

4. Next, ask everyone to list what they think the weaknesses are and stick them in the Anchors quarter. These are the things that are holding you back.

5. Finally, ask everyone to list what the threats are—both actual threats (just above the water) and possible threats (under the water)—and stick these up in the Mines quarter.

6. As a group, analyze the output and visually prioritize the elements in each quarter:

   · What are your biggest strengths? Sketch these as larger puffs of wind. How might you capitalize on these strengths more?

   · What are your biggest weaknesses? Sketch these as larger anchors with chains connecting them to the boat. How might you break those chains?

   · What are the most significant opportunities? Sketch these as larger stars. How might you "change course" to get to those opportunities sooner?

   · What are the most significant threats? Sketch these as larger mines, and think about how close they are to your boat. How might you avoid them?

After your group activity, try to sketch a more finessed version onto a large piece of paper, and keep it up on the wall so that your team can constantly refer to it.

Understanding an Organization's Place in the World by Using the PESTLE Canvas

The SWAM Canvas is great for understanding what's going on inside your organization, whereas the PESTLE Canvas is really useful for understanding the lay of the land *around* your organization.

PESTLE stands for political, economic, social, technological, legal, and environmental. It's derived from PEST (political, economic, social, and technological) analysis and is thought to have been invented by revered Harvard professor Francis Aguilar.[13]

PESTLE is a convenient framework for understanding the changes happening around your organization or product. The PESTLE Canvas, shown in Figure 10-19, helps you to look at the "big picture" of your chosen business, product, or service in the context of the forces in motion around it. It helps you and your team to see any potential gaps in your understanding that might either affect your organization or be opportunities for your organization.

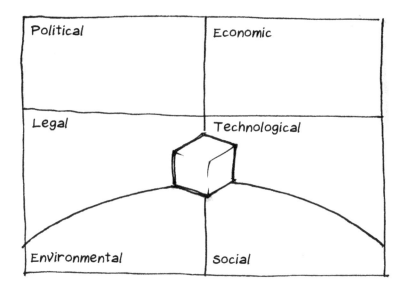

FIGURE 10-19

The PESTLE Canvas: There are a few PESTLE Canvases around, but I like mine to be a little more visual, with icons to help people remember what each factor represents.

---

13 His landmark book *Scanning the Business Environment* (Macmillan) is about how companies can use information about external events and trends. It still stands as a brilliant reference for any business consultant.

There's usually a lot of research sitting behind each of the segments in the PESTLE Canvas. It's only meant to display a distilled, synthesized version in each segment; the detail should live (and be readily accessible) elsewhere.

Use this pattern when you want to do the following:

- Uncover potential threats or market opportunities for your business.

- Spot differences in one market versus another, especially if you're looking to take your product into new markets.

- Help resolve internal discussions about longer-term business direction.

- Educate a set of stakeholders and uncover any unconscious biases about how your business will fare in the market.

This set of steps assumes that you're doing a PESTLE Canvas with a group. Before starting the canvas, it's best to have carried out research into each of the six areas and/or invited a group of people who are subject matter experts (SMEs) in these areas. The blend of roles that these experts have—and the information they can gather—will vary depending on your organization, but here is a handy guide:

Political (senior management, solicitors)
What is the political situation of the the country/state your organization is operating in or wants to move into, and how could it affect your business?

Economic (marketing and sales, business analysts, accountants)
What are the economic factors that are important for your business?

Social (senior management)
What social and cultural factors does the business need to be aware of, both within and around it?

Technological (senior technical management, developers, architects)
What technical innovations in the market could affect your business?

Legal (human resources management, solicitors and lawyers, senior management, accountants)

Are there any laws or regulations that could affect your business in the future?

Environmental (senior management)

What are the environmental concerns that your business needs to be aware of?

This preparation is very important; the last thing you want to do is create an echo chamber of a small amount of information or, worse, erroneous information. With that in mind, don't be afraid to stop at a point at which you don't know the answers and need to go and do some further work. Here's how to create your PESTLE Canvas:

1. Gather your group of SMEs and find a large wall or whiteboard. Begin by drawing up the canvas shown in Figure 10-19, with something representing your organization in the middle. The bigger, the better! You might need to quickly introduce each factor to ensure a shared understanding.

2. Make sure that everyone has plenty of sticky notes, preferably in three colors, and help them mentally prepare by telling them that they will look at each section through three different lenses, represented by the three different colors of sticky notes.

3. Ask everyone to write down and then stick up as many ideas as possible related to each of the factors using the first color. This is for all the top-of-mind stuff. Expect to capture broad topics like "AI" and "bots" in the Technological area, "election" in the Political area, and so on.

4. Next, ask everyone to grab a different color of sticky notes and write and stick up *opportunities* in each area.

5. Repeat this step for *threats*.

6. As a group, analyze what you have all generated. What are the densest couple of areas? Is this because the people in the room happen to know a lot about these areas, or because there are lots more opportunities or threats there? Are there any important connections that you can make between areas? Are there any significant gaps?

7. As a group, discuss the following:

- *What:* What does this analysis mean for your product or organization?

- *When:* What is the time factor on this? Is there anything that needs to be tackled urgently?

- *Who:* Who needs to own this and make any important decisions?

- *Why:* What reasons are you going to give to influence any stakeholders about what actions should be taken?

- *Where:* Where does this analysis belong? Should it be displayed on the wall for a particular product team?

- *How:* How should this analysis be shared to those who matter? Note: this PESTLE Canvas session isn't about *how you need to tackle the opportunities and threats*; that's a whole other set of activities for another time.[14]

8. Lastly, it's up to you to synthesize the board or wall as a neatened-up sketch. At this point, it might not be useful to keep it in the format of the PESTLE Canvas; you might need a different visual approach to communicate one or more insights that the group found. Here are some suggestions:

- Visualize specific threats and opportunities using your newfound (or greatly enhanced) visual metaphor skills (Chapter 7), and include them in a "Top 5 opportunities and threats" presentation.

- Plot specific actions on a visual timeline, with details about who is going to tackle each action and how, and keep it up on the wall for the business to refer to.

- Display a summarized course of action using the Team Purpose Map (Chapter 12).

---

14 The Build-a-Bridge sketch and the Goal Barriers sketch in Chapter 11 can certainly help.

SOME QUESTIONS FOR YOU

What keeps your customers up at night?

What are your customers' goals, hopes, dreams, and hassles? Does your entire team (nay, your entire organization!) have a central reference for that, and does everyone know where to find it? How might empathy mapping help you to get a shared, clear understanding about how your product or service connects to what your customers care about?

Do you have any silos in your organization?

One of the many things that I enjoy about journey mapping is that it really does help unite a lot of different parts of an organization around a common goal. It's an opportunity to align separate internal functions—like marketing, product, technical writing, and support—and help them have a common conversation about the customer experience.

How might a journey mapping session help unite your silos? What issues and "elephants in the room" have been simmering that journey mapping could assist in revealing in a helpful way?

What diagrams could you simplify to help communicate your system?

If yours is like a lot of businesses, you're probably drowning in intranet pages, product specification documents, flowcharts, presentation decks, and so on, but you're missing something that encapsulates all of that complexity into one easy-to-understand, common reference.

What existing assets could you synthesize and simplify into a conceptual model, to help you and your team understand your system?

How quickly can a new hire get up and running?

Suppose that I've just been hired at your business. I'm going to need some induction into the organization and into what you make and do. I'm going to want to know how I can begin adding value as soon as I can.

How long does it take to get everything across to new employees, so they feel really confident?[15] How might sketching some conceptual models help to synthesize and simplify your systems to help accelerate understanding and increase confidence?

Have you done something like a SWAM Canvas recently?

When was the last time people from across your business got together in a room and had a shared, clear understanding of your organization's strengths, weaknesses, threats, and opportunities? Is this displayed somewhere for everyone in the organization to refer to? Are there some specific factors from that analysis that are driving your organization's areas of strategic focus? Are those clear to everyone?

If not, could now be a good time for you to do a SWAM Canvas with your management?

Could you give me a compelling elevator pitch for your product?

If we met in an elevator and I asked you what your product (or service or business) did, could you pique my interest before I got out? If we both asked everyone in your team why people should switch from a competitor's product over to your product, would we get the same answer from everyone?

Could now be a good time to do a Value Proposition Canvas with them?

Interview with John Tutt

There's no need for a product disclosure statement or legal disclaimer with this sketching advice! John talks about how a little bit of sketching can go a long way.

JT: I'm a financial planner at PrimeWealth, a financial advisory firm, and our clients range from young professionals to business owners to retirees. One thing that they all have in common is that they haven't really done enough planning for their future, or their family's future, and so that's where I come in.

---

15 And dare I ask: are *you* confident?

Some of the financial concepts that I introduce to people—like super-annuation, taxation, and so on—can be quite difficult for them to grasp. Even if they've done a bit of research themselves first, it's easy for them to get lost. Sketching lets me simplify these concepts, as well as complex scenarios that my clients might be dealing with.

Most of the diagrams I do are on a whiteboard in front of the client. The client likes it when you get up, grab a marker, and draw on the whiteboard. There's this simple table that I usually draw that shows people the difference between income and superannuation, and how they attract tax in different ways. Most people see superannuation as a bit of a beast that they don't know much about, but it's just another tax structure; the table diagram I draw helps them understand that. If I *don't* draw this table, I lose them pretty early on. I have to say, I like that moment when their eyes light up when they see the boxes that say "nil tax"!

I often draw a simple graph that shows how money increases over time with compound interest. It's a common enough graph, and people get the idea of compound interest pretty quickly, but getting them to see it on the page in front of them as I draw it increases their engagement.

John on making difficult concepts easier to grasp: "Even if they've done a bit of research themselves first, it's easy for [my clients] to get lost. Sketching lets me simplify these concepts, as well as complex scenarios that my clients might be dealing with."

There's also this one-page snapshot that I draw for them; it's like a whole financial plan on a page. One side of the page has a box for each person, with their assets and liabilities listed on the left and right. Along the bottom are their goals, and some strategies for achieving those goals. On the other side of the page I draw a family tree, so we can keep track of relationships and how those circumstances might change over time. It's all visual.

There was this one lady who lives in a wealthy area of Sydney. She works freelance, not earning a lot. At the time we met, she couldn't afford to buy a house in that area, even though she really wanted to, but she didn't want to move out of the area either. Drawing her situation and strategies as that one-page snapshot was the first time she had really taken stock of her situation properly, and thought hard about what she could do about her situation.

She liked it so much that she asked for a copy of it for her to keep herself, plus a copy to go into the official paperwork of her financial plan. PrimeWealth is the first place I've seen this technique done, and I do it all the time now.

Drawing makes you a better listener. Drawing removes a lot of the dialog that would otherwise take up the first 15 minutes in a monologue. When you draw a picture, that picture is out in front of them to look at and think about, and it's then something you can use to ask questions.

It's easy to fall into the trap of doing too much talking, and not enough listening. There's so much information in your head that you think you need to say to convince the other person, but you don't have to show the client you know everything. It's more about asking the right questions, and then listening.

It doesn't have to be flash. Give it a crack. Find what works for you, but just get up and do it.

Drawing makes you a better listener.

[11]

Designing the Future

CHAPTER 10 USED SOME conceptual representation techniques to help you understand the *present state* better: who you're designing for, the world they're in, and the problems and situations that they face. Better understanding leads to better solutions.

This chapter is about using visual thinking and communication to envision the *future state*. What solution are you going to create, and how will it change that present state? This area is a mix of conceptual and literal representation, with a bit of visual metaphor thrown in. Let's see how it applies to the following:

- Helping your team rally around a common future with the Team Purpose Map

- Envisioning the future state of your customers with the Superhero Booth sketch

- Exploring goals with the Build-a-Bridge sketch

- Knocking down the barriers with the Goal Barriers sketch

- Envisioning a future product with the Experience Canvas

- Bringing future experiences to life with storyboarding

Rallying Around a Common Future with the Team Purpose Map

Setting out to create a new product or service is one of the most exciting things you can ever do. But sometimes it's worth parking that for a spell to first check how you as a team are functioning.

If you're part of a startup business, it's common to think of your business and your product as one and the same thing, having one and the same purpose. If you're part of a larger business with one or more products or services, your team purpose might need to be expressed in a different way (e.g., the purpose of a product support team is different from that of the development team).

Or maybe you have had some staff changes in the team, and it's been a while since the team's purpose was really said out loud.

In any case, the Team Purpose Map, which you can see in Figure 11-1, is a large-format template that you can use to visually guide and capture a team's discussions about its identity, purpose, and direction.

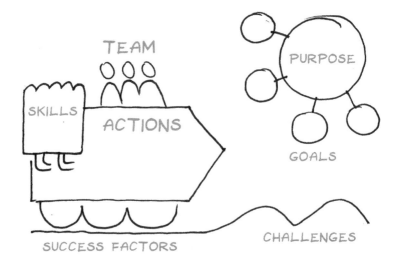

FIGURE 11-1

The Team Purpose Map: This is a fun visual activity to do with your team, especially if it's a new team and you need to form a shared understanding together of who you are, your purpose, and your destination.

There are loads of different kinds of these large-format graphic facilitation templates for capturing strategic outputs of large group discussions.[1] The version you see in Figure 11-1 is my version, based on refining a template through lots of different strategic sessions. As with all of these visual patterns, do feel free to adapt it to your team's needs.

Use this pattern when you want to do the following:

- Set (or reset) a team's identity, purpose, and direction, and get a shared understanding and sense of ownership.

- Expose any hidden assumptions or anxieties in a new team or a new project.

- Align several stakeholders, teams, or organizations around a common purpose and direction.

Here's how to do it:

1. Gather your group and draw the Team Purpose Map on the biggest whiteboard or wall you can find.

2. You might want to have the boss or a senior stakeholder establish the intent of the strategic discussion and provide some background that may be helpful for everyone.

3. Start everyone off with something fun: get them to draw themselves in the space where you see Team displayed. This definitely shows everyone that this isn't your regular sort of meeting, plus it gets them used to using their hands, not just their mouths.

4. Ask everyone to take a sticky note and write what they think is the purpose of the team (or product, or whatever you are focused on) and stick it in the Purpose area. As a group, reflect on any differences that have been posted up. The aim here is to establish a shared understanding of the higher purpose you're working toward, not the "down in the weeds" tasks.

   Sometimes it's worth asking everyone *why* they've written what they've written. This provokes deeper thinking.

---

1 Notable organizations that produce and use these sorts of templates (and a lot of brilliant bespoke patterns) are XPLANE, Grove, Kaospilot, and Lane Change Consulting.

5. Next, ask everyone to write what they think are the team's goals and stick them in the Goals area. This is what the team is going to do to fulfill that purpose.

6. This is a good time to ask your group what they think the *success factors* will be for achieving those goals. How will the team ensure that it reaches those goals? Depending on your context, this could be anything from "can-do attitude" to "special sales campaigns."

7. As a facilitator, it's worth pausing and reflecting on the story unfolding on the Team Purpose Map so far. You have a team with a specific purpose, and to achieve that purpose, there are several goals. There are also several things that must happen for this to be a success. But now, you need to equip yourselves for what lies ahead by calling out the *challenges*. Go ahead and get the group to write those up on the Team Purpose Map, too.

8. Now that your group knows *what* it must do, members should now fill the Actions area with notes about *how* they're going to do it. This might take some rearranging, but see if you can map it in a sequence of some sort.

9. The last part is to check if your group has the right *skills* to be able to achieve all those actions. Get your group to write down and stick up what skills are necessary and then reflect on that set to see if your group does indeed have those skills. If ever there were a time to call out any skills gaps that need to be filled to achieve those goals, it's now!

10. It's a nice idea to end your strategic discussion session by getting everyone to reflect on the overall story that the Team Purpose Map is telling. Ask everyone to summarize it in their own words. This helps people to really internalize that story, rather than staying mentally "at arm's length" from it.

Envisioning the Future State of Your Customers with the Superhero Booth Sketch

As Samuel Hulick of Useronboard.com has wisely said: "People don't buy products; they buy better versions of themselves." In all the flap and flurry of working out what features to include in a product, it's really worthwhile reframing that conversation into two questions: what *is* that better version of your customer, and how might your product achieve that?

To help with this, I use a visual pattern I like to call the Superhero Booth sketch (Figure 11-2). If you have done a good job at articulating who your customer is and what that customer is thinking, feeling, and doing in his job and life, you can use the Superhero Booth sketch to help you envision what a "super" version of your customer would be.

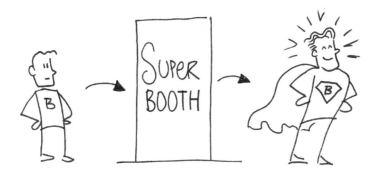

FIGURE 11-2

The Superhero Booth sketch: You can use this to envision what your customers would be like if they were to achieve their goals and resolve their problems.

Use this pattern when you want to do the following:

- Develop more empathy for your customers.

- Inject some fresh thinking and creativity into how you and your team think about your customers and your product.

- Help prioritize a list of possible features, or feature improvements.

You can do this either by yourself or with a group. Either way, you'll need to bone up on any research you have about your customers and their goals and habits,[2] and you'll need a whiteboard. Here's how to do it:

1. Sketch a figure on the left side representing a target customer type. If it helps, write her goals and needs above the figure.

---

2   By now, you'll have done Empathy Maps for all your target customers, right?

2. Sketch another figure on the right that represents the "super" version of that customer type. Based on the existing information that you have, what would she be like if her goals were achieved and her needs fulfilled? What else would happen for her? It's really important that you look at that super customer through the lens of her situation, *not your product*. Write or sketch what her life could be like.

3. Now, sketch a box in between the two figures that represents a booth that the regular customer steps through to become the super customer.

4. Metaphorically, what happened in that booth for her to become that super person? What did she do? What benefits did she get? And now, the clincher: how might your product help to achieve all that?

This is a great creative activity for you and your team when applied to customers. But it also works equally as well for you in your own life: what would a "super" *you* be like? And what is in that booth for that to happen?

Exploring Goals with the Build-a-Bridge Sketch

This is a really neat visual pattern that you can apply to lots of different situations. Whether you're thinking about improving a product or helping a team reach a certain objective, or trying to tackle a personal objective of your own, the Build-a-Bridge sketch is a way to visualize a goal and then visualize how to get there, as demonstrated in Figure 11-3.

FIGURE 11-3

The Build-a-Bridge sketch: You can use this for your own individual goals or as a group for your team's or product's goals.

Use this pattern when you want to do the following:

- Rally a group of people around how to achieve a certain goal.

- Map out specific steps for achieving a goal that up until now has seemed vague and out of reach.

Here's how to do it:

1. Sketch a figure on the left side of a page or whiteboard. On the right side, sketch a flag (representing a known goal). You might actually want to visualize that goal in more real terms by sketching more detail.

2. Sketch in two platforms with a gap between them, as shown in Figure 11-3.

3. Sketch a curved line joining the two. This is the metaphorical bridge from where you are now to where you want to be. You might want to use the line of the bridge itself to communicate what it's like to get to that goal. Is it a straight line, representing something that's straightforward? Or is it a gentle curve? Or a steep curve?

4. Either by yourself or as a group, talk about what specific steps you'd need to take to get across that bridge. Is there a specific order? Are the earlier steps easier than the later steps?

5. Finally, think about what is going to distract you from that goal. For every distraction, sketch in a crocodile below the bridge. Think about how you are going to ward off those distractions.

Just like with all of these patterns, keep your sketches handy to refer back to every now and then so that you can track your progress.

VARIATIONS

The Build-a-Bridge sketch is a really versatile visual pattern. You can adapt it in loads of ways, but here are a couple you might want to consider. You might want to try stringing several bridges together to visualize goals over several stages, as shown in Figure 11-4, or make the bridge a little heftier and put the stages within the same bridge, as depicted in Figure 11-5.

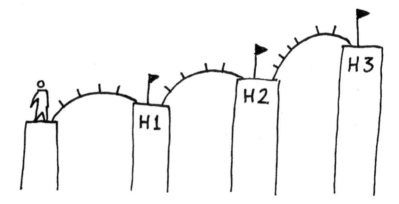

FIGURE 11-4
Multiple bridges for the Build-a-Bridge sketch: You can actually construct further visual bridges if you need to visualize how you or your team are going to tackle several goals over several quarters or time horizons.

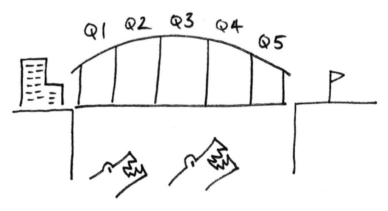

FIGURE 11-5
Corporate bridge with corporate crocodiles: You can use the Build-a-Bridge sketch to visually summarize an entire program of work for an organization over a series of quarters.

The bridge is a wonderful metaphor that you can take in many different visual and meaningful directions!

Knocking Down the Barriers with the Goal Barriers Sketch

Mapping out goals and how to get there is one thing, but I'm sure you can think of lots of challenges and obstacles in the way of your goals. Well, guess what? There's a visual pattern for that, too.

I don't like loading too much into one sketch to explain something, because it loses clarity. The Goal Barriers sketch is a separate sketch (Figure 11-6); it's a way to map each and every challenge you can think of, to make them visible and more tangible, and then to begin breaking them down.

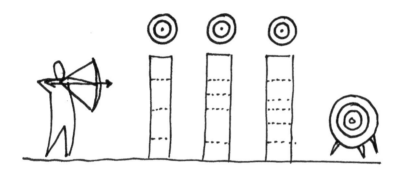

FIGURE 11-6

The Goal Barriers sketch: You can use this to call out and size up any barriers between you (or your team) and your goal. This helps you to see each barrier as a challenge to knock down.

Use this pattern when you want to do the following:

- Tackle that sense of "it's all too hard!" and break your challenges down into manageable chunks.

- Help a team articulate and quantify any barriers to achieving something that it needs to do.

This is a natural follow-on visual pattern from the Build-a-Bridge sketch, or you can use it in isolation, as long as you have a specific goal in mind. Here's how to do it:

1. Sketch a figure on the left side of the page or whiteboard. If you're feeling adventurous, you can sketch the figure with a bow and arrow.

2. Sketch a target on the right side, representing your goal, as shown in Figure 11-7.

3. Now, sketch in walls to represent every barrier you can think of (Figure 11-8). It can be incredibly insightful simply thinking about and visualizing exactly what barriers there are to achieving your goal. Try to be specific and write what the barrier is above each wall. It's probably a good idea to make every wall the same height, just as long as it's clear that the figure you sketched won't be able to hit the target with the arrow.

Take those walls a step further. Just like a wall is made up of bricks, each barrier is probably made up of parts. Draw a few lines across each wall to signify the subparts.

4. Add a question above each wall about how you can break down that wall. For example, if the target is to lose weight and the first wall is "No time to exercise," the question can be "How might I

get some time to exercise?" Now—and here's another useful thing about visualizing barriers and cutting them down—*you don't need to remove the wall entirely, but just lower it enough for the arrow to go over it.*

5. Visualize some things you could do to begin chipping away at those walls. You might even want to sketch those on the same piece of paper or whiteboard, too. Pretty soon, your walls could look like the ones in Figure 11-9, and you can then hit your target.

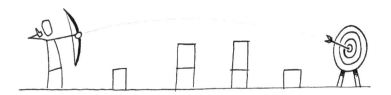

FIGURE 11-9

The Goal Barriers sketch with barriers reduced: It's satisfying to sketch what it would look like if you were to lower the barriers. Remember: you don't have to remove all of each barrier; you just need to remove enough to see and hit the target.

Envisioning a Future Product with the Experience Canvas

The Experience Canvas is adapted from Ash Maurya's Lean Canvas,[3] which itself is based on Alexander Osterwalder's Business Model Canvas.[4] The Business Model Canvas contains the essence of how a business can provide a product or service in a sustainable way.

---

3   Find out all about the Lean Canvas and how to use it in Ash Maurya's book *Running Lean* (O'Reilly).

4   The Business Model Canvas is itself derived from Michael Porter's value chain maps and Peter Drucker's theories of the business. Get your fix of the Business Model Canvas in *Business Model Generation* (John Wiley and Sons) by Alexander Osterwalder and Yves Pigneur. If you really want go deep on business thinking, *Competitive Advantage: Creating and Sustaining Superior Performance* (Free Press) by Michael Porter and *The Theory of the Business* (Harvard Business Review Press) by Peter Drucker are both outstanding.

But—and it's a big but—sometimes looking at a customer problem through the lens of an existing idea for a product isn't the best way to go. I've seen many times when there have been big assumptions made about a product or a feature being designed; instead, everyone needed to take a step back and analyze the *actual value and experience they wanted to achieve.*

As you saw previously, the Value Proposition Canvas gets us halfway there; it helps us clarify the unique value of what we can offer to customers. But what is the best way for customers to *experience* that value? Is it the existing product? Is it a new product altogether? Is it a new feature or a complementary add-on? Is it a better support service or "onboarding" (i.e., getting to know the product first) sequence?

That's where the Experience Canvas, shown in Figure 11-10, is really effective; by focusing on the *desired experience first*, you might come up with a different kind of product or service altogether. And because the experience comes first, it turns out that this canvas suits itself well to internal process and service improvements, too.

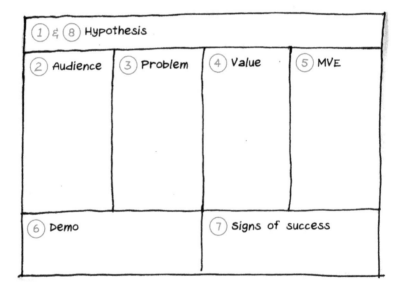

FIGURE 11-10

The Experience Canvas: This Experience Canvas is a lighter version of the Experience Canvas used at Atlassian and created by Dr. Marie-Claire Dean.

Use this pattern when you want to do the following:

- Move a discussion with a team from an idea about a product or service to its *value to the customer.*

- Clarify what problem is being solved by a product, service, process, or team.

- Clarify the difference between a solution to a problem and how that solution will translate to what is experienced by customers.

- Apply lean product thinking to internal team and process improvement.

Here's how to do it:

1. If you already have a hypothesis (or a hunch) in mind about the best experience you can provide your customers, begin by writing it in the top section. If not, it's fine to do it at the end; in fact, even if you *do* fill it in at the beginning, you might need to revise it by the time you complete the rest of this canvas anyway.

   There are few ways that you can write a hypothesis, but it's important to use this as a way to add rigor to your thinking about the way you're going to solve a customer's problem or increase the value of your business rather than just filling in the box.

   Any hypothesis you write in there should be testable, and it should help you clarify what you want to learn and what you would *do* with what you learn.

   I really like these formats:

   - We believe that [this audience] will [do this thing/use this thing] because [this reason]. We'll know we're right when [test result].

   - We believe that [this audience] has [this problem]. We can help them with [this solution]. We'll know we're right when [test result].

2. Just like the other canvases, fill in each section and use each section to clarify your thinking. Which particular audience are you focusing on? Or is there more than one? What's the actual problem that it has? If that's the case, what value can your product or service offer this audience? Use the Empathy Map and Journey Map as

separate thinking activities to help you clarify the Audience and Problem sections, and use the Value Proposition Canvas to help you clarify the Value section.

3. After you have clarified what value your product or service will provide to which audience experiencing which problem, ask yourself and your team: "What's the minimum that we could do to solve *that* problem and give *that* value to *that* audience?" This is your *minimum viable experience* (MVE). The way you fill this section in is up to you; it can be bullet points or sketches. You might even want to sketch things out on separate pieces of paper and then write or sketch a synthesized, combined version into each section of the canvas. Part of the limitation of space on these canvases to is to force you to distill and refine.

4. Now that you have an idea of the MVE that you could give your audience, what would a *demo* of that be? This is to help you and your team clarify what you would build to test with customers before committing to the time and expense of coding or final production.

5. The last section is all about how you are going to know that your MVE is a *success*; what is needed in the MVE itself for you to know whether it's successful?

6. Finally, go back to the hypothesis and check whether it is consistent with the rest of the canvas; it's not uncommon for this Experience Canvas activity to move into a different idea space and for the hypothesis to have to change a bit.

Bringing Future Experiences to Life with Storyboarding

Storyboards (Figure 11-11) are one of the classier design artifacts you're likely to come across in product and service design, as well as other domains like events, architecture, and obviously film and television. In all of these domains, they act as a prototype to think through and communicate the experience that a team of people will go on to make.

FIGURE 11-11

Storyboards take you from problem to solution to experience: Storyboards are prototypes for a future experience, and an ideal technique to help you and a team hash out problems and directions early on.

For my money, there's no better technique for bringing a potential product or service experience to life than storyboards. You can be director, scriptwriter, cinematographer, lighting technician, background artist, as well as all the actors and props! You can design the entire experience.

Although a lot of design and development assets can abstract the customer from the day-to-day work of making products, storyboards are an evocative way of connecting clients and stakeholders to the issues that their customers face. They're also a great way to visualize insights derived from research: presenting them as a story, with pictures of people in real places, with real goals, real behaviors, and real reactions puts the heart of the issue back into our communications.

Sometimes, storyboards can actually be the main prototype to aid previsualization, problem solving, communication, prioritizing, and planning work. Not bad for a bunch of sketched pictures, eh? In fact, it might come as a surprise to you that the movie production studio Pixar does not begin new movies with a script; instead the entire story is fleshed out through storyboarding. In some cases, storyboards can become the "source of truth" for production, too, rather than just for previsualization.[5]

It can be pretty daunting to even begin thinking about drawing any storyboards yourself. But if you apply your Presto Sketching skills of sketching the essence and visual metaphor, you'll be surprised at the storyboards you'll be able to generate.

And let me say straight up: I've seen some storyboards that weren't that useful, even though they were sketched by people who are "good at drawing," because the *story* didn't make sense.

THE ANATOMY OF STORYBOARDS

Storyboards are a form of sequential art, which is an eloquent way of saying that they're chains of framed images that communicate a story. As we touched on briefly back in Chapter 5, storyboards are made up of frames, and each frame is like a window cut out of the substrate that you're looking at that lets you peer into the world of the story, as demonstrated in Figure 11-12.

FIGURE 11-12
The anatomy of the storyboard: If you keep these few elements in mind and are neat with how you sketch them, you can't go wrong.

Think of each frame (or panel) you draw as a particular scene in the movie of the experience that you want to bring to life. Within each frame, you can have one or more elements:

---

5   The Wachowski twins (of *The Matrix* trilogy fame) were (in)famous for not letting cinematography deviate from the storyboard. Catherine Lewis's slideshow (*http://www. slideshare.net/catherinelewis/storyboards-for-the-matrix*) offers a glimpse of how close the final cut is to the storyboards drawn by comic book artists Steve Skroce and Geof Darrow.

Narration blocks

This is typically one line of text to set the context of the scene (e.g., "Meanwhile, back in the office...").

Speech balloons

Anything that a character says is contained within a speech balloon (Figure 11-13). The format can vary in style, as long as it has some way of indicating who is saying what.[6]

Thought balloons

Anything that a character thinks is contained within a thought balloon. Conventionally, thought balloons tend to be fluffy cloud–like lines with little bubbles instead of a hook descending from them.

FIGURE 11-13

A range of speech balloons and thought balloons: Varying the way you show speech, thought, and narration in your storyboards adds visual interest.

Gutters

The space between each frame is called the *gutter,* and it's a good idea to keep your gutters a consistent width. Gutters are a visual convention that gives audiences cues to move from one scene to the next.

---

6   Although it might be important to your story that it's not clear where a particular voice is coming from. In this case, the text can just appear to hang in the air without an "owner."

Reading flow

Be aware that people read storyboards the same way they do any text, which applies to each individual frame as well as the entire storyboard. So, if your audience is used to reading left-to-right, starting at the upper-left corner and moving down, make sure what you sketch adheres to this flow (Figure 11-14).

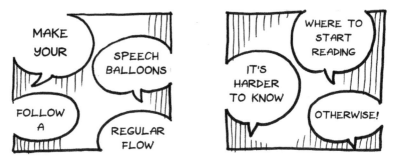

FIGURE 11-14

Make your speech balloons follow a conventional flow: People (in Western countries) read top to bottom, left to right; make sure your speech balloons are arranged in a way that helps reading flow.

Staging and focus

Staging is all about how you place the subject of focus within the environment you're showing in each of your storyboard frames. Make it easy for your audience to focus on one subject per frame (which could be anything from a figure or a screen to the way a hand is using a mobile phone) by using one or more of these techniques:

The Rule of Thirds

In your mind's eye, mark out each frame into horizontal and vertical thirds, as illustrated in Figure 11-15. Then, place whatever is meant to be in focus on one of the four points of intersection.

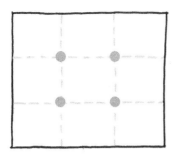 

FIGURE 11-15
The Rule of Thirds: place your subject at one of the four points of intersection in a frame that's divided into imaginary thirds.

Give the subject room to breathe

Leave some white space around the subject to help draw the eye to it, as shown in Figure 11-16.

FIGURE 11-16
Give your subject room to breathe: Note the difference in these two frames. The one on the left is visually cluttered and difficult to parse quickly; the one on the right makes it clear what we should be looking at.

Change the thickness of your line

You can imply three-dimensional space by paying attention to the thickness of your lines. By varying line weight you can add a lot of perspective and a feel of distance to each frame with very little effort (Figure 11-17).

FIGURE 11-17
Line thickness helps with focus and distance: You can imply a sense of distance by sketching a subject in the foreground with thicker lines and objects in the background with thinner lines.

Angles and shots

As a storyboard sketcher, you also have an incredible array of camera angles and shots you can take of your subject, which can communicate a lot about your story and how you want your viewers to feel about it.

Viewing something from lower than regular eye level tends to imply drama and tension, because it can make the central subject appear larger than it actually is. Viewing the subject from higher than regular eye level can imply anything from serenity to malevolence, depending on what's going on in the scene. Take a look at the different viewing angles of the same scene in Figure 11-18.

FIGURE 11-18
Different angles, different meanings: Here are three separate sketches of the same scene from different angles.

Showing something close up also implies great importance to it, especially if there are smaller details that you are drawing, like a furrowed brow on a character, or the strands of a rope beginning to fray and snap apart. Likewise, showing something far away can lend a sense of space and isolation, as demonstrated in Figure 11-19.

ESTABLISHING SHOT

FULL SHOT

THREE-QUARTER SHOT

CLOSE-UP SHOT

FIGURE 11-19
Use a variety of shots to emphasize different meanings: Even if you're sketching only basic shapes, you can vary the distance between the viewer and subject to add interest and drama.

One thing's for sure: playing with angles and shots in your storyboards is a great way to create more interest and make your ideas more memorable.

EXERCISES

INTERMEDIATE **Exercise 11-1: Play all the angles**

Sketch a cup of tea from a number of different angles and distances. Get creative, and remember that it's not necessary for the angles and distances you sketch to all make sense; this is to get you practicing sketching in ways that you haven't sketched before.

TRICKY **Exercise 11-2: Your work, from all the angles**

Do the first exercise again, but this time, sketch yourself at your desk (or whatever your natural work habitat is) from a number of different angles and distances.

The power of storytelling

Storyboards would be just a jumble of boxes and random objects were it not for the story that joins them all together. It's the story that makes your audience care. It's the story that feeds their curiosity, and keeps them reading to find out what happens next. It's the story that activates their imagination, and lets them fill in all the gaps that your storyboard doesn't specifically show.

And just as visual metaphor helps your audiences understand your concepts based on other concepts, the story helps them connect with your idea based on their existing experiences. As Nancy Duarte says in her book *Resonate: Present Visual Stories that Transform Audiences* (John Wiley and Sons), "Stories are the most powerful delivery tool for information, more powerful and enduring than any other art form."

The Presto Sketching version of the Hero's Journey

A lot of analysis of stories has been done over the years to help us understand the power they have over us. In his 1894 book *Technique of the Drama* (Scott, Foresman), Gustav Freytag rationalized stories into five acts: exposition, rising action, climax, falling action (or final suspense and resolution), and dénouement (conclusion). Another pattern is the Hero's Journey, a narrative convention made popular by Joseph Campbell in his book *The Hero with a Thousand Faces* (New World Library).

Designers, brand and marketing managers, product managers, and entrepreneurs have known for a long time how important storytelling is to connect people with their products. References about hero's journeys and story arcs, however, have often seemed a little academic and technical, and I've seen a lot of people struggle with trying to apply them to product design and marketing. I think the main reason for this is because too often we look only at the *mechanics* of the story, rather than the true *heart* of what's going on in the story itself.

What's actually most important about the Hero's Journey (as a convention) is not the steps the hero goes through, but what the hero finds *is most important to himself*: in *Lord of the Rings*, Frodo finds his courage; in *Star Wars*, Luke fulfills his destiny as a Jedi among Jedi. These heroes become who they are really meant to be by achieving an intrinsic emotional goal of some sort (as well as slaying countless orcs and saving galaxies, of course). And what can be more compelling to watch than that?

So with that in mind, here is a user experience story cycle that I find much more useful for applying to storytelling in user experience design in general, and storyboarding in particular (Figure 11-20). Consider it the Presto Sketching version of the Hero's Journey.

FIGURE 11-20

The user experience story cycle: This is adapted from the Hero's Journey and concentrates on how the hero of the story achieves both a tactical goal and an emotional goal.

It goes like this:

Tactical goal

The user (main character) has a goal in mind, to get something done. Examples might be booking flights for her and her family, or applying for a job online.

Emotional goal

This is why the user *really* wants to achieve that tactical goal, and this is where the richest part of your story will lie; it's also the part that your audience will connect with the most. Examples (to follow the preceding examples): because she hasn't seen her parents since they moved back to Italy 20 years ago; or because this is the 20th job she's applied for, and *maybe this time*, using this new jobs' website, she'll land that position she's after.

We then take the user on their journey:

1. *The trigger:* The event or problem that has kicked the user into action.

2. *The search:* How she is led toward your product or feature (note: it's not just using a search box on a website).

3. *The key:* The moment the user thinks she has found a path that will lead her to her tactical goal.

4. *The struggle:* The chain of challenges and steps, in which each step has to give her enough of a sense of desire and achievement to outweigh the anxiety of change and the itch of habit.

5. *The win:* The user has achieved the tactical goal! But as we now know, what's more important is that she has also achieved her emotional goal.

What this cycle does is explain to your audience how the experience of your product or service connects the user with her goals and needs, through a story.

Now let's apply this cycle to sketching some storyboards.

HOW TO SKETCH STORYBOARDS TO EXPLORE AND EXPLAIN A PROBLEM

Step 1: Get clear on an authentic problem at the right moment

Work on your story first, by thinking about these points:

Authenticity

Make your character and his journey as real as you can, and your audience will empathize with him. Make it clear what your character's tactical goal is ("I want to...") as well as his emotional goal ("So that..."). Also, ensure that the way you represent the story has its own internal logic. In other words, in the world of this story, it has to "make sense" for your audience to take your message seriously.

Moments

If you're going to show a character having a problem with a product, there are always several touchpoints or events in that experience where triggers, decisions, actions, changes in emotional state, and behavior reinforcement occur. Think about your character and journey in terms of these "moments," and pick the one or two most compelling moments.

Emotion

It's essential to communicate the emotional state of your character throughout the experience. Simple emoticon faces like the ones we sketched in Chapter 5 are perfect for adding the character and emotion your story needs to come alive in the hearts and minds of your audience.

Step 2: Write the story first

Yep, that's right. It's much easier and more efficient to write the journey that your character takes *first*. The main thing is to break the story up according to the aforementioned user experience story cycle. Write some bullet points that describe what the character says, thinks, feels, and does, according to the following:

1. *The trigger:* What's the event or problem that has kicked the user into action in the first place?

2. *The search:* How is she led toward your product or feature? Or, is this where the main problem begins?

3. *The key:* What's the moment at which the character thinks she has found a path that will lead her to her tactical goal? Or, again, is this the problem?

4. *The struggle:* What's the main pain point in this part of her experience? Is there enough benefit to outweigh the anxiety of change and the itch of habit?

5. *The win:* Because we're illustrating a problem here, how has the problem prevented her from achieving her goal? What's the physical and emotional impact of that?

However you describe your character's problem journey, try to end the storyboard on the impact of the problem. Was it a "showstopper" for her? Is she only mildly annoyed, or has the problem caused a major disruption?

Step 3: Get your story in touch with its emotions

Go back over your written story and sketch a face to show the character's emotional state at each step, as a simple expression. This will help you to maximize the empathy value of your story and also give you more hints about how to break up your story into storyboard frames.

Step 4: Roll camera

By now you should have a sense of the steps involved in your story. Here's where you bring all of the Presto Sketching skills you have learned so far to bear (as well as the points mentioned before about the anatomy of storyboards), and translate each step of your written story into separate storyboard frames (or panels).

For each frame, think about the following:

Figures and faces
   The poses of your character can convey a lot, so you don't need to use so many words.

Simple objects
   Set the scene by sketching just enough objects with just enough detail.

Visual metaphor
   Is there a visual metaphor that you could use to get the point of the problem or pain point across?

Here are some techniques to help you get started with frames:

Six-up technique

Grab a piece of blank paper and fold it in half, lengthways, and then in thirds, widthways. This gives you six frames in which to tell your story. If you need more, grab a second piece of paper, and so on, but try to keep it short.

Sticky note technique

Draw each frame of your storyboard on a separate square sticky note. That way, you can begin in the middle if you want to, you can move your "scenes" around, and you can add or remove other scenes to suit.

End impact technique

Begin with the end in mind. Think about the impact of the problem that your character is experiencing: what is he thinking, feeling, or doing? Make this the final frame of your storyboard; draw that first, and then work back from there.

Example of an existing scenario

Let's apply these steps to a fictional yet authentic-sounding scenario:

It's the weekend, and Ethan's in-laws have flown in for a visit. No one really wants to cook, so Ethan decides to order some dinner for him and the family from that great new Texan barbecue place. He searches for the restaurant online, orders from the menu, and chooses the home delivery option (rather than pick-up).

After entering his credit card details and submitting the order, he's informed that he'll receive a text message on his phone letting him know how long the order will take. When the text arrives, he nearly has a heart attack: delivery is one and a half hours away! His in-laws aren't going to like that.

Gathering himself, Ethan calls the restaurant to change the order so that he can pick it up instead. Hopefully that won't take as long. When he finally gets through to the restaurant, they tell him that they can't control that online ordering system from where they are, and he'll just have to wait. Ethan is furious! He can't even cancel the order, so now he feels trapped. Stabbing the "End Call" button on his phone, he turns to see his in-laws glaring at him. They don't look impressed.

Let's tackle this, step by step.

Step 1: Get clear on an authentic problem at the right moment

From the preceding scenario, I immediately pick out the main character (Ethan) and his goal (order food to be home delivered, and to impress the in-laws).

There are three big moments here: the shock of finding out how long the delivery is going to take, the outrage at not being able to change the order, and *then* the shame in front of the in-laws.

Step 2: Write the story first

Writing the story according to the steps in the user experience story cycle helps me to construct a flow (Figure 11-21). In writing this out, I get some ideas for dialog and some of the shots I'll end up drawing.

1 The trigger	Everyone's hungry, and Ethan decides to order in
2 The search	He searches online using his laptop
3 The key	He already knows the restaurant, but the key is nailing the menu choices for the family
4 The struggle	Delivery is MUCH longer than expected. THEN he can't even change the order from delivery to pick-up
5 The win	There is no win! Ethan feels frustrated and humiliated

FIGURE 11-21

Write out your story: Here's a brief account of the story, according to the five stages of the user experience story cycle.

Step 3: Get your story in touch with its emotions

I go back and draw faces at each step, to capture the emotion going on (Figure 11-22).

	1 The trigger	Everyone's hungry, and Ethan decides to order in. **Feeling self-assured.**
	2 The search	He searches online using his laptop
	3 The key	He already knows the restaurant, but the key is nailing the menu choices for the family
	4 The struggle	Delivery is MUCH longer than expected. THEN he can't even change the order from delivery to pick-up
	5 The win	There is no win! Ethan feels frustrated and humiliated

FIGURE 11-22

Add emoticons to your story: Going back over your existing story and adding little emojis is a great way to inject drama into your story and really bring out those significant moments.

Step 4: Roll camera

I begin with a very rough draft of the storyboard, according to the story and moments I've extracted (Figure 11-23). Sketching this out helps me to think of how to fit various parts of the dialog into each scene.

FIGURE 11-23

Draft storyboard: Here's a (very) rough draft I've done of two-thirds of the story. Visualize the steps of your story as a set of draft storyboard frames. Use this step to write in dialog and to try out different options for arrangement of shots, figures, and objects.

I then sketch a final version of the storyboard, according to the first draft (Figure 11-24). I alter some of the shots and add some along the way. If I wanted to add more visual interest and contrast at this point, I could also add in some color with a Copic art marker.

FIGURE 11-24

Final storyboard: Here's my take on visualizing the story. A bit of neatness in your sketches goes a long, long way in storyboarding. Neat writing for the dialog is perfectly fine, or you might want to make it even neater with a comic text font using software like Photoshop.

HOW TO SKETCH STORYBOARDS TO EXPLAIN A SOLUTION

I hope by now you can see that your ideas will be more compelling to clients and stakeholders if you package them in a storyboard, and get them to empathize with your character. Just as it's important for clients to feel the impact of a problem, it's also important for them to feel the benefit of a new solution.

I get particularly excited about sketching storyboards to show benefits, because this is exactly an area where *just* sketching user interfaces won't cut it. User interfaces are perfect for illustrating features, but to see and feel the benefits of those features we need to see people *using* those interfaces and *experiencing* the result.

So, here's how we can sketch storyboards to bring our solutions—and their benefits—to life.

Step 1: Get clear on the benefit at the proper moment

Just as before, work on your story first by thinking about these points:

Authenticity

Make it clear what your character's tactical goal is ("I want to...") as well as his emotional goal ("So that..."). Again, ensure that the way you represent the story has its own internal logic. Most important, ensure that the benefit you want to illustrate is *really a benefit*, not a feature in disguise. If in doubt, ask yourself, "So what?"

Here's an example I see fairly regularly. Suppose that I have to sketch a storyboard to show that a project management software product has tons of add-ons available. If I ask "So what?" I have to come up with an authentic reason why my character would care about tons of add-ons.

Moments

Every movie has its "promo shot"; that scene that gets used on the posters and in the trailers, and the scene that you want to stick in audiences' heads long after they see the movie. What's your storyboard's promo shot? Pick a moment that really showcases the benefit of your solution, and make that the best frame of your storyboard.

Emotion

Never assume that your audience will fill in all the blanks of what the solution and benefit mean to your character; make sure you show the connection of the benefit back to your character's goals.

Step 2: Write the story first

As before, try to write your story in bullet form first, and break your story up according to the user experience story cycle. Capture what the character says, thinks, feels, and does according to the following:

1. *The trigger:* What's the event or problem that has kicked the user into action in the first place?

2. *The search:* How is he led toward your product or feature?

3. *The key:* What's the moment at which the character thinks he has found a path that will lead him to his tactical goal?

4. *The struggle:* What's the "promo shot" in the experience here? Are there any problems that the character might anticipate that now don't happen? How is the experience beyond his expectations?

5. *The win:* What's the benefit of your solution to your character, and why should your audience care? How is his goal achieved? And how does it connect to his emotional goal?

However you describe your character's problem journey, try to end the storyboard on the benefit of your solution.

Step 3: Get your story in touch with its emotions

Go back over your written story and sketch a face to show the character's emotional state at each step, as a simple expression. This will help you to maximize the empathy value of your story and also give you more hints about how to break up your story into storyboard frames.

Step 4: Roll camera

As before, think about how you can flex those Presto Sketching skills to translate each step of your written story into separate storyboard frames.

Example of an envisioned scenario

Let's apply these steps to the preceding scenario but this time envision a better future for Ethan, our humiliated hero...

It's the weekend, and Ethan's in-laws have flown in for a visit. No one really wants to cook, so Ethan decides to order some dinner for him and the family from that great new Texan barbecue. He searches for the restaurant online, orders from the menu, and chooses the home delivery option (rather than pick-up).

This time, the online ordering platform tells him ahead of time that the wait time is going to be an hour and a half. It then gives him two options: Ethan can either pay an extra $10 for express delivery (wait time 30 minutes) or change his order to pick-up, instead.

Ethan decides to pay the extra $10 for 30 minutes' wait; that way, he doesn't need to leave the house and miss out on anything his in-laws are saying. After entering his credit card details and submitting the order, he's informed that he'll receive a text message to his mobile phone when his order is five minutes away.

When the text arrives, he checks to see if the table is set for dinner, and his partner has taken care of that nicely. Go team! His prepaid dinner arrives on time, and his in-laws love the Texan BBQ.

Let's tackle this envisioned scenario as a storyboard, step by step, as before.

Step 1: Get clear on the benefit at the proper moment

In the preceding envisioned scenario, the benefit is all about *keeping Ethan in control of the situation*: rather than the shock of finding out he must wait for an hour and a half, he now has *options*. Prompt home delivery is preferable to him than having to hop in the car and pick it up himself.

By the way, did you notice how we have now included the express delivery option, which is a way for the online delivery platform to make more money? I can imagine there'd be arguments about whether customers would use it; *showing the emotional benefit* about why a customer would fork out an extra $10 using a storyboard is a compelling way to justify having this feature.

Step 2: Write the story first

In this instance, steps 1 to 3 of the user experience story cycle are the same. Step 4 (the struggle) is really just about what delivery option to choose. Being in control is much better than having unwelcome bad news. Also, this time we definitely have a win (step 5): Ethan gets to look good in front of the in-laws. I want to make sure that this is clear in the story (Figure 11-25).

4 The struggle   Ethan decides to pay an extra $10 for the
                  benefit of faster home delivery

5 The win   Ethan looks great in front of his partner
                  and her parents

FIGURE 11-25

Write out your envisioned story: In this image, I've omitted steps 1 to 3 of the user experience story cycle because they're the same.

Step 3: Get your story in touch with its emotions

Again, I go back and draw faces at each step, to capture the emotion going on (Figure 11-26).

 4 The struggle Ethan decides to pay an extra $10 for the benefit of faster home delivery

 5 The win Ethan looks great in front of his partner and her parents

FIGURE 11-26

Add emojis to your envisioned story: Going back over this envisioned story makes me realize that we get to basically keep Ethan in the same emotional state; he's now feeling empowered the entire time.

Step 4: Roll camera

If you've already done a storyboard of an existing experience that you are reimagining, it might not be a bad idea to reuse parts of it, especially to reinforce with your audience the parts that remain the same. I'll omit the draft stage at this point—you probably get the idea now—and instead I'll jump straight to my version of the final storyboard of the envisioned scenario, which you can see in Figure 11-27.

FIGURE 11-27

Final envisioned storyboard: As you can see, I've reused the top row, and retold the story of how Ethan orders the meal. In storyboards that illustrate an envisioned solution, it's good to end on a clear benefit.

EXERCISES

TRICKY **Exercise 11-3: The relief of having a "smart home"**

Follow the steps outlined in "How to Sketch Storyboards to Explore and Explain a Problem" on page 273 and try sketching a storyboard to illustrate the following scenario:

> Tegan longs for an organized home; it makes her feel she's in control. To her, an organized home is the calm oasis she's always dreamed of. Which is why right now she's really stressed! Tegan is driving her daughter to soccer, and she suddenly panics: "I think I left the stove on!"

Tegan remembers the new HomeHelper 3000 system that she and her partner installed. Not wanting to take her attention from the road, she says to her smartphone (on the seat next to her): "Hey, Kori![7] Run the HomeHelper 3000 diagnostic!"

Her smartphone opens the HomeHelper 3000 app, which then starts a diagnostic routine. Meanwhile, back inside Tegan's house, a small console in the kitchen comes to life with a series of green LED pulses. One LED briefly pulses red and then switches to green.

Back in the car, a notification appears on Tegan's smartphone. Waiting at the lights, she reads it: "HomeHelper report: All systems checked and OK. Front-right burner of stove was on and unused for 5 minutes, and has now been switched off."

A wave of relief washes over Tegan. Tegan's daughter calls from the back: "Is everything okay, Mum?" Tegan smiles at her, "Everything's fine, honey. Everything's fine."

INTERMEDIATE **Exercise 11-4: What is the "super" you?**

Do the Superhero Booth sketch for yourself. What would a "super" you be like? And what needs to be in the superhero booth for that transformation to happen?

INTERMEDIATE **Exercise 11-5: What's your main goal, and how will you get there?**

Do the Build-a-Bridge sketch for yourself. What does the flag on the other side represent? What are the steps along the bridge for you to achieve that goal? And what are the distractions below the bridge that you have to guard yourself against?

INTERMEDIATE **Exercise 11-6: How will you knock down your barriers?**

Do the Goal Barriers sketch to sketch out what the barriers are between you and your goal. How could you minimize those barriers so that you can hit that target?

---

7   Kori: not the AI assistant's real name.

SOME QUESTIONS FOR YOU

Does your team have a shared, clear purpose?
It's easy to assume that everyone is thinking the same as you about your product, the latest release, the latest sprint, and so on. An hour spent looking at the strategic stuff by doing the Team Purpose Map activity can save days of inefficiency down the track. When was the last time you all got together to synchronize your understanding?

Are you chasing the feature and not the benefit?
Do you have a sneaking suspicion that others in your team are too focused on features rather than benefits? Or do you find that you're having the same old arguments about what to prioritize?

What arguments or roadblocks might be resolved if you were to do an Experience Canvas activity with your team?

What experience could you bring to life as a storyboard?
Are there any concepts that you and your team are noodling on that can't seem to get from abstract language to a physical prototype? What concepts could do with better explaining by displaying them as storyboards?

Who else could do with these helpful tools?
What other teams or individuals could use these tools to help them design their future? If you mentor anyone, these are great tools to pass on to them or, better yet, use with them. If you don't mentor anyone, is now maybe a good time to start?

Plotting the Course

As you've probably picked up by now, to better see a problem is to better solve a problem. Likewise, it's better to visualize our options about how to execute on our ideas and plans, to help teams discuss them and to help make decisions.

This chapter fills in that foggy space between the ideas and the project plan that gets an idea done. It uses a few simple visual patterns to help you prioritize and organize what work should be done, and why. Let's take a look at the following:

- Generating actionable options with the Concept Canvas

- Prioritizing action with the Hurdle Track sketch

- Prioritizing resources with the Resource Tank sketch

Generating Actionable Ideas with the Concept Canvas

A little bit of visual structure can not only help you and your team form your ideas, but also communicate and compare those ideas in a much more practical way.

PLEASE BE CAREFUL SAYING "QR CODES" AROUND ME

I remember having a brainstorming session from hell once. I was part of a team that had been brought in, along with another team, to help a telecommunications company redesign several of its systems and integrate them into a seamless customer experience.

The stakes were high, and the number of stakeholders in the room was high, too. Way too high for a brainstorming session like this, I thought.

The facilitator—a project manager from another agency—started us off by describing the state of the existing systems, and then, with whiteboard marker in hand, he asked us for ideas.

My heart sank. I love brainstorming, I really do. I know some people will gnash their teeth and snarl that brainstorming never works, but I guarantee you that brainstorming *does* work *if* you ask the right questions and have just a bit of structure.

But alas, that time at that telecommunications company, we had neither the right questions nor a bit of structure. It was a tepid, tedious, aimless, dreary talkfest. And the only thing I remember that vaguely approached a passing resemblance of an idea was written on the whiteboard: QR codes.

That was it, really. QR codes.

I'm sure it made perfect sense to the regional manager that clanked on and on about it, but that's all we had to go on by the end. QR Code Guy smugly left the room, and I remember thinking that QR codes weren't connected to the problem at hand—nor to the customers and their situations—at all.

Maybe you've had a similar experience.

GENERATE ACTIONABLE CONCEPTS, NOT VAGUE IDEAS

As great as it is to have lots of ideas in projects like these, what we usually need are *concepts*. To me, an idea can be as vague and unrelated to anything as—yes—QR codes, or as grand and bold as democracy itself. A concept contains a lot more information in it; it fleshes out the idea in such a way that you could actually execute on it, and maybe estimate time and resources for it, as illustrated in Figure 12-1.

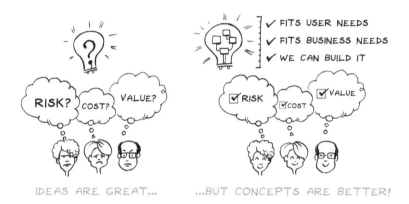

FIGURE 12-1

Ideas versus concepts: If you just generate vague ideas, people won't be able to make decisions based on any of them. Instead, show how it fits user needs and business needs.

That's what the Concept Canvas is for (Figure 12-2). It gives you and your team a way to add enough structure all of your ideas so that you can evaluate them more confidently.

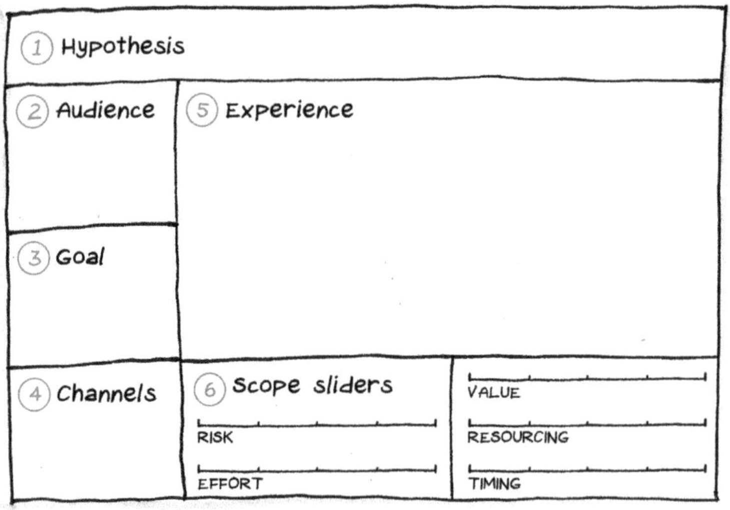

```
┌─────────────────────────────────────────────────────────┐
│ ① Hypothesis                                              │
├──────────────┬────────────────────────────────────────────┤
│ ② Audience   │ ⑤ Experience                               │
│              │                                             │
│              │                                             │
│ ③ Goal       │                                             │
│              │                                             │
├──────────────┼─────────────────────┬──────────────────────┤
│ ④ Channels   │ ⑥ Scope sliders     │ VALUE                │
│              │  RISK               │ RESOURCING           │
│              │  EFFORT             │ TIMING               │
└──────────────┴─────────────────────┴──────────────────────┘
```

FIGURE 12-2

The Concept Canvas: This is an easy template to use to turn several vague ideas into a consistently structured set that you can then compare for value, risk, or any other factor that you need.

Use this pattern when you want to do the following:

- Flesh out a bunch of loose ideas into a consistent set of concepts to investigate and prioritize.

- Keep a "line of sight" from your value proposition to your Experience Canvas to any ideas you have for executing on that minimum viable experience (MVE).

This visual pattern assumes that you have a group of people who have to come up with several ideas to solve a problem, or several ways to provide a new type of product, feature, or experience. For the sake of convenience, let's call that a brainstorming session.

Before your brainstorming session, draw the Concept Canvas template shown in Figure 12-2 onto a large piece of paper and copy it several times, enough to give several copies to each group that will be brainstorming. Here's how to do it:

1. Start your brainstorming session with a clear problem statement or hypothesis[1] that the group must tackle. Write it up on a whiteboard if you can.

   Example: *"We believe that people under 25 want to invest in property, but find it too expensive to even begin. We can help by selling them small pieces of existing properties and then giving them a proportional share of any net rental income. We'll know we're right when first-time buyers return to buy more pieces."*

2. Decide if you want people to come up with concepts individually or in small groups, and help to organize any groups necessary. Give everyone the goal that they must come up with as many concepts as they can to execute on that hypothesis. Help them get started with a targeted creative "How...?" question, like the following:

   - How can we attract prospective customers who have never considered this as a service?

   - How can we encourage existing customers to buy more pieces?

   - How do existing customers sell their pieces?

   Obviously, this will depend on the scope and nature of what you want the concepts to be about.

3. Now, of course people will (hopefully) come up with all sorts of random ideas early on, and it's great to capture all of those (using sticky notes, and/or writing on whiteboards). But watch out for ideas that are just one word. For example, I can just imagine my QR Code Guy blurting out "Referrals!"

   If this happens, ask the person to add a bit more detail according to the "How...?" question, the audience, and its goal.

   Example brainstorming question: *"How can we attract prospective customers who have never considered this as a service?"*

   Idea, short version: *Referrals*

   Ideas, detailed versions:

---

[1] You can read more about hypotheses in the section about the Experience Canvas on page 261.

- *Offer existing customers their next transaction fee-free for every referral they send that signs up.*

- *Find out which customers have more than 1,000 followers on any given social media platform, and offer them a special if they promote your business to their network.*

- *Hold a ritzy waterside evening event and invite top customers who can bring someone along who is not yet a customer.*

4. Ask each person (or group) to nominate their strongest three ideas. For each idea, use the Concept Canvas as a way to flesh out the initial idea into a more realized concept.

5. Begin by copying the hypothesis into the Hypothesis section of the canvas.

6. Write in who the particular audience type is in the Audience section (e.g., "Project manager" or "Brand-new customer, never used the product before").

7. In the Goal section, write in what that audience type's goal is. The goal should be specific to the audience, not about your product.

8. In the Channels section, write in what channels are involved in the concept. How does this customer actually experience this concept? Is it through an app on her mobile phone first thing in the morning? Is it on her laptop at work?

9. Now, use the main area of the canvas (Experience) to describe and illustrate what the actual experience is. This could be a bulleted list, a flowchart, a storyboard...whatever helps to really bring the concept to life, and to add rigor to your group's thinking about how the experience starts, how it finishes, and what different parts are needed to achieve it. This can include hints of the Channels section, too.

10. Finally, put a mark on each of the sliding scales in the Scope Sliders section for how "big" the concept is. Just rough guesses is fine at this stage, but impress upon everyone that they can't mark all of the concepts' sliders at maximum.[2]

---

2 If this *does* happen, remind your group what the minimum viable experience is. Ask them: what could they remove from each concept, and still answer the original brainstorming question, *and* have it be valuable in some way to the audience type?

The sliders included are risk, effort, value, resourcing, and timing. You can use these, or replace them with other factors that are important to you.

11. Because of the common structure, the Concept Canvas makes it easier for people to read and understand other people's concepts. As a way of refining the output of a group, you can get each person to briefly pitch their concepts to everyone, and then give them all three sticky dots to "vote" on the concepts they think are the strongest.

What you should finish with is a refined "gallery" of Concept Canvases. Even though the contents of the main Experience section might visually vary, you've given everyone just enough structure to help you sort through them and start sizing them for risk, effort, value, resourcing, and timing (or any other factors).

And it's to these factors we now turn, in our last two visual patterns.

Prioritizing Action with the Hurdle Track Sketch

One of the toughest kinds of stakeholder discussions to have in any organization—be it about products, services, internal systems, or restructures—is without a doubt the one about prioritizing and deciding on different initiatives.

Should we zig or zag? Which of these 12 initiatives should we start first? Should we move this team to the Milwaukee office, or that team to the Melbourne office? Or open a new office on the beach? I'm certainly not qualified to shell out business advice, but there's one thing I do know for sure: if we can visualize our options better, we can make better decisions. With that in mind, I give you the Hurdle Track sketch (Figure 12-3).

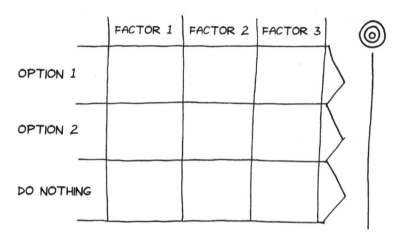

	FACTOR 1	FACTOR 2	FACTOR 3	◎
OPTION 1				
OPTION 2				
DO NOTHING				

FIGURE 12-3

The Hurdle Track sketch: Use this sketch to structure a group discussion about which option is strategically more favorable than others.

The Hurdle Track sketch is based on the visual metaphor of a set of runners on a track, where each runner represents an option before you and your business. They all have to "run the race" toward the same goal.

To finish the race, your "options" runners must jump over several hurdles that apply to them all. The hurdles represent different factors that go into the decision, and will vary depending on the problem at hand. Here are some examples:

- Cost of production

- Time to production

- Value to the customer

- Financial risk

Like all visual patterns, this ain't no silver bullet; it's a catalyst for a richer, more useful discussion.

Use this pattern when you want to do the following:

- Help yourself or a team to prioritize the value of several concepts.

- Help a group of stakeholders turn a long, aimless talkfest into a more structured strategic discussion.

- Help someone get "unstuck" on an important decision, if they're stuck in analysis paralysis.

The runners in your hurdles race are going to need a finish line, so the first thing you need is a *clear business objective*. Not the objective of the discussion itself, but the objective of the business, product, or service. Here are some examples:

- Increase the number of monthly active users of a digital product to one million by the end of the year.

- Increase NPS (net promoter score) by 30 points in 2 quarters.

- Increase the online product conversion rate to 11 percent by next quarter.

- Decrease the resolution time for top-tier customers' support requests by 20 percent this quarter.

The second task is to clarify what the options are that should be prioritized. The options themselves will be driven by whatever your project is; they could be a set of concepts that you created Concept Canvases for, or they could be more strategic options (like opening a new office on the beach). Try to keep the options to more than two, and less than five.[3]

Gather your group for the discussion, and ensure that you have plenty of whiteboard space for your Hurdle Track sketch. Here's how to do it:

1. Begin by drawing a target near the upper-right corner of the whiteboard and write up the business objective. Drop a vertical line down to represent the finish line.

2. On the left side, list the options up for discussion, and then draw some tracks from the options over to the finish line, as shown in Figure 12-4. Explain what you're doing to the group; this should increase their anticipation of reaching a decision by the end of the session.

---

3 I get suspicious when only two options are presented for stakeholders to decide on. I suspect it's because we're used to holding everything in our heads and then talking about our ideas rather than visualizing them, and so any more than two options is just too difficult. Even including a third "do nothing different" option will sometimes be a useful catalyst to help decision making. And any more than five options will just take too long to discuss.

NPS +30

FREE KITTENS
FOR EVERYONE

BETTER
ONBOARDING

GOOGLE
INTEGRATION

FIGURE 12-4
A demo Hurdle Track sketch with business objective and three options: In this scenario, a team has to decide which initiative to run with to increase their product's NPS by 30 points.

3. The next step is to list the factors that will affect decision making along the top. You might have these already, which is best. If not, be prepared to add "hurdles" to your track as the factors emerge from the discussion. You could begin with a couple of regular factors, like *cost* and *time to delivery* (depending on your context). Drop vertical lines down from each one, so that you begin to have a set of boxes appearing.

4. Ask your group which hurdle is the highest for the first factor, which is the second highest, and so on. It might seem a weird question, but this will be a catalyst to focus the discussion on one factor at a time. You can write notes in each box (depending on how much room you have on your whiteboard), but make sure that you draw a wall with whatever the "height" score is (see Figure 12-5). Make sure that each one is given a different number; that is, all options can't have the same factor of, say, "3."

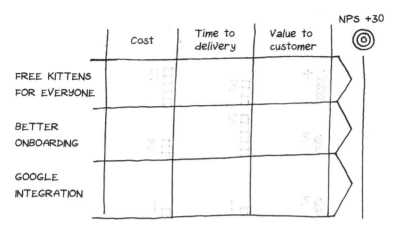

	Cost	Time to delivery	Value to customer	NPS +30 ◎
FREE KITTENS FOR EVERYONE				
BETTER ONBOARDING				
GOOGLE INTEGRATION				

FIGURE 12-5

A demo Hurdle Track sketch with three decision factors: In this scenario, giving kittens to everyone will cost the most, but yield the most value to customers. It might be more prudent to go with the Google integration option; it won't cost as much or take as long, but it will still provide decent value to customers.

5. Sometimes the factor might be more of an *advantage*. For example, if one option has a high score for "customer value," that score might push it ahead of the other options. If you have any of these factors, visualize them as "springs," and rate them accordingly, too.

6. The group discussion will probably ramble all over the matrix of boxes that you've drawn up. You can decide to either let it flow and jot notes and scores in each box as it happens, or add a bit more structure and perhaps break your group into smaller groups. You can ask each one to score the "height" of each option among themselves, and then share the results.

7. As the discussion develops, add any extra factors that arise along the top.

8. Make it clear that if the group can't add a height score in a box, it's better to say that it doesn't know and to mark it with a question mark for follow-up investigation.

9. Aim to fill in all the boxes with some time left for critical discussion of the results. As a group, look at the board and imagine each option "running the race." The higher the hurdles, the more each runner will slow down, and it might be visually clear which runner will win (i.e., reach the target of the business objective first).

10. Push your group to make a decision, based on the information visually displayed. Use your Hurdle Track sketch as a catalyst to help resolve some parts where you can, or expose some important trade-offs that your group will need to make.

Here are some scenarios I've seen, and what can help:

"You can't compare these options; they're apples and oranges!"

All options are in service of the same business objective and will be executed by the same organization, so they must have *some* things in common; for example, the team that will produce it, the budget that will pay for it, and so on.

"There are too many question marks on the board; we don't know enough to make a decision."

The group must decide if it knows enough to move ahead, or if it's worth taking the extra time to do the work necessary to fill in those gaps in understanding. Warning: it's easy for people to defer a decision by saying they don't have all the information. If this happens, ensure that you have a "do nothing" track in your Hurdle Track sketch, and emphasize the impact of not taking action.

"All of the hurdles are too high! None of the runners will win!"

The "runners" you have (e.g., concepts, strategic options) are either all too similar to one another, or just not up to the task of achieving your stated business objective. If this happens, the spread of options is not diverse enough. You should consider going back a step and coming up with better options. Keep in mind that you might need completely different people to achieve that.

Prioritizing Resources with the Resource Tank Sketch

Sometimes, the struggle with prioritizing isn't so much to do with the relative merit of various concepts or importance and urgency of various strategic options, but simply the time and resources we have to execute them.[4]

Indeed, our time is one of the most precious resources we have, and if you think back to Chapter 2, we need to keep a handle on what we're spending our attention on every day.

Or perhaps you're not so much concerned with your *individual* attention budget, but the resources of a *team*, and their skills, time, and current spread of work.

The Resource Tank sketch can help you manage how you prioritize these resources (Figure 12-6). And maybe it will even help you to get some of those resources back.

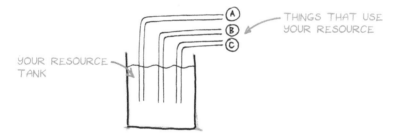

FIGURE 12-6

The Resource Tank sketch: This is a versatile sketch to help you think about how a resource is being spent, and how to manage that.

The Resource Tank sketch works on the visual metaphor of a tank that holds a finite amount of fuel. Different things draw resources out of that tank, at different rates. It's really helpful to visualize what those different things are, so that we can be better at managing them.

---

4   That said, I never like "lack of time and resources" being a reason for *not* executing on what is otherwise the best strategic option available. But hey, I'm also pragmatic enough to acknowledge that sometimes it *does* play a role in prioritizing.

For instance, when we run into a problem or need to make a decision, it draws from our "cognitive fuel tank." A few problems or a few decisions are okay, but when there are more and more, it can drain us dry.

But wait, there's more. By visualizing different "levels" in the tank, and straws that go to different depths, you can also explore how different things can drain more of the resource, whether you want them to or not, as demonstrated in Figure 12-7.

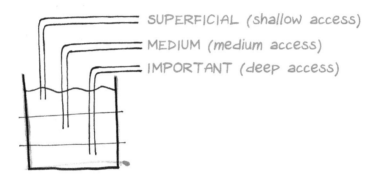

FIGURE 12-7
Level up your Resource Tank sketch: By adding levels, and straws going to different levels, you can visualize how "deeply" different things can draw on your resource.

This is a really neat visual metaphor that you can adapt and use in a variety of ways. For example, you can use a Resource Tank sketch to visualize any of the following:

Your attention

What are the things that matter the most to you? There should always be "fuel" for those things, which is why they get the deepest straw. There will also be things that matter a lot less, and you should only let them have a shallow straw, as shown in Figure 12-8.

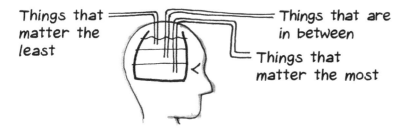

Things that matter the least

Things that are in between

Things that matter the most

FIGURE 12-8

Attention map: You can use the Resource Tank sketch to visualize the things that are taking up your own attention, and determine whether to make any changes to that.

Budget and expenses comparison

What would it look like if you compared what your budget expenditure should be to what it actually is (Figure 12-9)? Are there types of expenses that are crowding out other types, draining resources away from the things that matter?

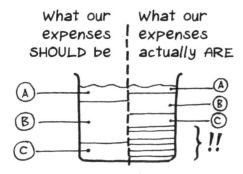

What our expenses SHOULD be

What our expenses actually ARE

FIGURE 12-9

Budget and expenses comparison map: You can use the Resource Tank sketch to visually compare how a resource should be used versus how it is actually being used. This is really just a stacked column chart pattern, but there's something about picturing it as a tank of fuel that brings insights to life a bit more.

Team resources and expenditure comparison

What would the fuel tank look like if it were your team (Figure 12-10)? Suppose that you manage a support team; are you leaving enough fuel in the tank for your premium clients? Or is energy being sapped by lots of seemingly urgent and important tasks?

FIGURE 12-10

Team resources map: You can also use the Resource Tank sketch to visualize how your team's time, resources, and attention should be spent.

Use this pattern when you want to do the following:

- Better understand where your own time and attention are spent so that you can be more effective.

- As a manager, better understand how your team's time, attention, and resources are being spread across its work.

- As a team, gain a shared understanding of where your time, energy, and budget are being spent, and where you would like to make changes.

This is a really versatile visual pattern (as you can see from the previous examples), so there's no one way to do it. However, it's best to break it down into two steps:

1. **Understanding what draws from your resource.** Sketch a tank and a wavy line representing liquid inside it (much like Figure 12-6). This is the resource. Write all the various things that are currently drawing from that resource above and on either side of the tank. Draw lines from each thing into the tank, to visualize them drawing from the resource through "straws."

   Sit back and take stock of what you've sketched. You might have drawn all of the "straws" going straight to the bottom of the tank. That's what it's like when you feel like everything sucks everything out of you (or everyone in your team is always running around being involved in everything all the time), and you have nothing left in the tank.

2. **Prioritizing what draws from your resource.** Sketch a tank and a wavy line as before, but this time, sketch some lines across the tank to visualize different levels (like in Figure 12-7). Write the various things that you want to draw from your resource. Maybe there are some things that you don't even want to write on there this time?

   Now, draw the straws for each thing, but this time decide the level to which you want each thing to draw. You should find that the most important things will have the longer straws, whereas the less important things will have shorter straws.

After you have visually explored *what* you want to prioritize, there's obviously some work to do in *how* you do that. But I've always found that visualizing what's going on in this way helps everyone to better understand what's going on, and to be better equipped to make choices.

SOME QUESTIONS FOR YOU

What's your team's attitude toward brainstorming?

Is anyone on your team skeptical about the value of brainstorming? I'd never want a team's skeptical (or negative!) attitude to the *idea* of brainstorming to get in the way of a potentially breakthrough concept. Would explaining the difference between "idea" and "concept" help in this situation?

What decisions could you help your team make with the Hurdle Track sketch?

If I had a dollar for every time someone said "Ah, *that* old chestnut!" I would...Well, I would have at *least* enough money to buy a coffee, and buy you one, too. The point is: I think we get used to carrying around unresolved problems and unmade decisions in organizations. And that's not okay.

What decisions could you help your team make by doing the Hurdle Track sketch with them?

How is your resource tank?

How is the "level of your tank" right now? If you were to do the Resource Tank sketch on yourself, how might you reprioritize some things that you're spending time on to give you more "fuel" to spend on what matters?

And what about your team? Or your colleagues? Are there people on your team who could benefit from doing the Resource Tank sketch on themselves?

Interview with Devon Bunce

Devon is a freelance graphic facilitator with a rich and varied education in her field. Here, she shares what it means to transform a group's conversation into a tangible, meaningful object.

Visual communication is an alternative language that creates space for multiple meanings and interpretations. When I'm scribing, I think about creating that space for all of the voices in the room to exist, and for me to be as neutral as possible (I don't believe in total neutrality).

I first learned about visualization from Grove in San Francisco, a consultancy that uses visual environments to help a group move forward and have a better conversation. I also learned a toolkit for visual language, from a Danish company called Bigger Picture, which included simple objects like signposts and arrows. But there was more to it than just scribing technique; I learned a lot about listening, leadership, and personal development through Kaospilots, my education in Denmark.

I committed to taking my notes visually. I got a blank notebook without lines, picked four colors I liked, and just started doodling. Oh, and gray! Discovering grays was a really poignant moment for me. Shadows added dimension to my drawings. It really stood out for me!

I realized over time that I listen a lot better when I doodle. There are three levels of listening. The first level is listening and interpreting what the content means to me. The second level is listening with an attentive focus on another person. The third level of listening is about paying attention to the whole group, the environment they're in, and what is happening to the energy in the room. Third-level listening incorporates your intuition, and can also be seen as supporting a *third entity*: what is seeking to emerge in this space? And how can I best support what is seeking to emerge?

I'm really into the idea of engaging with the whole of my body. My work at Global Leadership Foundation has taught me about the three brains in the body, also referred to as "centers": the head gives us insight, the heart gives us intuition, and the gut gives us instinct. Usually we rely on just two of those centers at a time, but the key is to use all of them. When you're engaging with all three of these centers you're *present*, you're in flow. When I find this flow, I'm able to remain focused and engaged throughout conversations that can span multiple days.

The pictures I draw help participants relate to content differently, and spark new perspectives and opportunities for thinking differently (see Devon at work in Figure 12-11). Introducing visual language to a conversation gives permission to expand the way we are doing things. And seeing the progression of thinking, conversing, and activity amongst a group mapped out in a collective journey creates a sense of oneness. The illustration brings content to life in a playful way. It allows us to access our heart center.

When I'm working, I'm trying to pay attention to what is emerging in me, or what is igniting something in me based on my own experiences, and what I see to be important, versus what might be relevant for the group. I'm often asked about the process of making a choice about what to visualize and record, and this is where attention to the third entity is required. However, I must admit that it can be easy to get swept into the emotion of a conversation when the subject is American politics!

FIGURE 12-11
Devon on the pens, hard at work: "The pictures I draw help participants relate to content differently, and spark new perspectives and opportunities for thinking differently."

This is something that's really important to me. It's so important to continuously think: how can I be in service of what is seeking to emerge in the room, rather than just me? As you scribe, you will have an engaged body center. So, aim to pay attention to when the other centers, the head and the heart, are dominating the airwaves. It's about being in balance. That's when I'm at my best. That's when I'm present, I'm in flow. I'm just exactly where I am.

> It's so important to continuously think: how can I be in service of what is seeking to emerge in the room?

[13]

Sharing Your Sketches with Others

As fantastic as it is to bring sketching into your product direction, management, and design work, the last thing you want is to be stuck doing lots of sketching while everyone else in the team has finished up and gone for cocktails to celebrate.

Let's look at how we can be efficient in the way we sketch at work. This chapter is packed with tips for to do the following:

- Capturing your sketches professionally

- Storing and sharing your sketches

- Reusing and getting the most out of your sketches

There's Magic in the Making, Not Just What's Made

Sketching in product management and design, like a lot of things, is best done with others rather than just alone.

It's well established that involving others in a solution is the best way to get their endorsement and approval. But I'm not talking about the well-worn phrases of the workplace, like "collaboration" and "stakeholder buy-in." I'm talking about involving *all* types of people on whom your product is going to have an impact. Your customers. The sales staff. The call center staff.

And I'm not just talking meetings and pitching sessions. I'm talking about involving their *hands* as well as their ears, minds, and mouths. It's one thing to show a room full of stakeholders your lovely storyboards, but it's quite another to get them sketching storyboards, too.

So, when it comes to sharing your sketches, think about how you might *share the experience of sketching* with others, as well as sharing your actual sketches. There's magic in the making, not just what's made.

Capturing Your Sketches

Whether you're sketching alone or with others, you'll want to capture what you've sketched as efficiently as possible so that the rest of your team can see it, use it, and reuse it. So, what are the best ways of capturing what we sketch, and getting it into formats we can use and share?

IS IT TIME FOR YOU TO SWAP TO DIGITAL SKETCHING?

Efficiency is a big advantage of sketching digitally in the first place rather than scanning or taking photos of a paper or whiteboard sketch to then process it as digital files. Digital sketching techniques can take some getting used to, but if you're finding that you have to capture and digitize a lot of sketches, it might be time to roll up your sleeves and get good at sketching on a tablet.[1]

---

1   Don't forget, Chapter 4 has a rundown of digital products to use as well as a discussion on blending the material and digital worlds.

THINK ABOUT HOW YOU'RE GOING TO USE THE SKETCHES

That said, it's good to think about why you want to capture your sketches (Figure 13-1). It's all about where your sketches will end up:

High-resolution printing
You're going to need to scan your sketches for maximum quality.

Instant sharing on social media or your intranet
Snap away! That camera on your smartphone is fine.

Capturing for project work or for a presentation
You'll want your images nice, white, and clean, in a way that fits your workflow.

Enhancing, coloring, and editing
A smooth vectorized image is best.

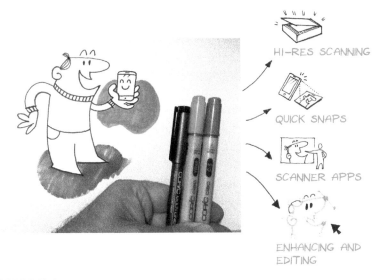

FIGURE 13-1
Think about how you're going to use your sketches: How you're going to use your sketches can drive how you capture them, whether it's a high-resolution scan or a quick snap using a smartphone camera or scanner app.

High-resolution printing

Nothing beats a good quality desktop scanner—or office printer with a scanning function—for capturing your sketches in a nice, crisp 300 dpi (or higher) format. Always check the glass for blemishes, and invest in a scanner that can either send you the scans via email or save them to a network drive for more convenient access.

Instant sharing

If you just want an image of your sketches to share on Instagram, Twitter, and so on[2] (or maybe your work intranet or chat room), the camera app on your smartphone is fine. Here are some pro tips:

- Go for maximum light; always photograph your sketch in as much light as possible.

- Watch out for shadows of either you or your smartphone.

- Try dynamic angles for added interest.

- Show a bit of process behind your magic. Include the edges of the paper or sketchbook, and the markers you used; people love to know more about how you created that sketch.

Capturing for project work or for a presentation

The camera on your smartphone probably won't give you a sharp, clean, bright, squared-off image, so go for a scanner app like CamScanner or Office Lens.[3] Both of these are mainly meant for document scanning (as well as receipts and business cards), but their image scanning is great, too. Both have great edge detection and perspective fixing (Figure 13-2), so no more wonky images at odd angles to tidy up!

---

2   And, y'know, tag them with #prestosketching so that we can all see how awesome they are!

3   For links to these apps and others (like Scanbot, TinyScanner, and Evernote's Scannable) in Mac, Android, and Windows flavors, see the Presto Sketching blog post "Capture Photos of Your Sketches like a Pro" (*http://prestosketching.com/blog/2017/04/03/capture-photos-of-your-sketches-like-a-pro/*). New and improved scanning apps are coming out all the time, so try searching your platform's app store for "scanning" for other apps available.

FIGURE 13-2

Capturing a sketch using CamScanner: Note the edge detection for squaring up the image (left). The picture retains the color nicely (middle), and the close-up shows nice enough resolution to be useful for screen presentations (right).

What's more, both include optical character recognition (OCR) capability, so depending on how neat your writing is, they will automatically capture that in an editable format, too.

Office Lens is perfect if you already use OneNote or OneDrive, and you can export your scans as editable Office files. It also has a great feature of being able to toggle between Photo, Document, and Whiteboard modes. The Whiteboard mode view can give amazing results of your scrawls on a whiteboard, even in a dim room. But beware! As you can see in the image in Figure 13-3, colored shapes end up looking pretty janky.

FIGURE 13-3

Capturing a sketch using Office Lens: The Whiteboard mode is very useful for enhancing a picture of dry erase ink on a whiteboard (middle), but can struggle with colored shapes (right).

Enhancing, coloring, and editing

If you need to capture your sketches to refine in an image editing application, or create something that combines several sketches together, any of the aforementioned scanning apps are fine—but if you can, try Adobe Capture CC and capture your sketches as vectorized images. It does a tremendous job of cleaning up, clarifying, and smoothing out the lines of the sketch (Figure 13-4).

FIGURE 13-4

Capturing a sketch using Adobe Capture CC: This app knocks out the color, but cleans, clarifies, and processes your sketch as a vector image. Lovely!

Perhaps you need to augment an existing sketch with further digital sketching over the top (or underneath)? There are loads of digital drawing apps that let you import existing images (either from the camera or the albums on your smartphone), but a favorite of mine is SketchBook by Autodesk. SketchBook not only lets you import an image as a new shot from your camera, it lets you erase the color of the paper behind the sketch so that it sits on a transparent background. This is super useful if you want to add layers of color "behind" your sketch.

Storing and Sharing Your Sketches

If you're sketching regularly at work, before too long you'll have a growing stack of sketchbooks and sketches on loose-leaf paper lying around. If you're doing lots of whiteboarding, your smartphone will rapidly fill up with photos, too.

Before things get out of hand, it's a good idea to plan how you'd like to store your sketches for referral and reuse later on. If you're in the habit of filling sketchbooks with sketches (and what a commendable habit that is), consider dating the front of each one, or make up a color-coding system using colored sticky dots, where each dot represents a different subject or project.

If you're storing your sketches digitally, there are loads of places you can keep them securely in cloud storage, depending on what you're after:

For you and you only

Personal cloud storage solutions like Box, OneDrive, and Dropbox are great, but you might not get to see thumbnails of your images. With services like Flickr, Google Photos, Photobucket, Apple iCloud, and Amazon Prime Photos, you can set up private folders of images. Look for services that automatically synchronize content across your devices, like OneDrive, Google Drive, Dropbox, and Evernote.

For you and your team

Your sketches will love having a home on whatever online collaboration platform your team happens to use, like Confluence, Yammer, Slack, or SharePoint. If you've worked hard at helping your team explore problems and generate concepts visually, ensure that all that hard work doesn't die in obscurity; keep it alive by including sketches in your online chats and work documentation, as well as links throughout relevant intranet pages to your sketches.

For you and an audience

Unless your sketches are confidential to your business and clients, it's a great idea to store and share them online for others to see and say nice things about them. There are loads of hugely popular services you can use, like Flickr, Twitter, Facebook, Pinterest, and Instagram, but consider using more niche creative places like Behance and DeviantArt. All of them allow hashtagging, so you not only can index your own work, but you can make it available for others to find by searching by topic.

Popular hashtags include: #art, #dailydoodle, #dailydrawing, #doodle, #doodleaday, #doodles, #drawing, #graphicfacilitation, #graphicrecording, #realtimegraphics, #scribing, #sketch,

#sketchbook, #sketches, #sketching, #sketchnote, #sketchnotes, #sketchnoting, #todaysdoodle, #visualpractice, #visualthinking, #vizthink, #whiteboard, and #whiteboarding.[4]

For you to build a portfolio

Consider building up a groomed portfolio of your work (especially if there's a story you want to write about each sketch you've done), using any of the host of blogging platforms such as WordPress, Wix, Squarespace, or Tumblr.

For you to store and sell

There are some pretty sophisticated services around that let you store and sell your sketches (or anything visual, really), like Etsy, Zenfolio, SmugMug, Gumroad, PhotoShelter, and 500px.

Reusing Your Sketches

As you store (and share) more and more of your sketches, think about separating them into different collections that reflect the different types of work you do, and reasons why you might want to reuse them. Index all the collections in different ways (using tags or labels) to make it easier to search by topic across all of them.

Here are some ideas from how I catalog and reuse my sketches that might help you:

Sketched icons

Save each icon as a separate clean file (*.png* or *.jpg*), to duplicate and reuse in storyboards, slide presentations, Journey Maps, and other visual communication pieces (Figure 13-5).

---

4   And #prestosketching. Did I mention #prestosketching?

FIGURE 13-5
Store your sketches in a digital asset manager: Slice, dice, and store your sketches as separate assets in a digital asset manager, like Lingo (in this figure), Asset Bank, Smartimage, Evolphin, or Templafy.

User interface components

Turn your own hand-drawn sketches of screen frames, navigation elements, form elements, and other UI components into a reusable visual library to "build" interfaces in graphics and presentation software like Illustrator, Photoshop, and PowerPoint. That way, you can have the best of both worlds: a sketchy look and feel together with digital drag-and-drop speed.

Storyboards

Save all your storyboards together for future reference, especially if there are frames with particular shots, angles, poses, and so on of which you're particularly proud

Whiteboard conceptual sketches

The visual patterns you saw in Chapters 10 to 12 all came from various workshops and whiteboarding sessions I've done. At some point for each of them, I looked at photos from each whiteboarding session, redrew each new visual pattern in a neat, repeatable way, and saved it in a visual facilitation playbook for later reference.

Canvas templates

As you might have picked up on by now, I'm a bit of a nerd for visually organizing structured information about something as a canvas. In the same way as the aforementioned whiteboard conceptual sketches, I've formalized and saved each canvas I've either made up or borrowed from someone else (attribution notes included, of course) as a template sketch for use in later workshops and sessions.

If you're part of a team on which there are more than one of you sketching, consider pooling the best of your work and formalizing a "house style." The aim isn't to get everyone sketching *exactly the same*, as if they're a collective robotic source of the same icon library (that would be a bit weird); it's about agreeing on a certain visual voice and tone (formal versus friendly), markers and materials used, line style (smooth and even versus rough and textured), use of color (a restricted color palette used in a certain way), and visual contrast (large vivid blocks of color versus tints and washes of subtle color).

As you get better at capturing, storing, indexing, and reusing your sketches, you'll find that you truly will get the best of both worlds: the warmth and character of hand-drawn imagery with the speed and copy/paste efficiency of digital. You'll spend less time doing repetitive sketching and more time thinking and synthesizing.

And that, my dear Presto Sketcher, will be a huge win for visual thinking and communication.

SOME QUESTIONS FOR YOU

What treasures does your smartphone's photo app hold?

Go through the photos on your phone. Are there any photos of sketches (yours or anyone else's) that you would want to copy into a sketchbook to have them all in one place? Are there any screenshots or photos of anything else visually inspirational that you could turn into a sketch for your sketchbook?

Do you have the start of a sketch icon library?

Look over the sketches you've been doing while you've been reading this book. Are there any with which you want to start populating your own sketch icon library?

What sketches could you use in your work presentations?

I guarantee you that including your own sketches in your presentations at work will make them more appealing and more memorable. What text in the slides of your latest presentation could you replace with a sketch?

What recent sketch makes you proud?

Go through some recent sketches you've done. Which one stands out to you as one that you're pleased with, and why?

Why not share it on social media right now? Be sure to use hashtags so that we can all find it!

[14]

Spreading Your Wings

WELL, LOOK AT YOU! You've taken in a ton of learning, done the exercises, and answered some tricky questions along the way. Hopefully your eyes, mind, and hands have awoken to the amazing potential of visual thinking and visual communication through sketching. And if you were already on that journey, hopefully *Presto Sketching* has fleshed out those skills even more.

It's time we part company for now, and it's time for you take flight with your new turbocharged sketching skills. I want to leave you with some final words about the following:

- Looking for opportunity

- Trying new things

- Getting into the community of visual thinking and communication

- Setting yourself challenges

Keep Looking for Opportunity

There's one thing I always try to instill in everyone who comes along to my sketching classes near the end of each class: it's *you* who is in the best place to spot opportunities to use your Presto Sketching skills of visual thinking and visual communication, and it's *you* who is the best person to take up those opportunities (Figure 14-1).

IN MEETINGS

IN PRESENTATIONS

ON THE INTRANET

IN CLIENT REPORTS

FIGURE 14-1

Find ways of bringing your new sketching skills into your existing job: Before you know it, you could have your sketches on the whiteboard in meetings, in presentations, on your intranet, and in client reports.

It's unlikely that your boss or your boss's boss is going to walk up to you, give you a soft, chummy punch on the shoulder and say, "I know we're all spread really thin on <insert name of hugely important project here>, but why don't you step out for a few days and work on your sketching skills and confidence instead?"

That's just not going to happen! Instead, you need to find ways of inserting sketching into your regular work, your regular meetings, and your regular deliverables.

Keep Your Tools (and Your Mind) Sharp

I hope that in reading *Presto Sketching*, and in doing the various sketching activities throughout these pages, you've come to discover (or have a better sense of) the power that sketching gives you to think. I mean, really *think*.

From here on, you're going to notice patterns in things that other people don't. You're going to see insightful and useful connections in things that others don't. As technology changes the jobs we do,[1] your powers of thinking, critique, synthesis, and sense-making will be sought after more and more.

So, keep your mind sharp! Feed it the right diet of information in healthy proportions. Give it time to relax, reflect, and sift through the barrage of that information. And always sketch. Sketch to think, sketch to relax, sketch to express what your words can't, sketch to empty your mind, sketch to fill it up again, sketch to delight, sketch to encourage, sketch to uncover uncomfortable truths, and sketch to inspire others.

Try New Materials

The Google Tilt Brush was released just before I began writing this book. It's the first virtual reality drawing and painting app to give us a fluid, immersive three-dimensional drawing experience. And the first time I used it was another one of those tech mind-blowing experiences! You can even paint in smoke, fire, and snow—just thinking about it now makes me giddy.

As I finish writing this book, Google has updated JamBoard, a 55-inch cloud-linked interactive whiteboard that eight people can draw on at once. I got to play with one recently and marveled at how it has brought several interactions together in one smooth experience. The point is, new technology and new materials are coming out all the time. All these new products will all say that the only limits are our own

---

1   As it always has, whether it's the Jacquard loom of 1801, or bots and artificial intelligence.

imagination. But you know what? That has always been the case, from the ochre that our Paleolithic ancestors used to paint the animals they hunted in Lascaux, France, to the Google Tilt Brush.

They are nothing without our imagination.

Having said that, new tools certainly spark new creativity, so keep trying out new materials, new surfaces, new markers, and new apps. The list is endless, but here are a few random ideas:

Try a dive slate

If you find that you get ideas first thing in the morning while you're in the shower, why not have something in the shower to capture those thoughts and ideas? Dive slates are basically slates that scuba diver instructors use to write underwater. They're pretty cheap, and you can get them in a range of sizes from scuba diving stores or online.[2]

Try a 3D pen

If you can't get a VR headset and Google Tilt Brush, why not try something that writes in 3D in real life? Warning: these things are addictive; I have a Lix 3D pen, and I'm having loads of fun experimenting with different kinds of sculptures and subjects.

Try chalk and a blackboard

You can turn any wall into a hipster blackboard with blackboard paint (it's pretty cheap and available at most hardware stores). The roughness forces you to draw simple, sketchy, and large—a welcome change if you're used to always doing persnickety small drawings.

What Next?

Right now, I know you must be bursting with enthusiasm and chutzpah, relishing the idea of striding into a boardroom conversation and bringing awe-inspiring clarity and insight to the cliché-laden workspeak, with a Jedi-like stroke of a whiteboard marker. And so you

---

2 AquaNotes waterproof notepads are a similar product. You can write on them without them getting soggy in the shower, but they work like Post-It Notes, so when you're done you can rip one note off and take it with you. You can find them at *myaquanotes.com*.

should be! With that marker in your hand and the wind in your hair, you need to be thinking that there's no problem you can't solve, no concept you can't explain, and no path you can't chart.

Truly, you can redefine what you do, and the value you bring to the world, if you blend these visual thinking and visual communication skills into the job you already have.

So where to now? Here are a few ideas that have helped me a lot, and I hope they help you.

GET INTO THE COMMUNITY

As I mentioned in Chapter 13, it's a great idea to find a community of like-minded sketchers, to learn from them, be inspired by them, and share your work for feedback and advice.

Nothing beats getting together with real humans in real places for this,[3] but this is also where the anonymity of being online works in your favor: you don't need to be afraid of showing anything you sketch online, because most people who see it won't know you and never will.

I've always found that the online community of sketchers—especially on Twitter and Instagram—is incredibly kind and supportive.[4] You'll be amazed at the numbers of likes, hearts, and encouraging comments you'll receive on posts of your sketches, no matter how raw you think they are. And if you're lucky, every now and then you'll forge a real friendship or two, with people from whom you can get honest and useful feedback on your work to make it better.

There are also more official associations that are only too happy to bring you into the fold—such as the International Forum of Visual Practitioners (IFVP) (*https://www.ifvp.org*)—and websites that are hubs for like-minded individuals, like *sketchnotearmy.com*.

---

3   A quick search for "sketching" or "sketchnoting" on *meetup.com* will show you any meet-ups happening near you.

4   Search for others' sketches using the hashtags listed in "Storing and Sharing Your Sketches" on page 312.

SET YOURSELF CHALLENGES

Your Presto Sketching prowess ain't gonna walk out and get a job by itself: you have to be intentional about developing these skills. The easiest way to get that groove going is to set yourself challenges. They can start small and simple, and grow in effort and reward over time. Here are a few challenges to try:

- Challenge yourself to get into the sketchbook habit (if you're not already). Grab a sketchbook and commit to filling it with sketches, even if you just do 15 minutes a week to build up a cadence of sketching, enough so that it feels natural.

- Name your kryptonite, and deal with it. What is your kryptonite when it comes to sketching? What's the thing that you feel is holding you back? What freaks you out? What makes you nervous, just a little bit? Name it, and take steps to sketch your way out of it.

- Add your sketches to your own slide presentations. Even this can be a huge step for a lot of people, but you'll be pleasantly surprised at the healthy response you get from your audience.

- Sketch the conversation on the whiteboard during a meeting. Rather than tooling around on your phone or laptop like everyone else, quietly begin sketching what you pick up from the meeting around you. Even simple bullet points with the odd arrows connecting one thought with another will really increase everyone's engagement in the meeting.

- Keep your eye out for regular online challenges to be a part of. Popular ones include Inktober (draw something every day in the month of October), 100 drawings (draw something every day for 100 days), London Sketchnote Hangout's "Icon and Sketchnote Challenge" (commit to sketching an icon for every day of the month according to the descriptions given), and "daily doodle" (post a sketch every day on Twitter or Instagram and tag it #dailydoodle).

THE PARTING LINE

I want to leave you with a quick story.

A while back, I was invited to a class of design students to talk (and sketch) about sketching in design, during one of their lunch breaks. I sketched away, using several examples that you've now read about. One of the students in that class was really taken with this style of drawing. The style itself is of course not new; visual note-taking has been around arguably forever, but has become a thing since the mid-2000s.

Anyway, this student began sketchnoting and posting his sketches on Twitter. A longtime friend of his—a teacher—saw these sketches, and thought to himself that he'd like to try it. And try it he did, at the next teaching conference he went to. He just picked it up by himself, and before long he had a lot of others at the conference expressing their amazement and appreciation at what he was doing.

That teacher not only used sketchnoting in his own studies—indeed, it helped him land his next job—but also taught his students to sketchnote. Has their engagement in class increased? You bet it has. Has that teacher been asked back to those same teaching conferences to teach other teachers? Why, yes. Yes, he has.

In case you haven't picked it up, the student is Justin Cheong, and his interview is on page 70. His longtime friend is Andrew On Yi Lai, and his interview is on page 121.

Sketching for visual thinking, visual communication, and synthesis is an amazing key that has the power to unlock not only the solutions to whatever is holding you back, but a better livelihood for you and for those you care about.

This power is real, and it is quite literally in your hands.

So, keep on sketching, and keep on bringing your thinking, your ideas, and your vision out into the world. It needs it!

[A]

Concept-to-Metaphor Transfigurator

If you have a particular concept or theme in mind that you want to bring to life as a visual metaphor, use this table to look up which visual metaphor(s) to use, which you can then reference in Chapter 7.

IF YOU WANT TO ILLUSTRATE THIS CONCEPT...	USE THIS VISUAL METAPHOR...
Alone	Footprints, Island, Parachute
Angry	Cloud
Authority	Crown, Shield, Wand
Branching	Tree
Cause (and effect)	Arrow, Dominoes, Iceberg, Layers, Matryoshka doll, River, Road, Ruler, Sign, Steps, Tree
Challenge	Jigsaw puzzle, Mountain, Matryoshka doll, Milestone, Road, Steps, Target, Treadmill, Wall
Cold	Iceberg, Weather
Confusion	Maze, Treadmill
Connection	Arrow, Bridge, Handshake, Matryoshka doll, Vine
Courage	Boxing glove, Heart, Shield
Customization	Fingerprint
Cycle	Orbit, Stopwatch, Treadmill
Danger	Bones (Jolly Roger), Cliff, Fire, Gauge, Gravestone, Lightning, Sign, Trap, Waves
Death	Bones, Gravestone, Trap
Decision	Arrow, Compass, Milestone, Ruler, Sign, Steps, Tree, Vine
Dependability	Mountain
Depth	Iceberg, Ruler, Steps

IF YOU WANT TO ILLUSTRATE THIS CONCEPT...	USE THIS VISUAL METAPHOR...
Determination	Boxing glove, Dice/die, Dominoes, Milestone, Road, Rocket, Sign
Direction	Arrow, Compass, Horizon, Lighthouse, Map, Maze, Milestone, Road, Ruler, Sign, Steps, Stopwatch, Target, Thermometer
Disorientation	Maze, Treadmill
Emotional	Heart, Trap
Energy	Battery, Gauge, Lightning, River, Rocket, Spring, Sun (Weather), Thermometer
Enigma	Box, Gift, Footprints, Iceberg, Matryoshka doll, Maze, Tree
Enthusiasm	Lightning, Rocket, Spring
Eternity	Mountain, Orbit, River
Extinct	Bones, Dinosaur, Gravestone
Faith	Four-leaf clover, Sun (Weather)
Focus	Compass, Lens, Limelight, Sign, Target
Fragile	Egg
Freedom	Ballroom, Parachute, Road, Rocket, Wings
Fresh	Egg
Friendship	Gift, Handshake, Heart, Holding hands
Fun	Balloon, Dice/die, Gift, Parachute, Rocket, Spring, Wand
Goal	Flag, Milestone, Mountain, Prize ribbon, Road, Sign, Steps, Target, Trophy
Grandeur	Mountain, River, Tree
Growth	Ruler, Seed, Spring
Grumpy	Cloud
Happiness	Rainbow, Sun (Weather), Spring
Height	Mountain, Ruler, Spring, Steps, Thermometer
Hidden	Box, Gift, Iceberg, Matryoshka doll, Trap
Hope	Four-leaf clover, Treadmill
Idea	Light bulb, Matryoshka doll, Seed
Identity	Fingerprint

IF YOU WANT TO ILLUSTRATE THIS CONCEPT...	USE THIS VISUAL METAPHOR...
Imprisonment	Trap, Treadmill
Influence	Ripple
Information	Cogs and gears, Dam, Filter, Funnel, River, Ruler, Sign
Insight	Lens, Light bulb, Limelight, Sign, Trap
Inspiration	Cloud, Lightning, Light bulb, Spring, Sun (Weather)
Issue	Elephant, Flag, Sign
Journey	Bridge, Flag, Footprints, Horizon, Map, Maze, Milestone, Mountain, River, Road, Rocket, Rollercoaster, Sign, Steps, Welcome mat
Kindness	Gift, Heart
Loneliness	Island, Footprints
Long-term	Horizon, Mountain, Milestone, Road, Steps
Love	Four-leaf clover, Heart
Luck	Dice/die, Four-leaf clover, Gift
Magical	Box, Four-leaf clover, Matryoshka doll, Spring, Wand
Majesty	Iceberg, Mountain, River, Tree
Measurement	Ruler, Scales, Sign, Steps, Stopwatch, Target, Thermometer
Movement	Milestone, Ripples, Road, Spring
New	Egg, Gift, Rocket, Seed, Spring
Old	Bones, Cobwebs, Dinosaur, River
Organization	Engine, Factory, Tandem, Tree
Outdated	Bones, Cobwebs, Dinosaur, Stopwatch
Personalization	Fingerprint, Gift
Perspective	Horizon, Parachute, Reflection, Road, Steps
Power (authority)	See *Authority*
Power (energy)	See *Energy*
Power (strength)	See *Strength*
Premium	Prize ribbon, Shield, Trophy

IF YOU WANT TO ILLUSTRATE THIS CONCEPT...	USE THIS VISUAL METAPHOR...
Pressure	Gauge, Thermometer
Privacy	Padlock
Problem	Bones (Jolly Roger), Cliff, Flag, Jigsaw puzzle, Knot, Sign, Trap, Wall
Process	Arrow, Dominoes, Factory, Flag, Funnel, Jigsaw puzzle, Map, Milestone, Road, Ruler, Steps
Product	Box, Factory, Gift, Rocket
Progress, easy	Waterfall, Ladder, Map, Milestone, Road, Rocket, Steps
Progress, hard	Cliff, Ladder, Map, Milestone, Road, Steps
Protection	Padlock, Parachute, Shield, Wall
Proximity	Onion rings, Map, Matryoshka doll, Target
Rational	Head, Ruler
Rebellion	Bones (Jolly Roger)
Recognition	Prize ribbon, Trophy
Relationship	Belt, Bridge, Cogs and gears, Filter, Jigsaw puzzle, Map, Matryoshka doll, Onion rings, Steps, Target, Tree, Vine
Remote	Island, Map, Milestone, Road
Repetition	Orbit, Ruler, Steps, Stopwatch, Treadmill
Risk	Bones (Jolly Roger), Cliff, Flag, Gauge, Lightning, Parachute, Ruler, Target, Thermometer, Trap
Role	Hats
Rotten	Bones, Egg, Toilet
Safety	Bridge, Key and lock, Lighthouse, Parachute, Shield, Trap, Wall, Welcome mat
Security	Key and lock, Padlock, Shield, Trap, Wall
Shock	Lightning, Trap
Slow	Cobwebs, Parachute, Stopwatch
Speed	Lightning, Parachute, Stopwatch
Story	Footprints, Milestone, River, Road, Trap, Tree rings
Strategy	Lighthouse, Map, Meat-cut chart, Milestone, Road, Ruler, Scales, Silos, Steps, Target, Trap

IF YOU WANT TO ILLUSTRATE THIS CONCEPT...	USE THIS VISUAL METAPHOR...
Strength	Boxing glove, Crown, Dam, Iceberg, Lightning, Mountain, Muscles, Rocket, Thermometer, Tree, Trophy, Wall
Stubbornness	Anchor, Boxing glove, Dam, Mountain, Wall
Support	Holding hands, Parachute, Steps, Wall
Surprise	Box, Gift, Lightning, Spring, Trap
System	Cogs and gears, Engine, Filter, Funnel, Ruler, Steps, Stopwatch, Tandem, Wall
Tension	Knot, Thermometer, Trap
Terror	Dinosaur, Trap
Time	Stopwatch
Trust	Anchor, Handshake
Unconnected	Island, Ladder, Maze, Steps
Value	Gemstone, Prize ribbon, Ruler, Thermometer
Vision	Cloud, Horizon, Mountain, Sun (Weather)
Weakness	Anchor
Worthless	Toilet, Treadmill

Visual Pattern Reference-o-Tronic 3000

THIS APPENDIX GROUPS ALL of the visual patterns and techniques presented in this book according to what you want to achieve, either individually or as a team. There are seven groups, which you can see in Figure B-1.

FIGURE B-1

Your visual guide to the Visual Pattern Reference-o-Tronic 3000: Look up which visual patterns can help you, according to what you want to achieve.

Shared Clarity

IF YOU WANT TO DO THIS...	USE THIS VISUAL PATTERN	PAGE
Clarify what you know about your customers and separate facts from assumptions	Empathy Map	217
Get a shared understanding for what is driving your customers	Empathy Map	217
Get a shared understanding about how your product or service is used, from a customer's perspective	Journey Map	223
Clarify any messages, features, and benefits of your product according to different customer types	Value Proposition Canvas	229
Communicate an entire system in simple terms before delving into detail	Concept Modeling	232
Get a shared understanding of an organization's strategic position across a team (especially with new members)	SWAM Canvas	238
Clarify what problem is being solved by a product, service, process, or team	Experience Canvas	259
Clarify the difference between a vague idea and a workable solution	Concept Canvas	288
Get everyone seeing and understanding the impact of a problem to a customer	Storyboarding	262
Get everyone seeing and understanding the benefit of a solution to a customer	Storyboarding	262
Get a shared team understanding of where time, energy, and budget are being spent and where you would like to make changes	Resource Tank sketch	299

Fresh Thinking and Discovery

IF YOU WANT TO DO THIS...	USE THIS VISUAL PATTERN	PAGE
Unearth gaps in your understanding about your customers	Empathy Map	217
Get a better understanding of the value chain in a product or service	Value Relationship Map	221
Gain insights about unlocking new value in a system of people, products, and services	Value Relationship Map	221
Detect pain points, disconnections, or redundancies in how customers use your product or service	Journey Map	223
Find opportunities to improve customers' evaluation experience as well as opportunities for upselling and cross-selling	Journey Map	223
Uncover potential threats or market opportunities for your business	PESTLE Canvas	240
Spot differences in one market versus another, especially if you're looking to take your product into new markets	PESTLE Canvas	240
Expose any hidden assumptions or anxieties in a new team or a new project	Team Purpose Map	250
Inject some fresh thinking and creativity into how you and your team think about your customers and your product	Superhero Booth sketch	252
Inject some fresh thinking into internal process improvement	Storyboarding	262

Actionable Insights

IF YOU WANT TO DO THIS...	USE THIS VISUAL PATTERN	PAGE
Unearth gaps in your understanding about your customers	Empathy Map	217
Get a better understanding of the value chain in a product or service	Value Relationship Map	221
Get help in distilling customer research information into something actionable by a team	Empathy Map	217
Check if existing user stories align with tasks and goals that customers actually have	Journey Map	223
Illustrate research insights in a more compelling way to your team	Storyboarding	262

Invention

IF YOU WANT TO DO THIS...	USE THIS VISUAL PATTERN	PAGE
Develop more empathy for your customers	Empathy Map	217
Develop an imaginative mindset for what your customers could achieve with your product or service	Superhero Booth sketch	252
Generate ideas to improve particular pain points that customers face	Journey Map	223
Generate ideas for breaking down challenges into manageable chunks	Goal Barriers sketch	257
Apply lean product thinking to internal team and process improvement	Experience Canvas	259
Generate ideas for MVPs	Experience Canvas	259
Generate ideas into a consistent set of concepts to investigate and prioritize	Concept Canvas	288

Strategic Perspective

IF YOU WANT TO DO THIS...	USE THIS VISUAL PATTERN	PAGE
Move a team's thinking and discussion about a product from being about features to being about value	Value Proposition Canvas, Experience Canvas	229,
Get "up above" the level of screen designs and database schemas to show how several internal and external entities work together	Concept Modeling	232
Analyze the strategic position of a team, product, or organization	SWAM Canvas	238
Educate a set of stakeholders and uncover any unconscious biases about how your business will fare in the market	PESTLE Canvas	240
Keep a "line of sight" from your value proposition to your Experience Canvas to any ideas you have for executing on that minimum viable experience (MVE)	Concept Canvas	288

Prioritizing

IF YOU WANT TO DO THIS...	USE THIS VISUAL PATTERN	PAGE
Sort out what are the most important messages, features, and benefits of your product according to different customer types	Value Proposition Canvas	229
Prioritize what "bets" an organization should be making	SWAM Canvas	238
Clarify strategic priorities for an organization	PESTLE Canvas	240
Help prioritize a list of possible features or feature improvements	Superhero Booth sketch	252
Map out specific steps for a goal that until now has seemed vague and out of reach	Build-a-Bridge sketch	254
Help yourself or a team prioritize the value of several concepts	Hurdle Track sketch	293

IF YOU WANT TO DO THIS...	USE THIS VISUAL PATTERN	PAGE
Help someone get "unstuck" on an important decision, if they're stuck in analysis paralysis	Hurdle Track sketch	293
Better understand where your own time and attention is spent so that you can be more effective	Resource Tank sketch	299

Direction and Alignment

IF YOU WANT TO DO THIS...	USE THIS VISUAL PATTERN	PAGE
Get alignment on the value of your product or service with a team	Value Proposition Canvas	229
Get alignment on what "bets" an organization should be making	SWAM Canvas	238
Build an argument for a certain strategic direction	PESTLE Canvas	240
Help resolve internal discussions about longer-term business direction	PESTLE Canvas	240
Set (or reset) a team's identity, purpose, and direction, and get a shared understanding and sense of ownership	Team Purpose Map	250
Align several stakeholders, teams, or organizations around a common purpose and direction	Team Purpose Map	250
Rally a group of people around how to achieve a certain goal	Build-a-Bridge sketch	254
Help a team articulate and quantify any barriers to achieving something they need to get done	Goal Barriers sketch	257
Help a group of stakeholders turn a long, aimless talkfest into a more structured strategic discussion	Hurdle Track sketch	293
Help your team understand how its time, attention, and resources need to be modified to be healthier and more efficient	Resource Tank sketch	

[*Index*]

road (visual metaphor), 145, 165, 168–169
rocket (visual metaphor), 165
rock salute hand, 118
roles
    indicating in figure sketches, 81–82
    journey mapping teams, 224
rollercoaster (visual metaphor), 165
Roosevelt, Theodore, 238
Rule of Thirds, 268–269
ruler (visual metaphor), 165
Running Lean (Maurya), 261

S

Samsung tablets, 63–64
saturation (colors), 205
Say (Empathy Map), 218, 220
scales
    conveying with hands, 114–115
    sketching at different, 77–78
    visual metaphor using, 166
Scanning the Business Environment (Aguilar), 241
Scope sliders (Concept Canvas), 292, 294–295
search (user experience story cycle), 274–276, 282
secondary colors, 203–204
seed (visual metaphor), 147
See (Empathy Map), 218, 220
selling sketches, 316
separators and frames. See frames and separators
shade (colors), 205
shadows, adding to images, 198–200
shapes and lines
    complex objects, 106–121
    inside-out technique, 106–110
    marks and patterns, 76–77
    simple objects, 77–101
    in storyboards, 269–270
shapes in conversations, 216–217
sharing sketches, 311–316
shield (visual metaphor), 166
signpost (visual metaphor), 166
Signs of success (Experience Canvas), 262, 264
sign (visual metaphor), 165–166
silencing the inner critic, 46–49

silhouettes
    city skyline as, 96
    figure sketches as, 81, 83, 210
silos
    identifying in organization, 245–246
    visual metaphor using, 166
similes, 41
six-up technique, 277
Sketchbook (Audodesk), 314
sketchbooks and paper, 57–60
sketching. See basic sketching skills; complex objects, sketching; visual communication
sketchnoting, 121–123, 325–327
skills area (Team Purpose Map), 252, 254
Skroce, Steve, 266
smart pens, 65
Snook.ca Colour Contrast Check, 207
Social (PESTLE Canvas), 241–242
software
    hiding behind, during presentations, 46–47
    killing communication with, 16
space(s)
    in conceptual thinking and sketching, 186–190
    in storyboards, 267, 269–271
speech balloons
    in frames, 97
    in storyboards, 266–268
split-complementary colors, 205
springs (visual metaphor), 167
square colors, 205
squares, sketching, 96
staging in storyboards, 268–270
Stars (SWAM Canvas), 238–239
Stephenson, Glenn, 25–27
steps (visual metaphor), 167
stick figures, adding life to, 78–82
sticky note technique, 277
stopwatch (visual metaphor), 167
storing sketches, 315–317
storyboards and storyboarding
    about, 264–266
    anatomy of, 266–272
    example of existing scenario, 277–280
    exercises for, 272–273, 285–286

About the Author

Ben Crothers is a design strategist, facilitator, and visual thought partner. He has a constant passion for sketching, and helping others unlock their powers of creativity and synthesis through sketching.

Even before discovering design, he used to moonlight as a cartoonist for the Australian Army, and published a book of comics (*STAND EASY: The Best of Ben*) in 1994. Ever since, he has used all sorts of visual thinking and visual communication techniques to help others in consulting and strategy, product management, design, and innovation.

Colophon

The cover image is by Ben Crothers. The cover fonts are URW Typewriter and Guardian Sans. The text font is Scala Regular; and the heading font is Gotham Narrow Medium.

Learn from experts.
Find the answers you need

Sign up for a **10-day free trial** to get **unlimited access** to all of the content on Safari including Learning Paths, interactive tutorials, and curated playlists that draw from thousands of ebooks and training videos on a wide range of topics, including data, design, DevOps, management, business—and much more.

Start your free trial at:
oreilly.com/safari

(No credit card required.)